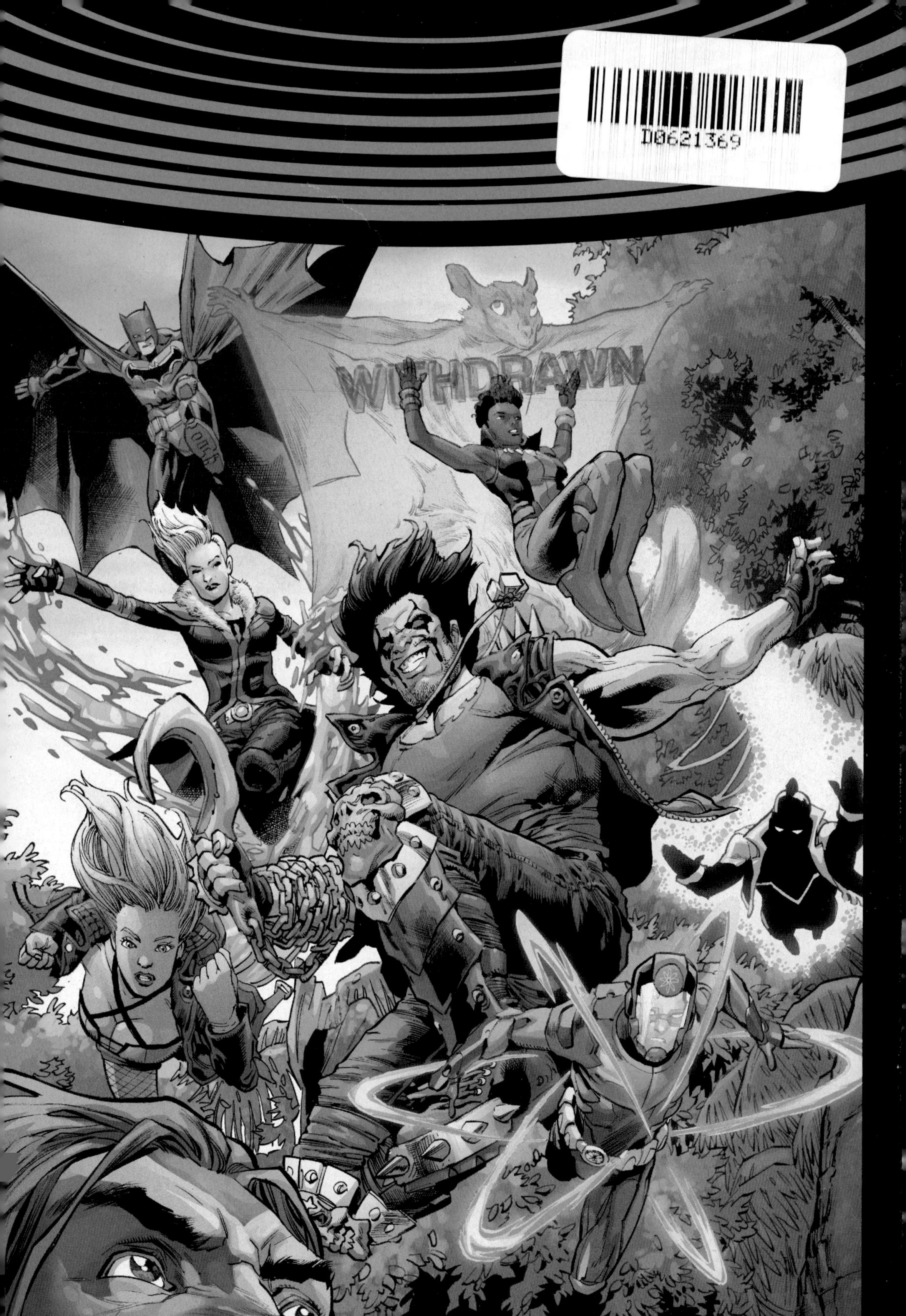

JUSTICE LEAGUE OF AMERICA

VOL.2 CURSE OF THE KINGBUTCHER

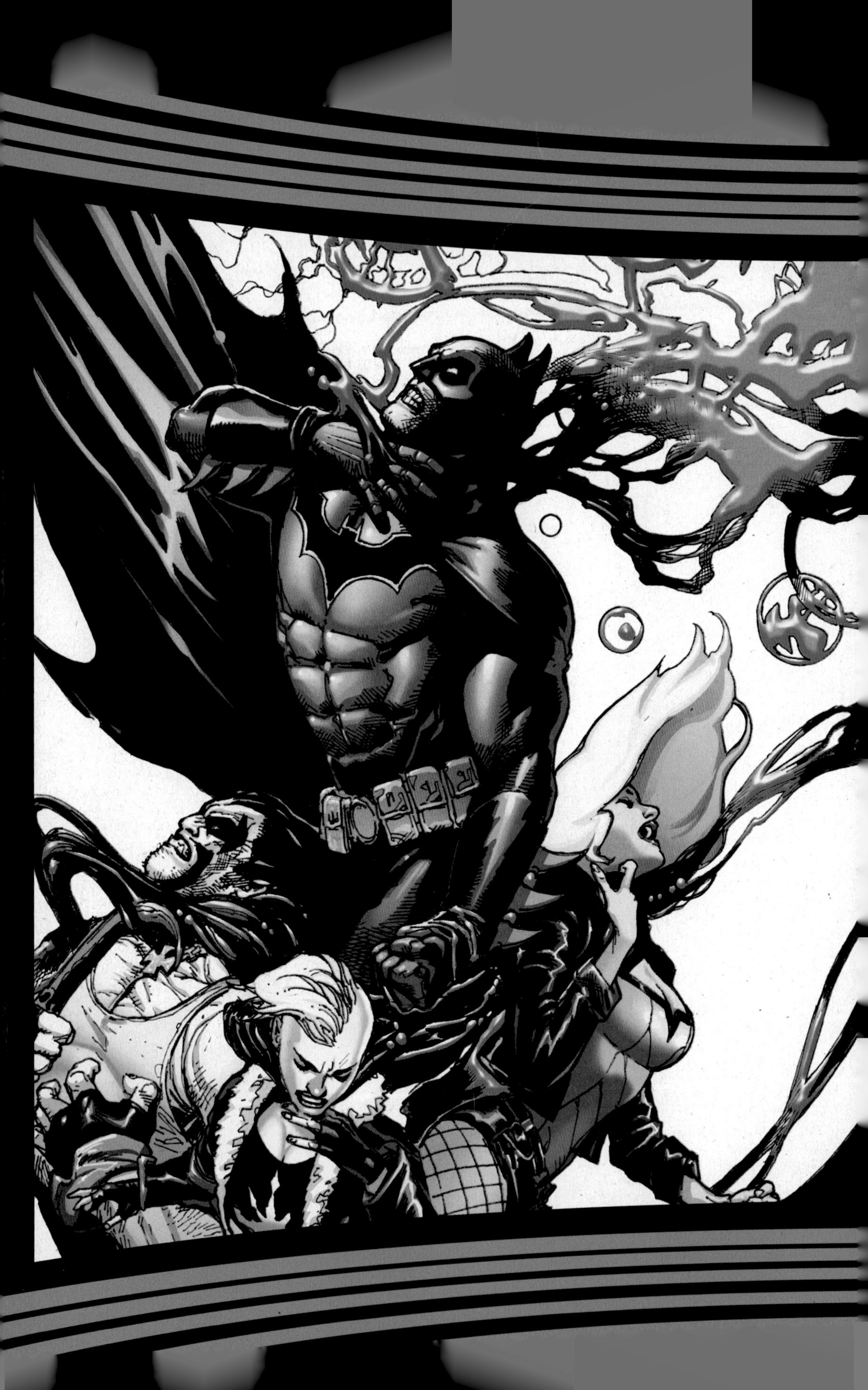

JUSTICE LEAGUE OF AMERICA
VOL.2 CURSE OF THE KINGBUTCHER

STEVE ORLANDO
writer

FELIPE WATANABE * **JAMAL CAMPBELL**
ANDY MacDONALD * **NEIL EDWARDS**
pencillers

SCOTT HANNA * **JAMAL CAMPBELL**
ANDY MacDONALD * **SANDU FLOREA**
inkers

HI-FI * **JAMAL CAMPBELL**
colorists

CLAYTON COWLES
letterer

FELIPE WATANABE and HI-FI
collection cover artists

BRIAN CUNNINGHAM Editor - Original Series ✷ **AMEDEO TURTURRO** Associate Editor ✷ **DIEGO LOPEZ** Assistant Editor - Original Series
JEB WOODARD Group Editor - Collected Editions ✷ **LIZ ERICKSON** Editor - Collected Edition
STEVE COOK Design Director - Books ✷ **MONIQUE NARBONETA** Publication Design

BOB HARRAS Senior VP - Editor-in-Chief, DC Comics
PAT McCALLUM Executive Editor, DC Comics

DIANE NELSON President ✷ **DAN DiDIO** Publisher ✷ **JIM LEE** Publisher ✷ **GEOFF JOHNS** President & Chief Creative Officer
AMIT DESAI Executive VP - Business & Marketing Strategy, Direct to Consumer & Global Franchise Management
SAM ADES Senior VP & General Manager, Digital Services ✷ **BOBBIE CHASE** VP & Executive Editor, Young Reader & Talent Development
MARK CHIARELLO Senior VP - Art, Design & Collected Editions ✷ **JOHN CUNNINGHAM** Senior VP - Sales & Trade Marketing
ANNE DePIES Senior VP - Business Strategy, Finance & Administration ✷ **DON FALLETTI** VP - Manufacturing Operations
LAWRENCE GANEM VP - Editorial Administration & Talent Relations ✷ **ALISON GILL** Senior VP - Manufacturing & Operations
HANK KANALZ Senior VP - Editorial Strategy & Administration ✷ **JAY KOGAN** VP - Legal Affairs ✷ **JACK MAHAN** VP - Business Affairs
NICK J. NAPOLITANO VP - Manufacturing Administration ✷ **EDDIE SCANNELL** VP - Consumer Marketing
COURTNEY SIMMONS Senior VP - Publicity & Communications ✷ **JIM (SKI) SOKOLOWSKI** VP - Comic Book Specialty Sales & Trade Marketing
NANCY SPEARS VP - Mass, Book, Digital Sales & Trade Marketing ✷ **MICHELE R. WELLS** VP - Content Strategy

JUSTICE LEAGUE OF AMERICA VOL. 2: CURSE OF THE KINGBUTCHER

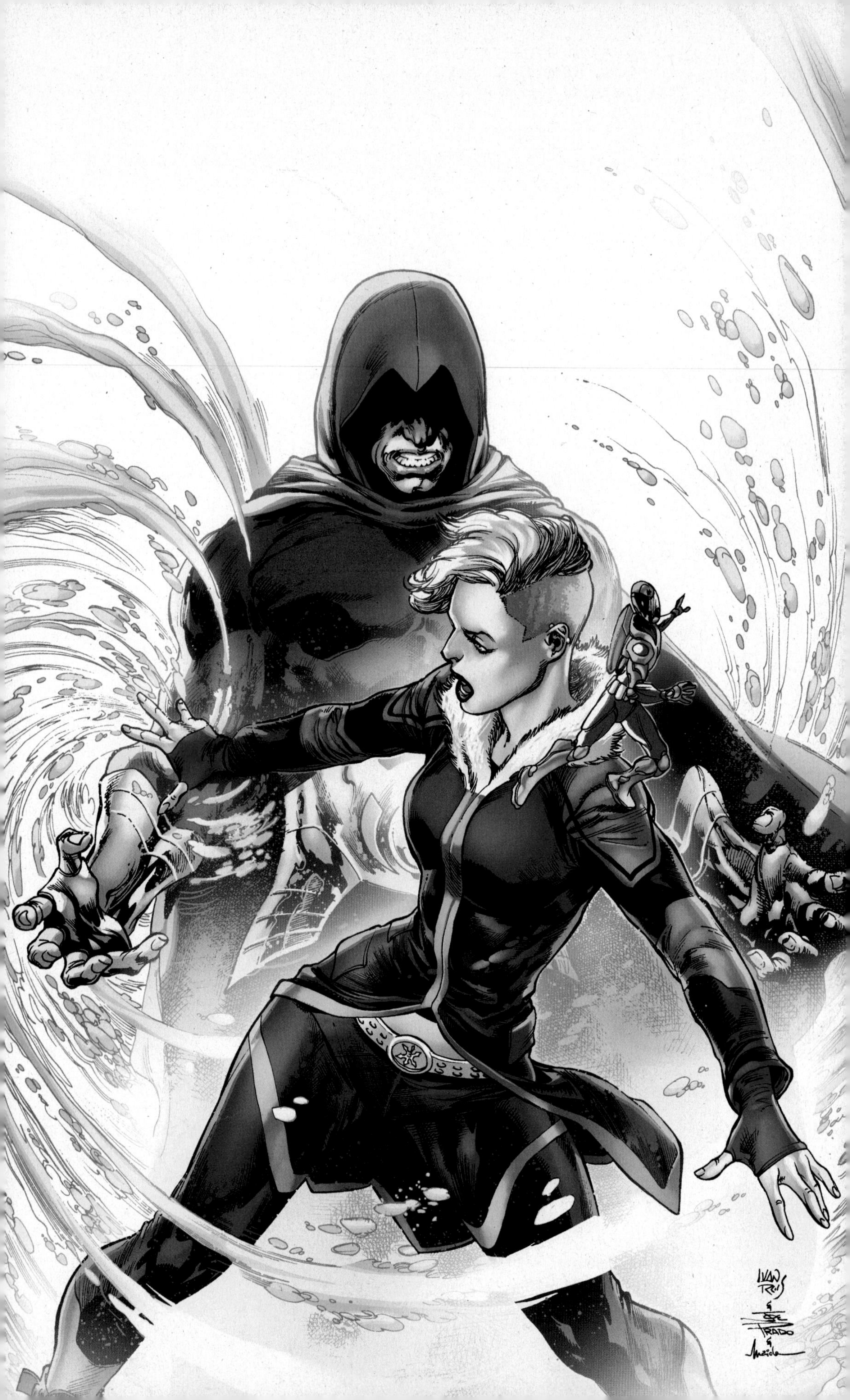

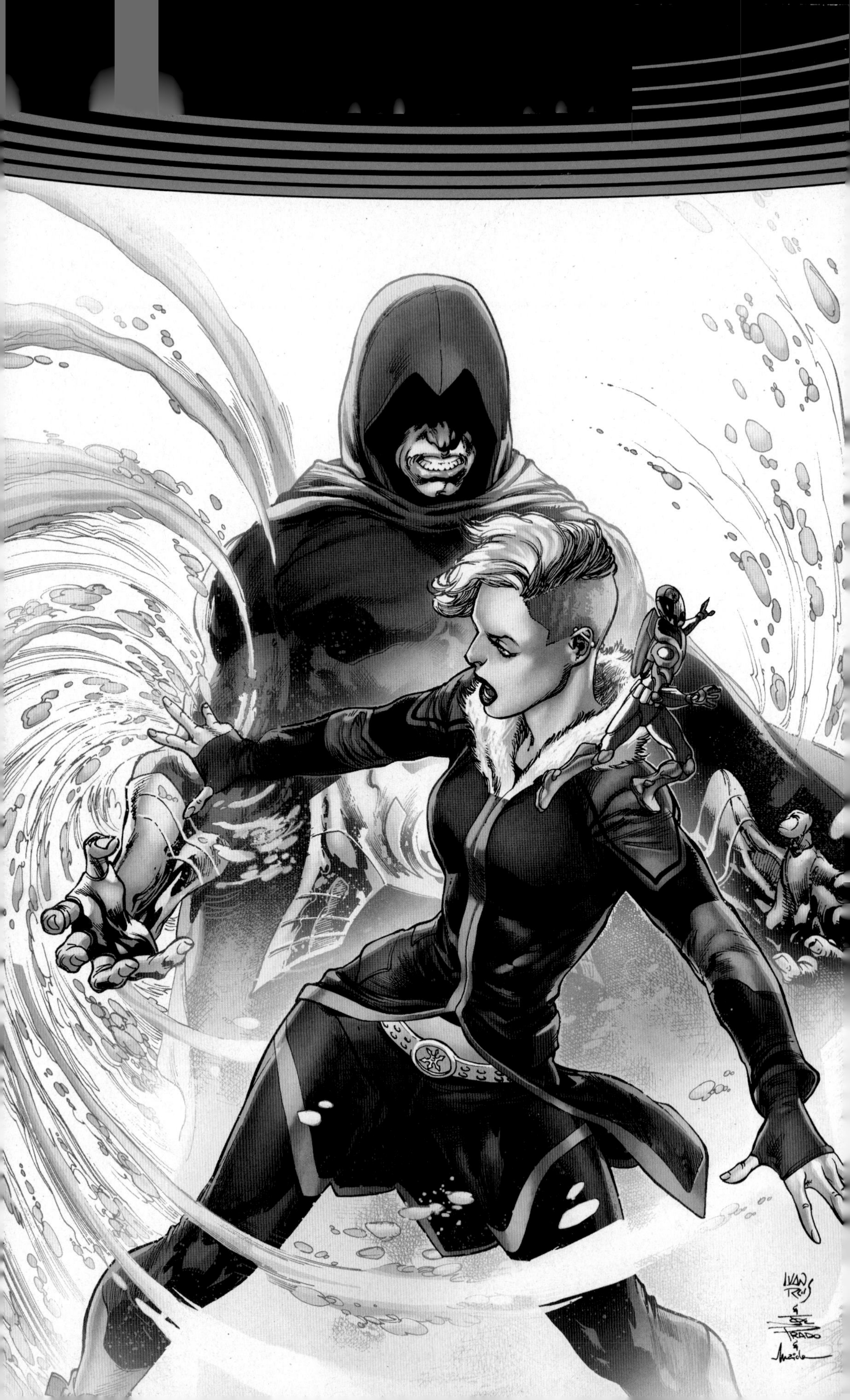

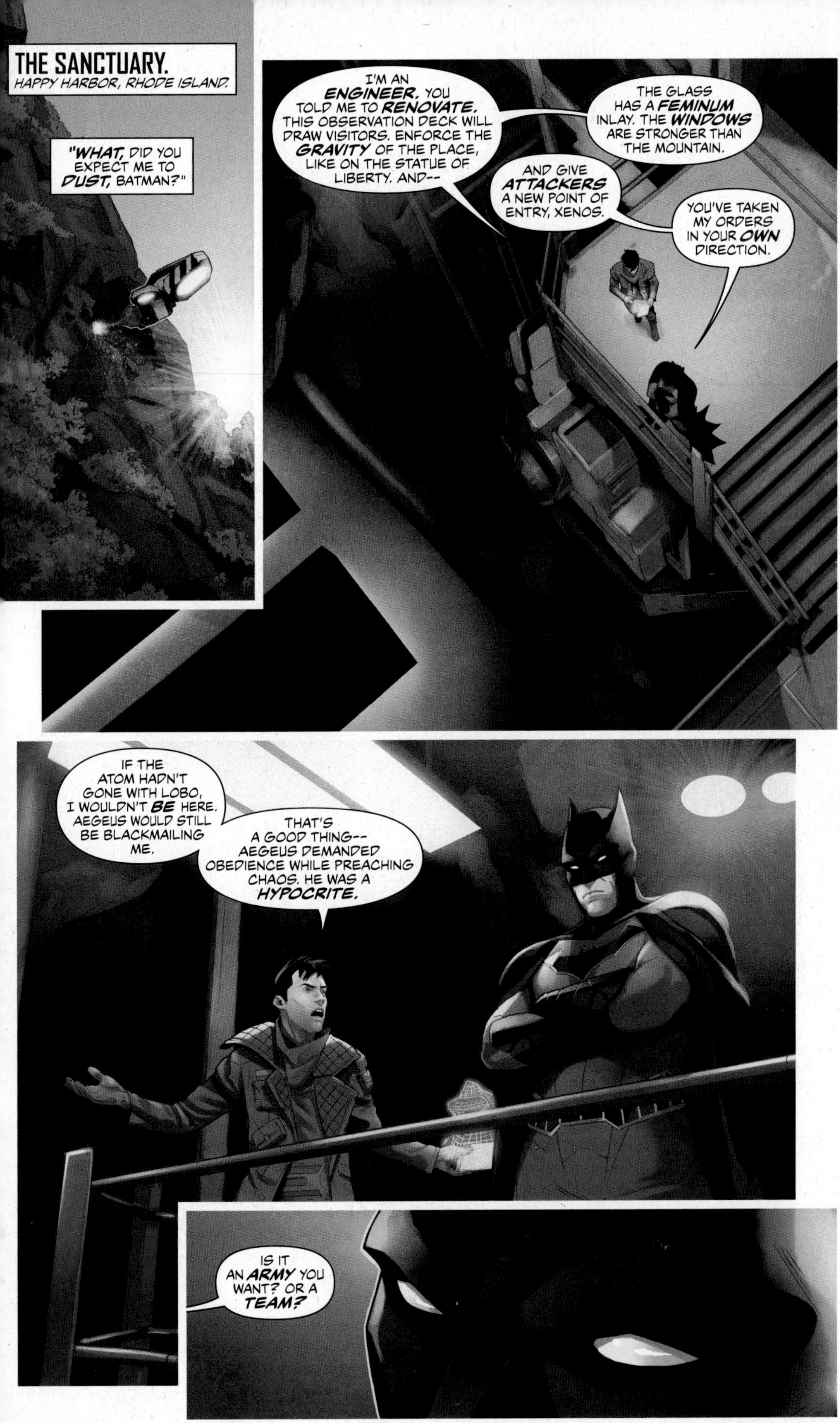
THE SANCTUARY.
HAPPY HARBOR, RHODE ISLAND.
"WHAT, DID YOU EXPECT ME TO DUST, BATMAN?"
I'M AN ENGINEER. YOU TOLD ME TO RENOVATE. THIS OBSERVATION DECK WILL DRAW VISITORS. ENFORCE THE GRAVITY OF THE PLACE, LIKE ON THE STATUE OF LIBERTY. AND--
THE GLASS HAS A FEMINUM INLAY. THE WINDOWS ARE STRONGER THAN THE MOUNTAIN.
AND GIVE ATTACKERS A NEW POINT OF ENTRY, XENOS.
YOU'VE TAKEN MY ORDERS IN YOUR OWN DIRECTION.
IF THE ATOM HADN'T GONE WITH LOBO, I WOULDN'T BE HERE. AEGEUS WOULD STILL BE BLACKMAILING ME.
THAT'S A GOOD THING-- AEGEUS DEMANDED OBEDIENCE WHILE PREACHING CHAOS. HE WAS A HYPOCRITE.
IS IT AN ARMY YOU WANT? OR A TEAM?

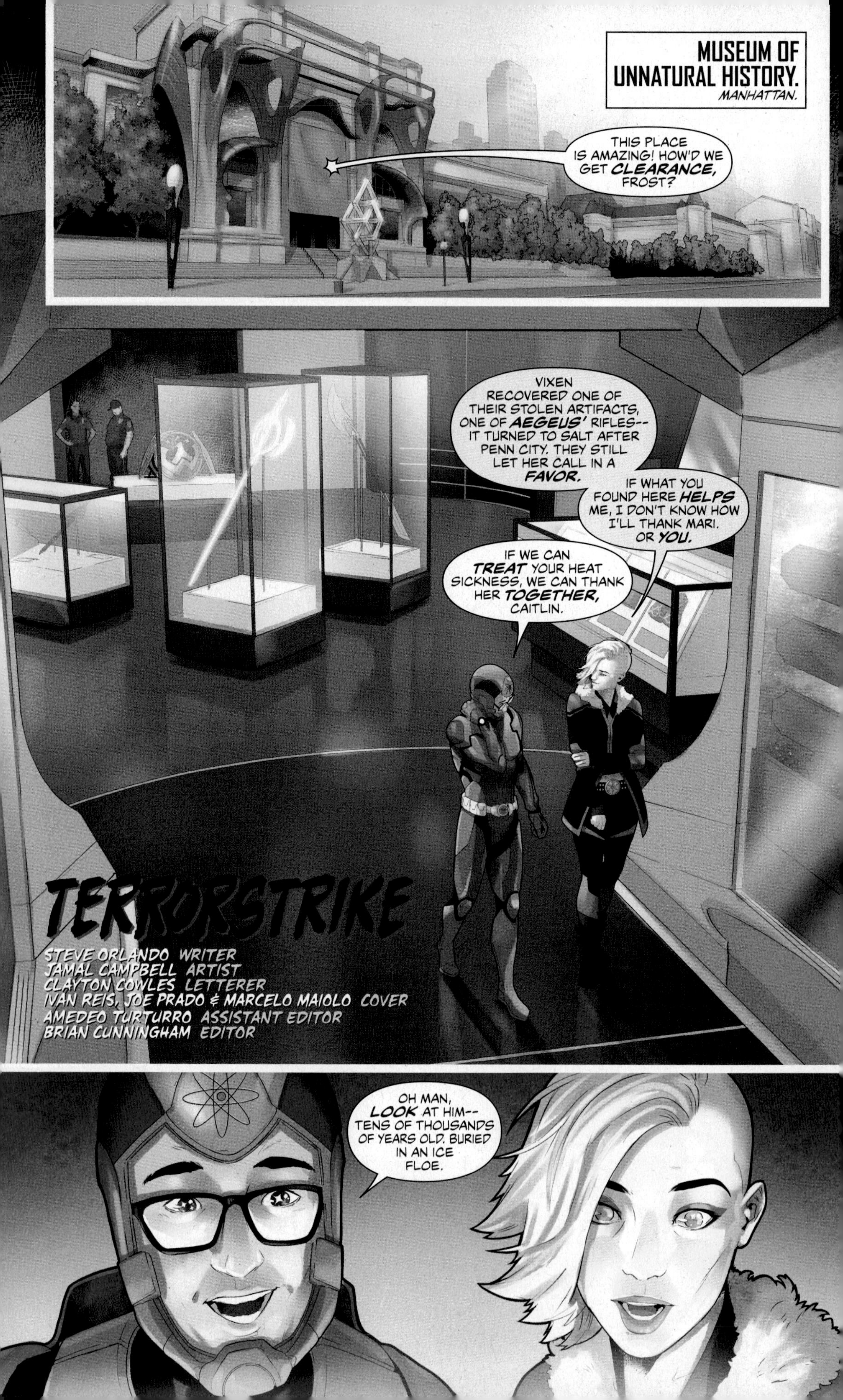
MUSEUM OF UNNATURAL HISTORY.
MANHATTAN.
THIS PLACE IS AMAZING! HOW'D WE GET CLEARANCE, FROST?
VIXEN RECOVERED ONE OF THEIR STOLEN ARTIFACTS, ONE OF AEGEUS' RIFLES--IT TURNED TO SALT AFTER PENN CITY. THEY STILL LET HER CALL IN A FAVOR.
IF WHAT YOU FOUND HERE HELPS ME, I DON'T KNOW HOW I'LL THANK MARI. OR YOU.
IF WE CAN TREAT YOUR HEAT SICKNESS, WE CAN THANK HER TOGETHER, CAITLIN.
TERRORSTRIKE
STEVE ORLANDO WRITER
JAMAL CAMPBELL ARTIST
CLAYTON COWLES LETTERER
IVAN REIS, JOE PRADO & MARCELO MAIOLO COVER
AMEDEO TURTURRO ASSISTANT EDITOR
BRIAN CUNNINGHAM EDITOR
OH MAN, LOOK AT HIM--TENS OF THOUSANDS OF YEARS OLD. BURIED IN AN ICE FLOE.

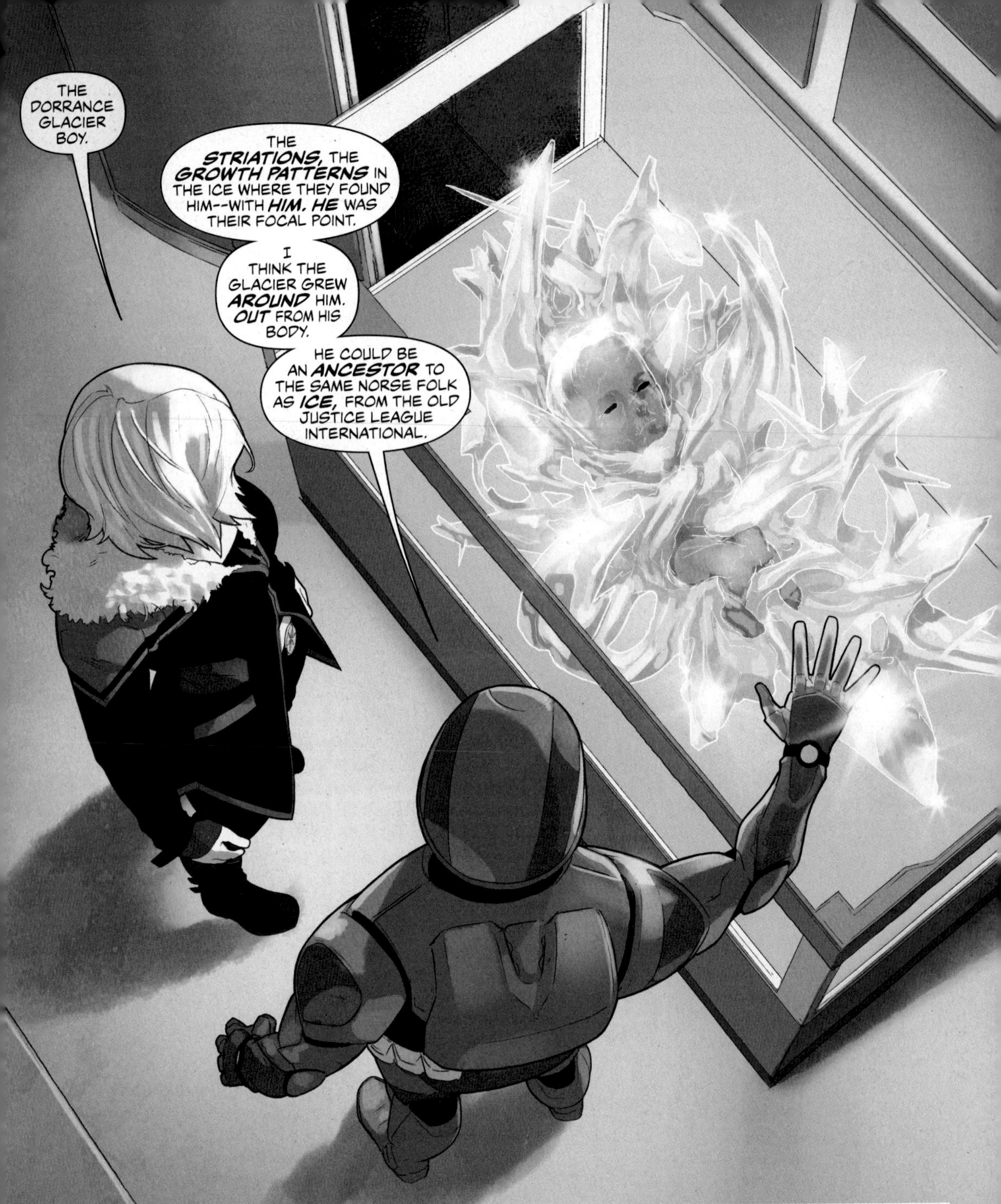
THE DORRANCE GLACIER BOY.
THE STRIATIONS, THE GROWTH PATTERNS IN THE ICE WHERE THEY FOUND HIM--WITH HIM. HE WAS THEIR FOCAL POINT.
I THINK THE GLACIER GREW AROUND HIM. OUT FROM HIS BODY.
HE COULD BE AN ANCESTOR TO THE SAME NORSE FOLK AS ICE, FROM THE OLD JUSTICE LEAGUE INTERNATIONAL.

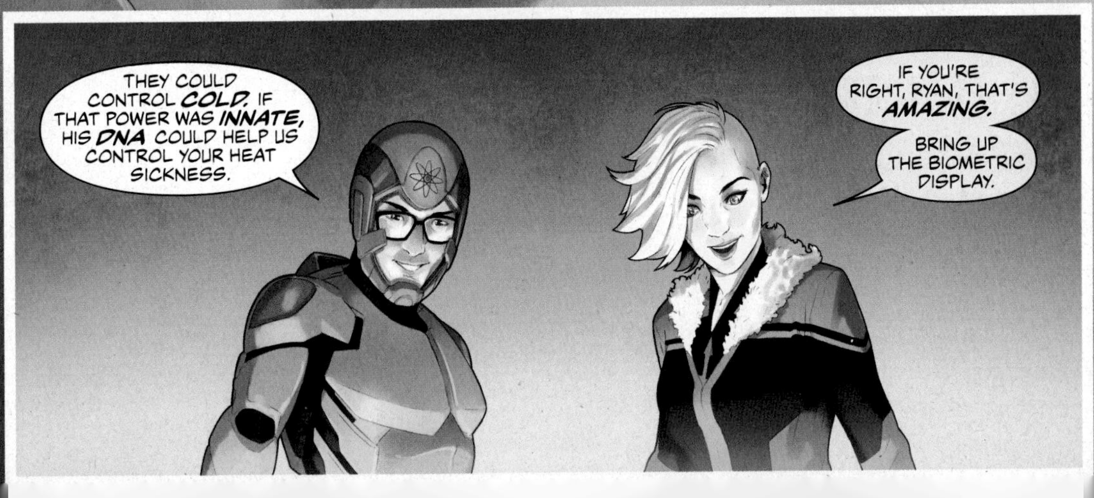
THEY COULD CONTROL COLD. IF THAT POWER WAS INNATE, HIS DNA COULD HELP US CONTROL YOUR HEAT SICKNESS.
IF YOU'RE RIGHT, RYAN, THAT'S AMAZING.
BRING UP THE BIOMETRIC DISPLAY.

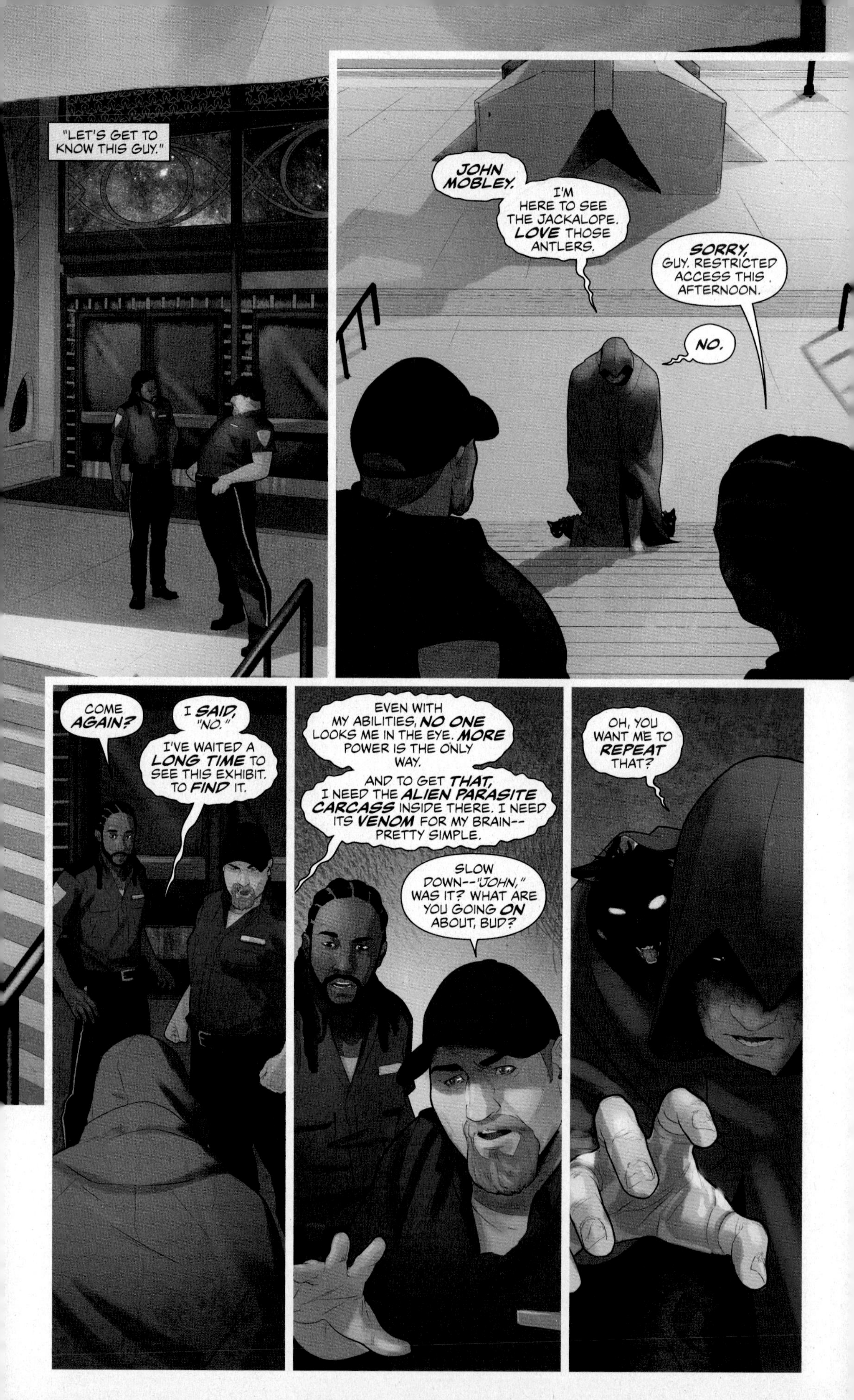
"LET'S GET TO KNOW THIS GUY."
JOHN MOBLEY.
I'M HERE TO SEE THE JACKALOPE. LOVE THOSE ANTLERS.
SORRY, GUY. RESTRICTED ACCESS THIS AFTERNOON.
NO.
COME AGAIN?
I SAID, "NO."
I'VE WAITED A LONG TIME TO SEE THIS EXHIBIT. TO FIND IT.
EVEN WITH MY ABILITIES, NO ONE LOOKS ME IN THE EYE. MORE POWER IS THE ONLY WAY.
AND TO GET THAT, I NEED THE ALIEN PARASITE CARCASS INSIDE THERE. I NEED ITS VENOM FOR MY BRAIN--PRETTY SIMPLE.
SLOW DOWN--"JOHN," WAS IT? WHAT ARE YOU GOING ON ABOUT, BUD?
OH, YOU WANT ME TO REPEAT THAT?

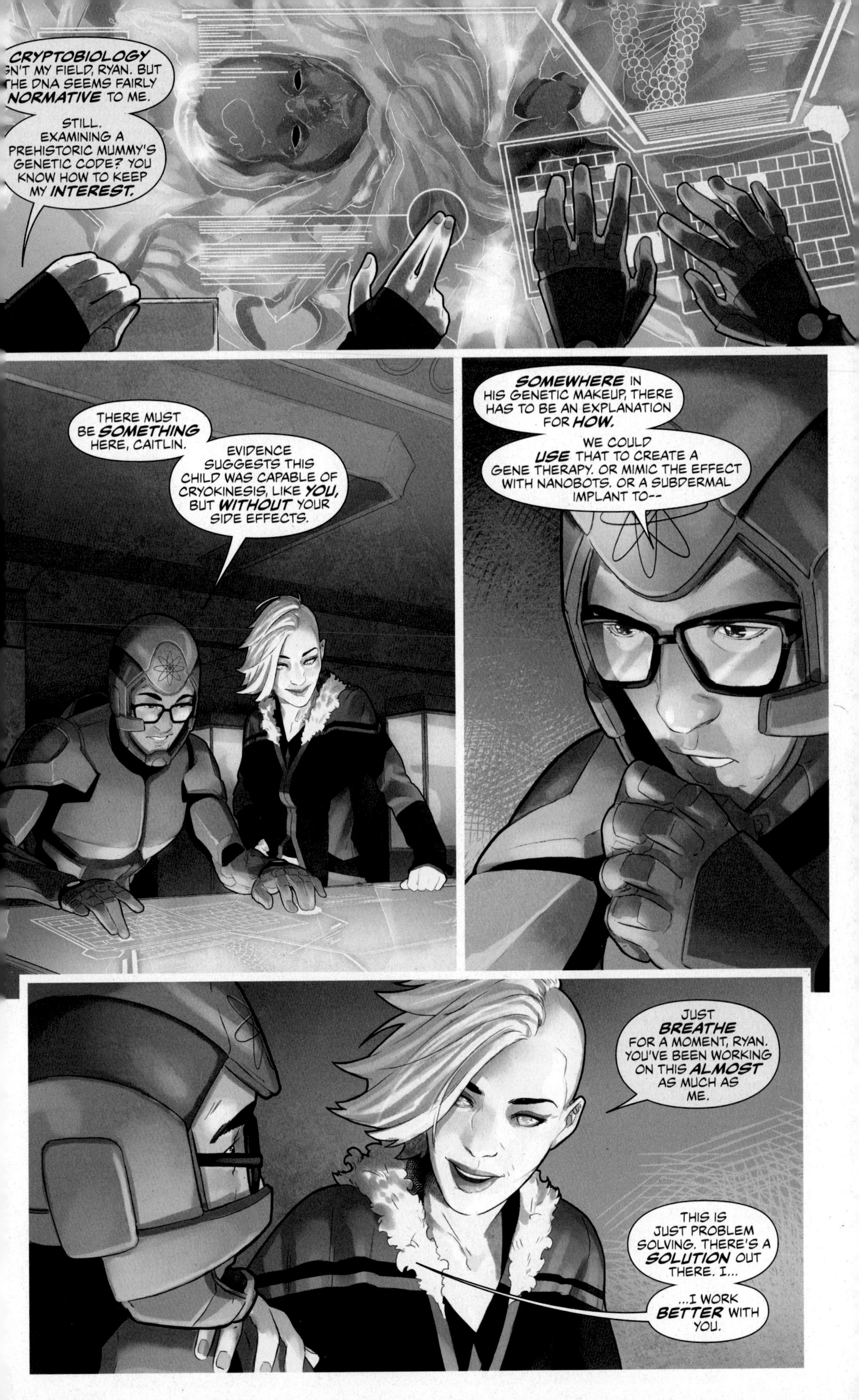

CRYPTOBIOLOGY ISN'T MY FIELD, RYAN. BUT THE DNA SEEMS FAIRLY NORMATIVE TO ME.
STILL. EXAMINING A PREHISTORIC MUMMY'S GENETIC CODE? YOU KNOW HOW TO KEEP MY INTEREST.
THERE MUST BE SOMETHING HERE, CAITLIN.
EVIDENCE SUGGESTS THIS CHILD WAS CAPABLE OF CRYOKINESIS, LIKE YOU, BUT WITHOUT YOUR SIDE EFFECTS.
SOMEWHERE IN HIS GENETIC MAKEUP, THERE HAS TO BE AN EXPLANATION FOR HOW.
WE COULD USE THAT TO CREATE A GENE THERAPY. OR MIMIC THE EFFECT WITH NANOBOTS. OR A SUBDERMAL IMPLANT TO--
JUST BREATHE FOR A MOMENT, RYAN. YOU'VE BEEN WORKING ON THIS ALMOST AS MUCH AS ME.
THIS IS JUST PROBLEM SOLVING. THERE'S A SOLUTION OUT THERE. I...
...I WORK BETTER WITH YOU.

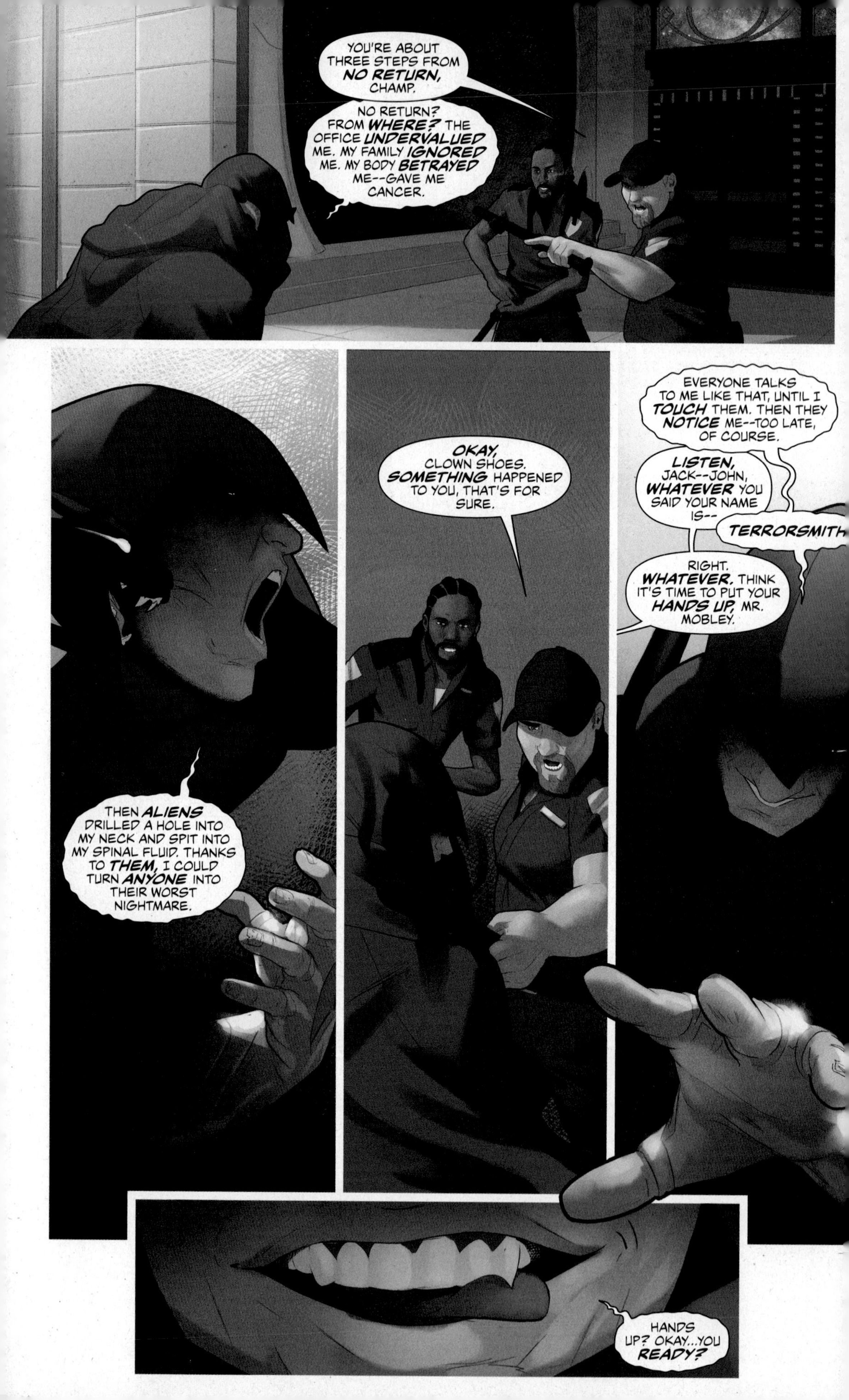
YOU'RE ABOUT THREE STEPS FROM NO RETURN, CHAMP.
NO RETURN? FROM WHERE? THE OFFICE UNDERVALUED ME. MY FAMILY IGNORED ME. MY BODY BETRAYED ME--GAVE ME CANCER.
THEN ALIENS DRILLED A HOLE INTO MY NECK AND SPIT INTO MY SPINAL FLUID. THANKS TO THEM, I COULD TURN ANYONE INTO THEIR WORST NIGHTMARE.
OKAY, CLOWN SHOES. SOMETHING HAPPENED TO YOU, THAT'S FOR SURE.
EVERYONE TALKS TO ME LIKE THAT, UNTIL I TOUCH THEM. THEN THEY NOTICE ME--TOO LATE, OF COURSE.
LISTEN, JACK--JOHN, WHATEVER YOU SAID YOUR NAME IS--
TERRORSMITH
RIGHT. WHATEVER. THINK IT'S TIME TO PUT YOUR HANDS UP, MR. MOBLEY.
HANDS UP? OKAY...YOU READY?

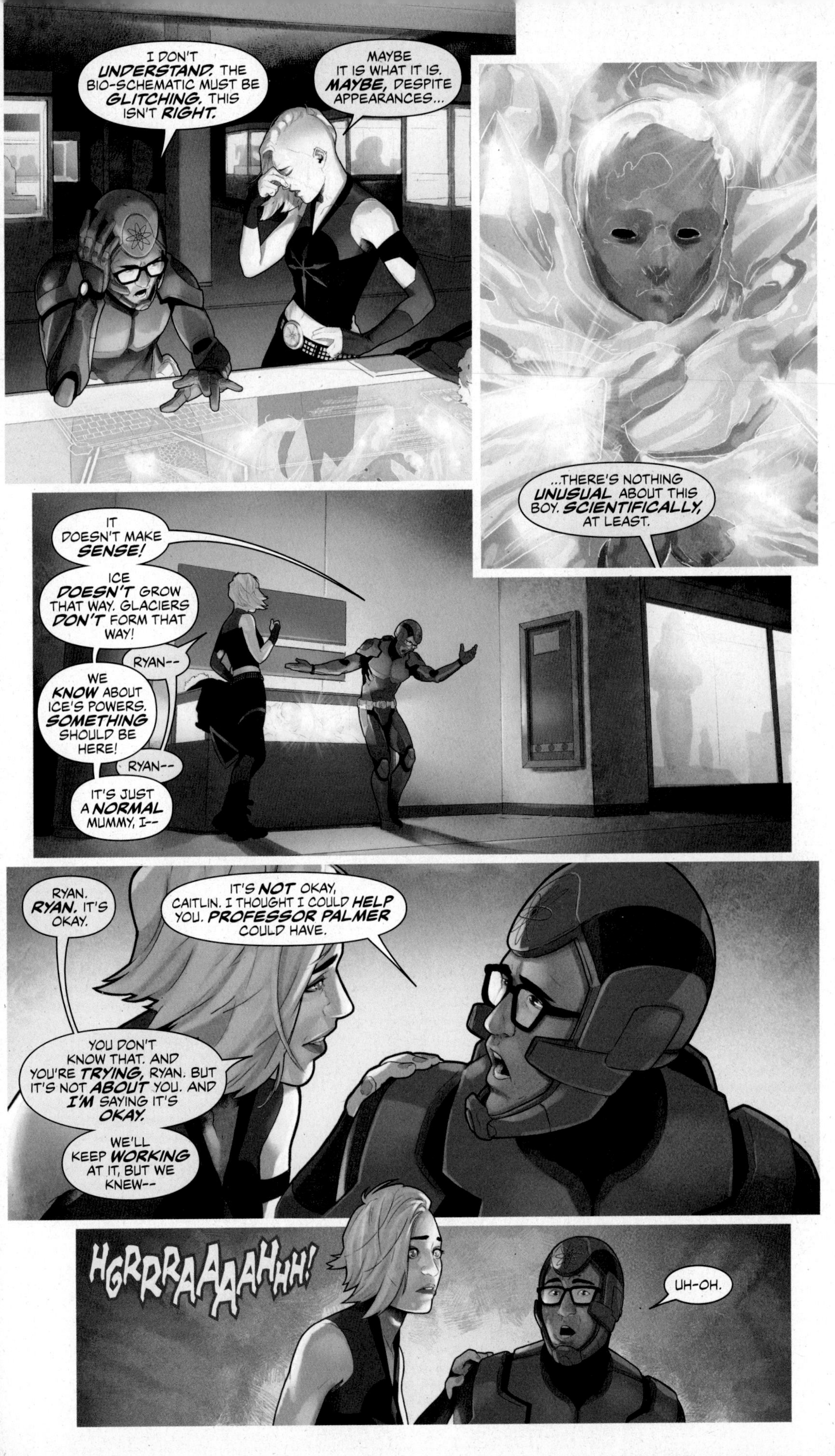

I DON'T UNDERSTAND. THE BIO-SCHEMATIC MUST BE GLITCHING. THIS ISN'T RIGHT.
MAYBE IT IS WHAT IT IS. MAYBE, DESPITE APPEARANCES...
...THERE'S NOTHING UNUSUAL ABOUT THIS BOY. SCIENTIFICALLY, AT LEAST.
IT DOESN'T MAKE SENSE!
ICE DOESN'T GROW THAT WAY. GLACIERS DON'T FORM THAT WAY!
RYAN--
WE KNOW ABOUT ICE'S POWERS. SOMETHING SHOULD BE HERE!
RYAN--
IT'S JUST A NORMAL MUMMY, I--
RYAN. RYAN. IT'S OKAY.
IT'S NOT OKAY, CAITLIN. I THOUGHT I COULD HELP YOU. PROFESSOR PALMER COULD HAVE.
YOU DON'T KNOW THAT. AND YOU'RE TRYING, RYAN. BUT IT'S NOT ABOUT YOU. AND I'M SAYING IT'S OKAY.
WE'LL KEEP WORKING AT IT, BUT WE KNEW--
HGRRRAAAAAHHH!
UH-OH.

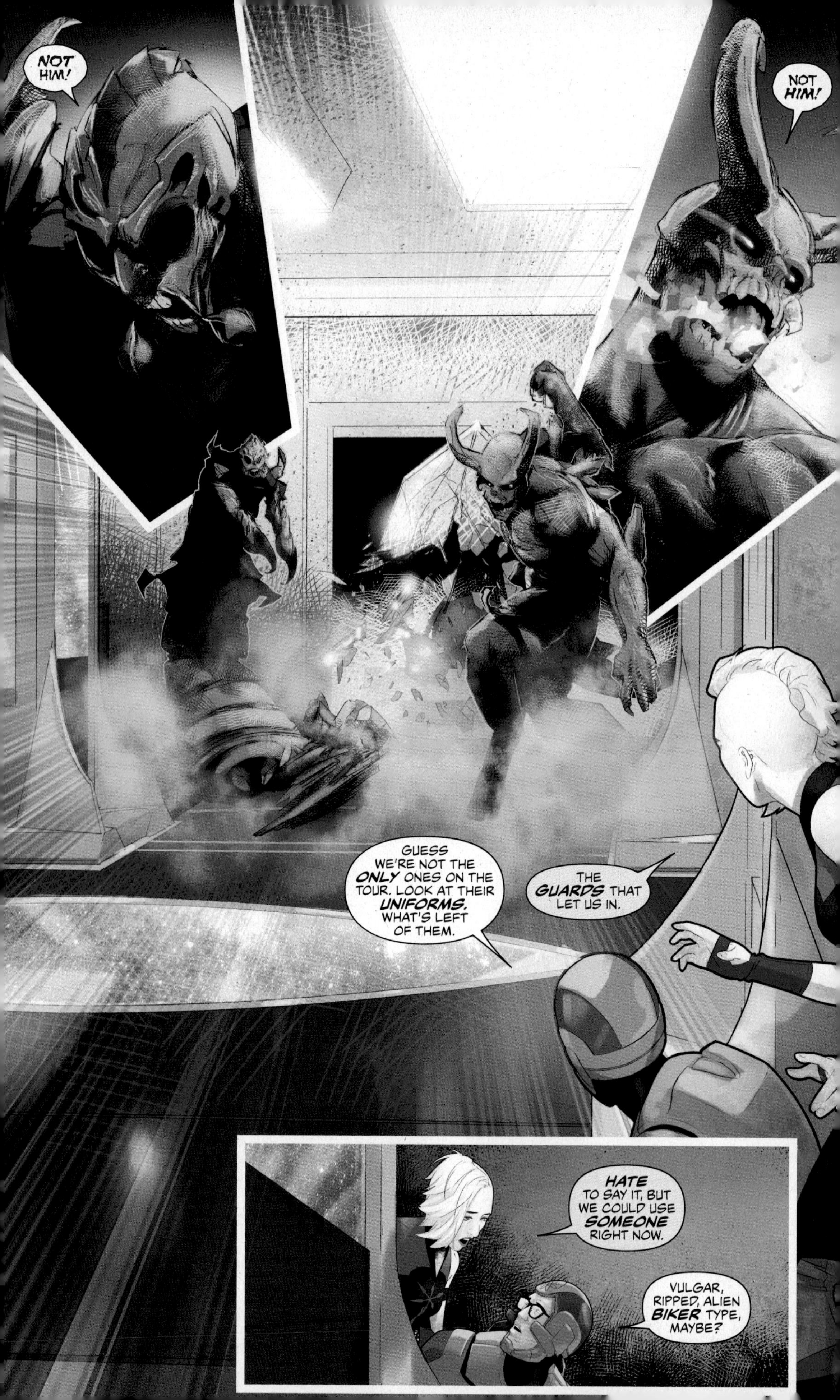
NOT HIM!
NOT HIM!
GUESS WE'RE NOT THE ONLY ONES ON THE TOUR. LOOK AT THEIR UNIFORMS. WHAT'S LEFT OF THEM.
THE GUARDS THAT LET US IN.
HATE TO SAY IT, BUT WE COULD USE SOMEONE RIGHT NOW.
VULGAR, RIPPED, ALIEN BIKER TYPE, MAYBE?

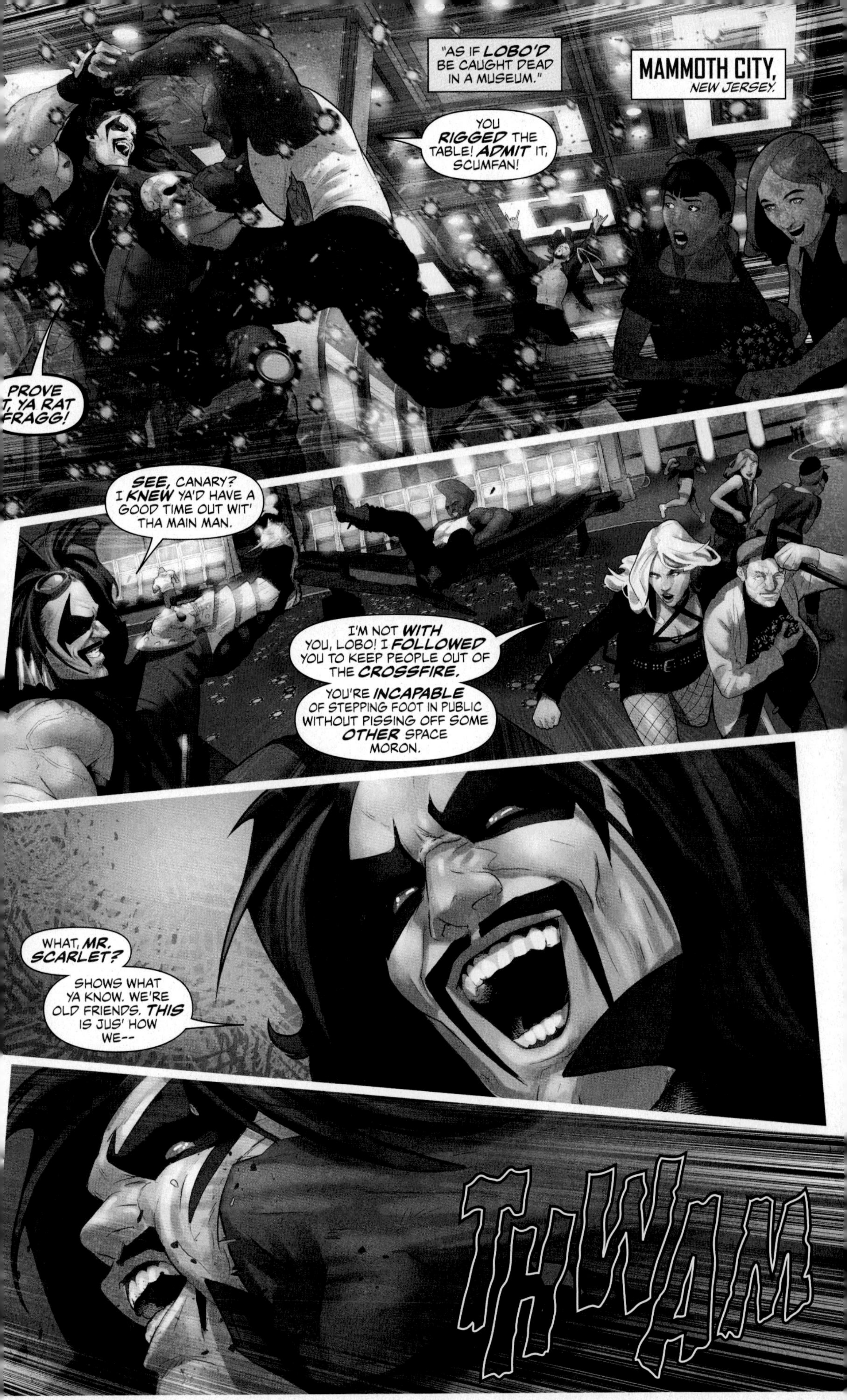

"AS IF LOBO'D BE CAUGHT DEAD IN A MUSEUM."
MAMMOTH CITY, NEW JERSEY.
YOU RIGGED THE TABLE! ADMIT IT, SCUMFAN!
PROVE IT, YA RAT FRAGG!
SEE, CANARY? I KNEW YA'D HAVE A GOOD TIME OUT WIT' THA MAIN MAN.
I'M NOT WITH YOU, LOBO! I FOLLOWED YOU TO KEEP PEOPLE OUT OF THE CROSSFIRE.
YOU'RE INCAPABLE OF STEPPING FOOT IN PUBLIC WITHOUT PISSING OFF SOME OTHER SPACE MORON.
WHAT, MR. SCARLET?
SHOWS WHAT YA KNOW. WE'RE OLD FRIENDS. THIS IS JUS' HOW WE--
THWAM

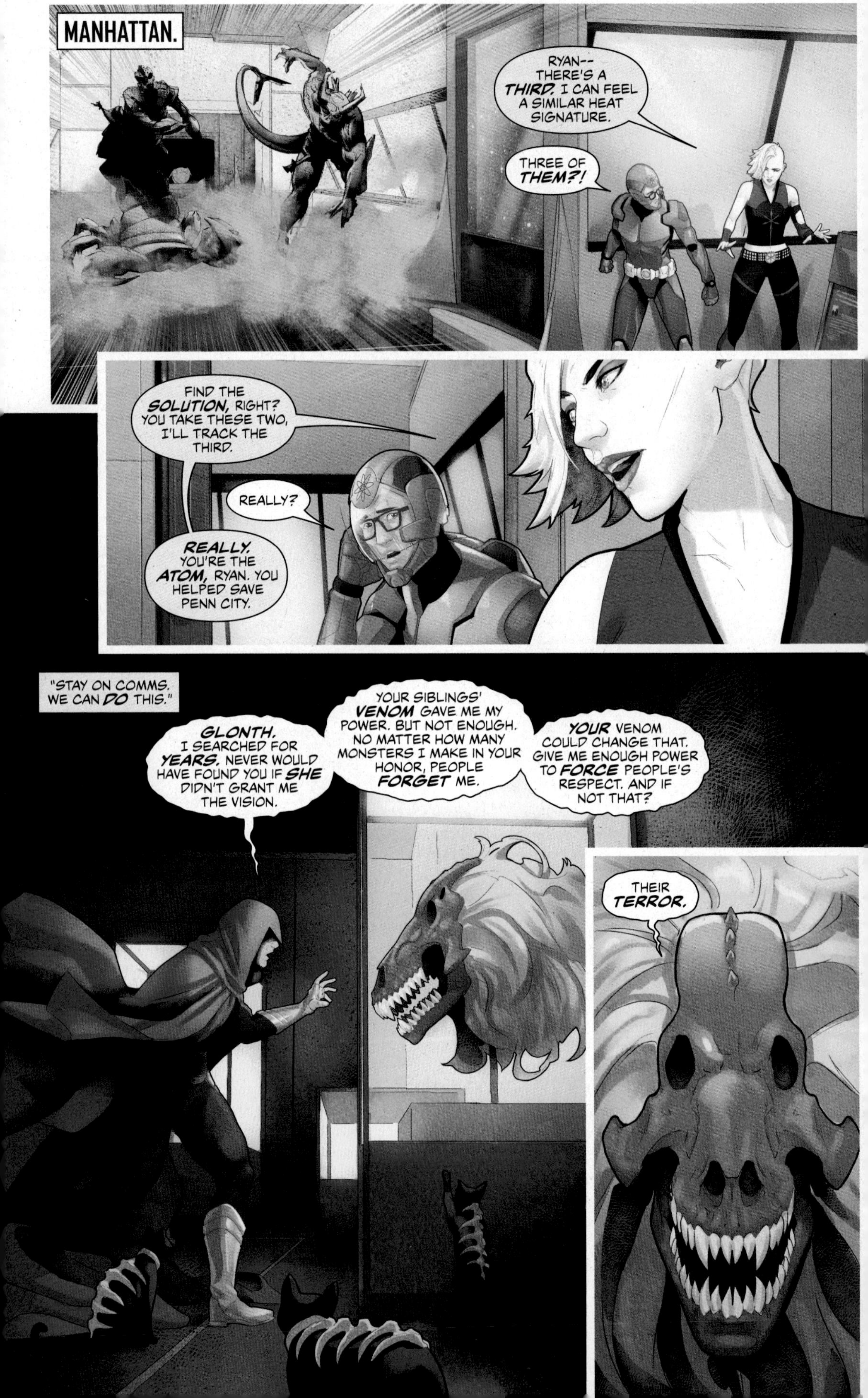
MANHATTAN.
RYAN-- THERE'S A THIRD. I CAN FEEL A SIMILAR HEAT SIGNATURE.
THREE OF THEM?!
FIND THE SOLUTION, RIGHT? YOU TAKE THESE TWO, I'LL TRACK THE THIRD.
REALLY?
REALLY. YOU'RE THE ATOM, RYAN. YOU HELPED SAVE PENN CITY.
"STAY ON COMMS. WE CAN DO THIS."
GLONTH. I SEARCHED FOR YEARS. NEVER WOULD HAVE FOUND YOU IF SHE DIDN'T GRANT ME THE VISION.
YOUR SIBLINGS' VENOM GAVE ME MY POWER. BUT NOT ENOUGH. NO MATTER HOW MANY MONSTERS I MAKE IN YOUR HONOR, PEOPLE FORGET ME.
YOUR VENOM COULD CHANGE THAT. GIVE ME ENOUGH POWER TO FORCE PEOPLE'S RESPECT. AND IF NOT THAT?
THEIR TERROR.

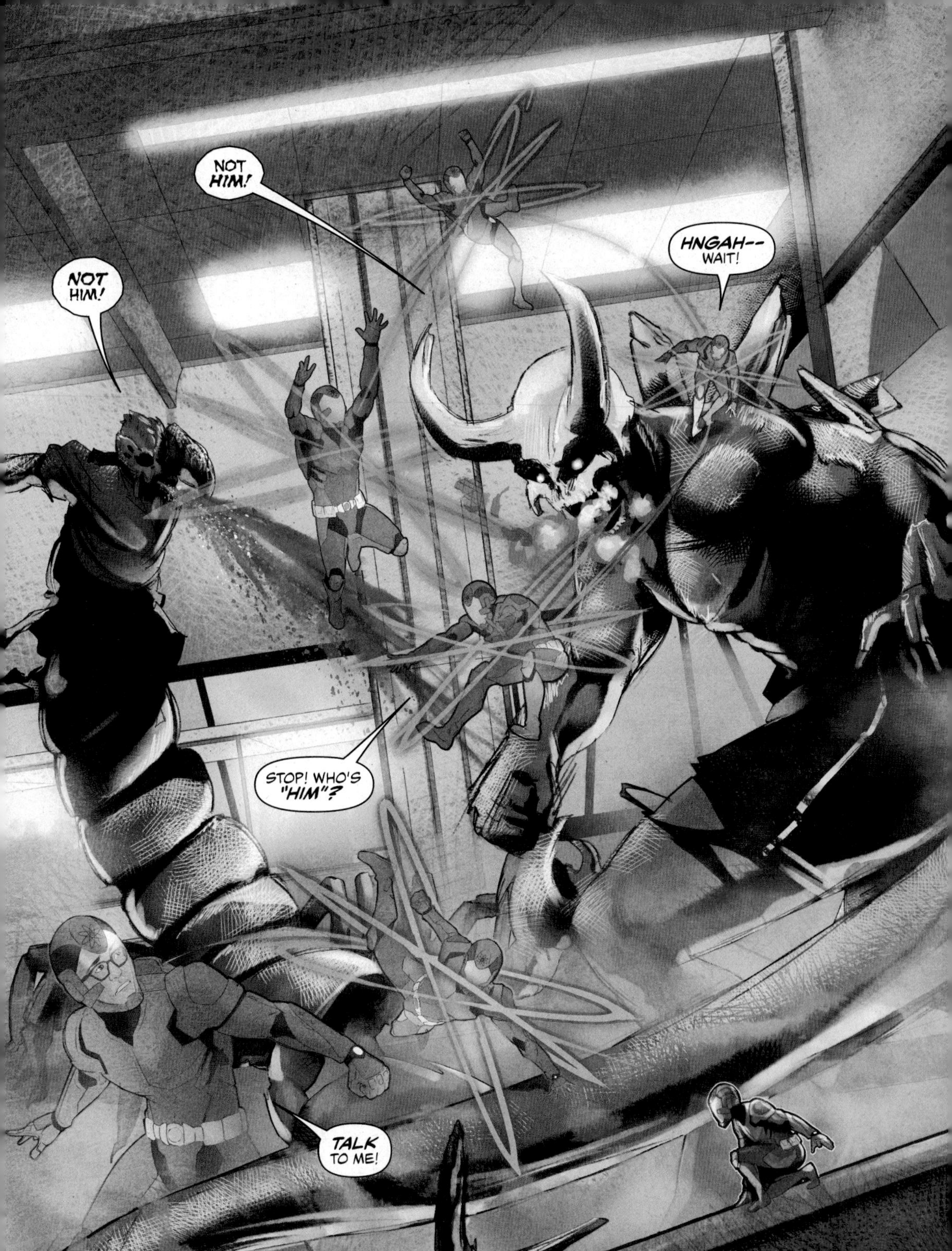

NOT HIM!
NOT HIM!
HNGAH-- WAIT!
STOP! WHO'S "HIM"?
TALK TO ME!

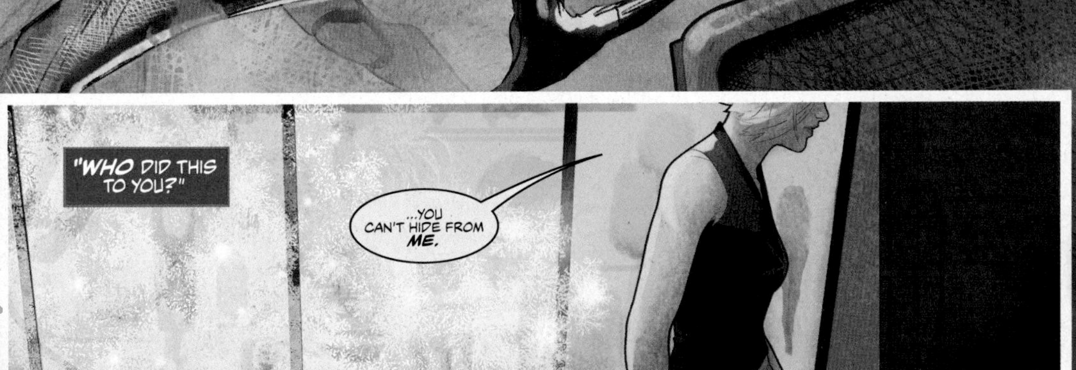

"WHO DID THIS TO YOU?"
...YOU CAN'T HIDE FROM ME.

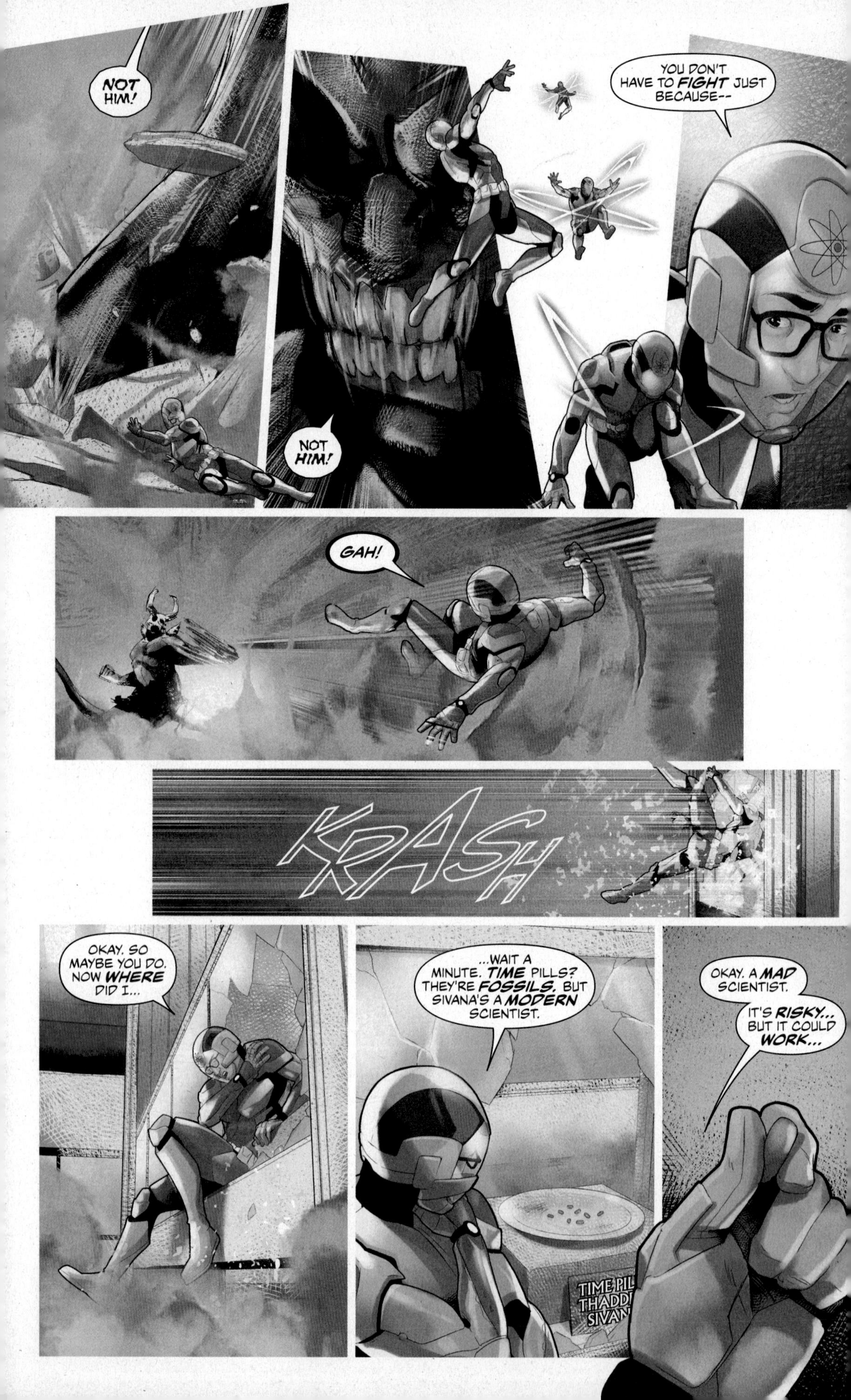

NOT HIM!
NOT HIM!
YOU DON'T HAVE TO FIGHT JUST BECAUSE--
GAH!
KRASH
OKAY. SO MAYBE YOU DO. NOW WHERE DID I...
...WAIT A MINUTE. TIME PILLS? THEY'RE FOSSILS. BUT SIVANA'S A MODERN SCIENTIST.
OKAY. A MAD SCIENTIST.
IT'S RISKY... BUT IT COULD WORK...

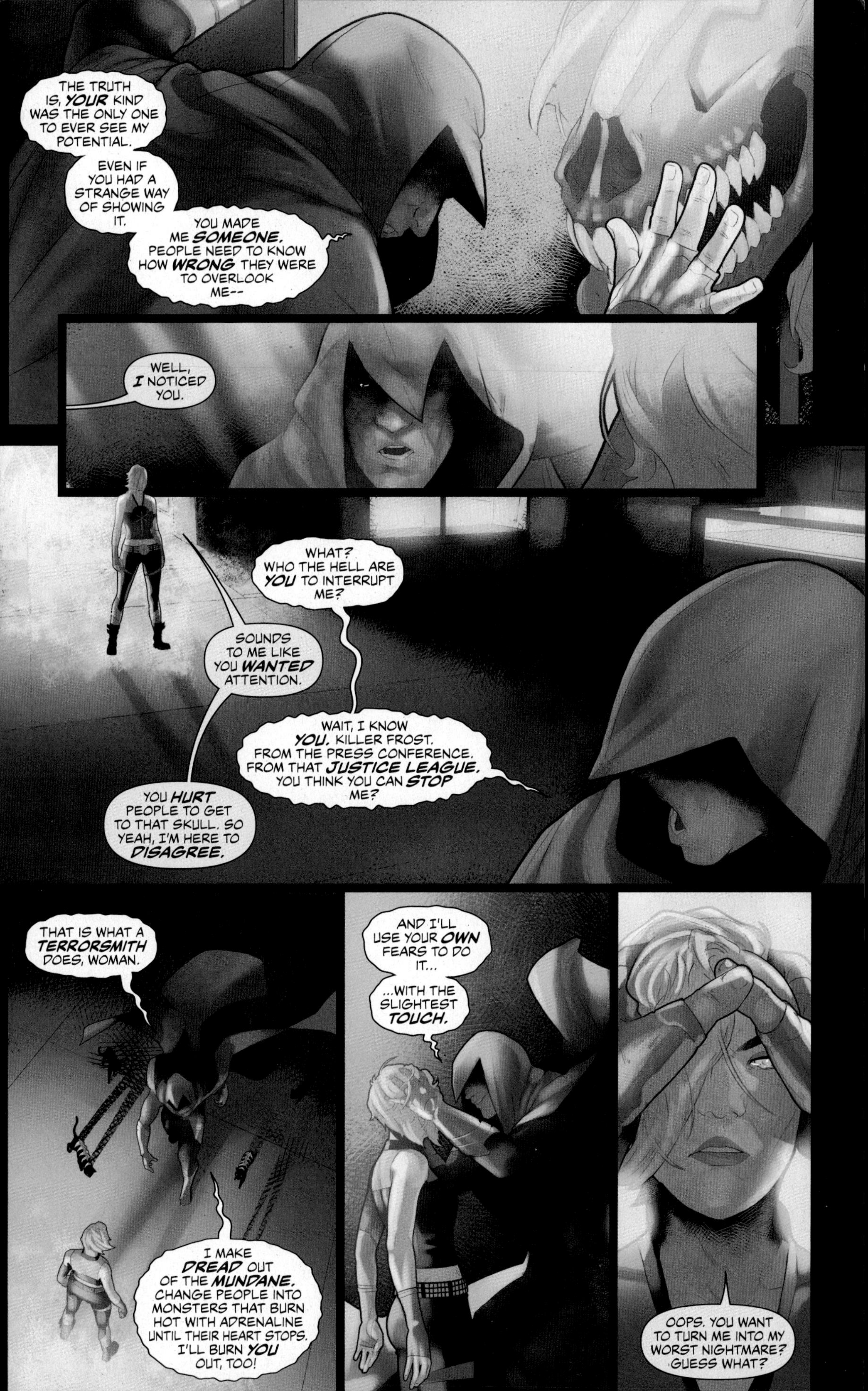
THE TRUTH IS, YOUR KIND WAS THE ONLY ONE TO EVER SEE MY POTENTIAL.
EVEN IF YOU HAD A STRANGE WAY OF SHOWING IT.
YOU MADE ME SOMEONE. PEOPLE NEED TO KNOW HOW WRONG THEY WERE TO OVERLOOK ME--
WELL, I NOTICED YOU.
WHAT? WHO THE HELL ARE YOU TO INTERRUPT ME?
SOUNDS TO ME LIKE YOU WANTED ATTENTION.
WAIT, I KNOW YOU. KILLER FROST. FROM THE PRESS CONFERENCE. FROM THAT JUSTICE LEAGUE. YOU THINK YOU CAN STOP ME?
YOU HURT PEOPLE TO GET TO THAT SKULL. SO YEAH, I'M HERE TO DISAGREE.
THAT IS WHAT A TERRORSMITH DOES, WOMAN.
I MAKE DREAD OUT OF THE MUNDANE. CHANGE PEOPLE INTO MONSTERS THAT BURN HOT WITH ADRENALINE UNTIL THEIR HEART STOPS. I'LL BURN YOU OUT, TOO!
AND I'LL USE YOUR OWN FEARS TO DO IT...
...WITH THE SLIGHTEST TOUCH.
OOPS. YOU WANT TO TURN ME INTO MY WORST NIGHTMARE? GUESS WHAT?

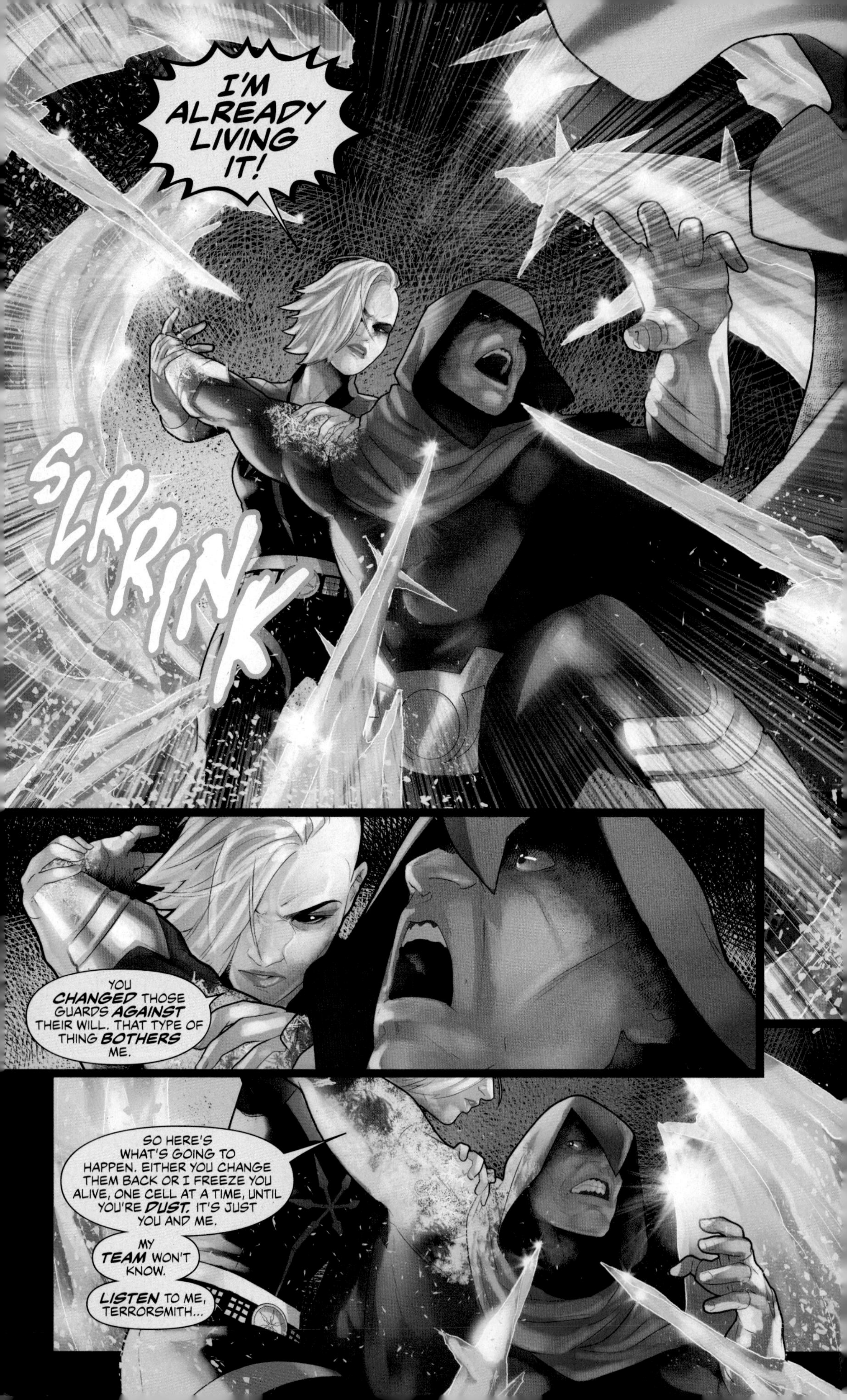
I'M ALREADY LIVING IT!
SLRRINK
YOU CHANGED THOSE GUARDS AGAINST THEIR WILL. THAT TYPE OF THING BOTHERS ME.
SO HERE'S WHAT'S GOING TO HAPPEN. EITHER YOU CHANGE THEM BACK OR I FREEZE YOU ALIVE, ONE CELL AT A TIME, UNTIL YOU'RE DUST. IT'S JUST YOU AND ME.
MY TEAM WON'T KNOW.
LISTEN TO ME, TERRORSMITH...

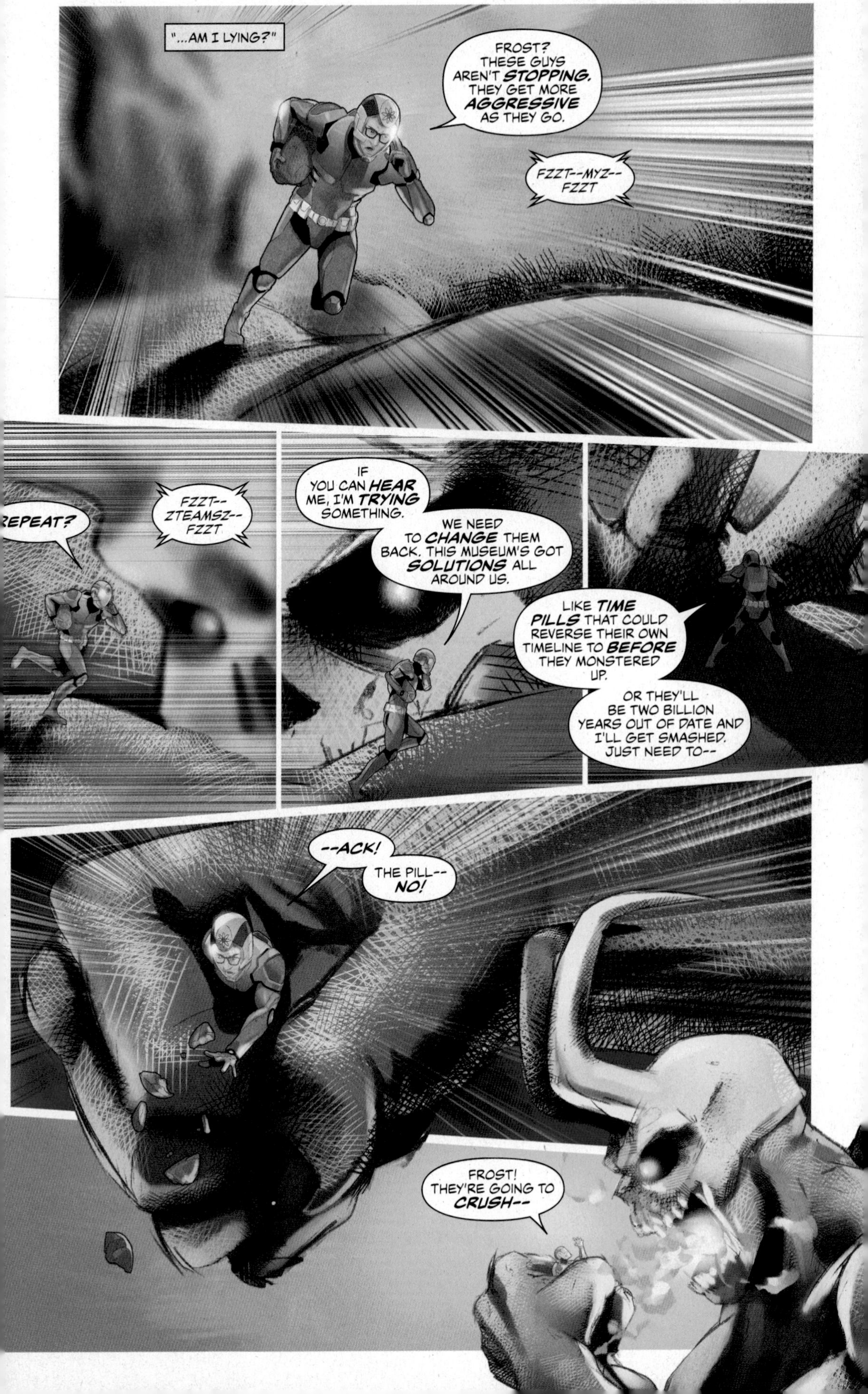
"...AM I LYING?"
FROST? THESE GUYS AREN'T STOPPING. THEY GET MORE AGGRESSIVE AS THEY GO.
FZZT--MYZ--FZZT
REPEAT?
FZZT--ZTEAMSZ--FZZT
IF YOU CAN HEAR ME, I'M TRYING SOMETHING.
WE NEED TO CHANGE THEM BACK. THIS MUSEUM'S GOT SOLUTIONS ALL AROUND US.
LIKE TIME PILLS THAT COULD REVERSE THEIR OWN TIMELINE TO BEFORE THEY MONSTERED UP.
OR THEY'LL BE TWO BILLION YEARS OUT OF DATE AND I'LL GET SMASHED. JUST NEED TO--
--ACK!
THE PILL-- NO!
FROST! THEY'RE GOING TO CRUSH--

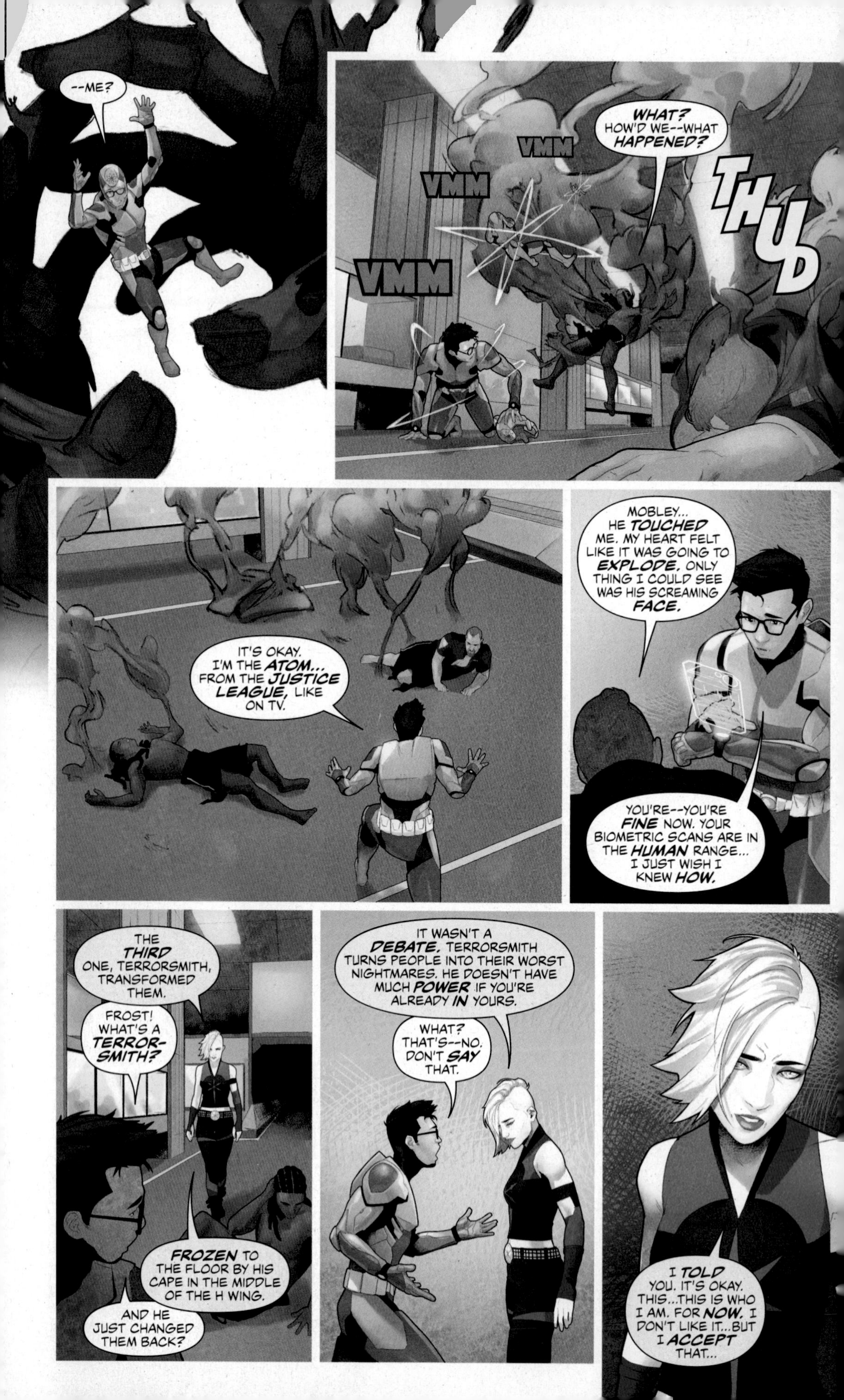
--ME?
WHAT? HOW'D WE--WHAT HAPPENED?
VMM
VMM
VMM
THUD
IT'S OKAY. I'M THE ATOM... FROM THE JUSTICE LEAGUE, LIKE ON TV.
MOBLEY... HE TOUCHED ME. MY HEART FELT LIKE IT WAS GOING TO EXPLODE. ONLY THING I COULD SEE WAS HIS SCREAMING FACE.
YOU'RE--YOU'RE FINE NOW. YOUR BIOMETRIC SCANS ARE IN THE HUMAN RANGE... I JUST WISH I KNEW HOW.
THE THIRD ONE, TERRORSMITH, TRANSFORMED THEM.
FROST! WHAT'S A TERROR-SMITH?
FROZEN TO THE FLOOR BY HIS CAPE IN THE MIDDLE OF THE H WING.
AND HE JUST CHANGED THEM BACK?
IT WASN'T A DEBATE. TERRORSMITH TURNS PEOPLE INTO THEIR WORST NIGHTMARES. HE DOESN'T HAVE MUCH POWER IF YOU'RE ALREADY IN YOURS.
WHAT? THAT'S--NO. DON'T SAY THAT.
I TOLD YOU. IT'S OKAY. THIS...THIS IS WHO I AM. FOR NOW. I DON'T LIKE IT...BUT I ACCEPT THAT...

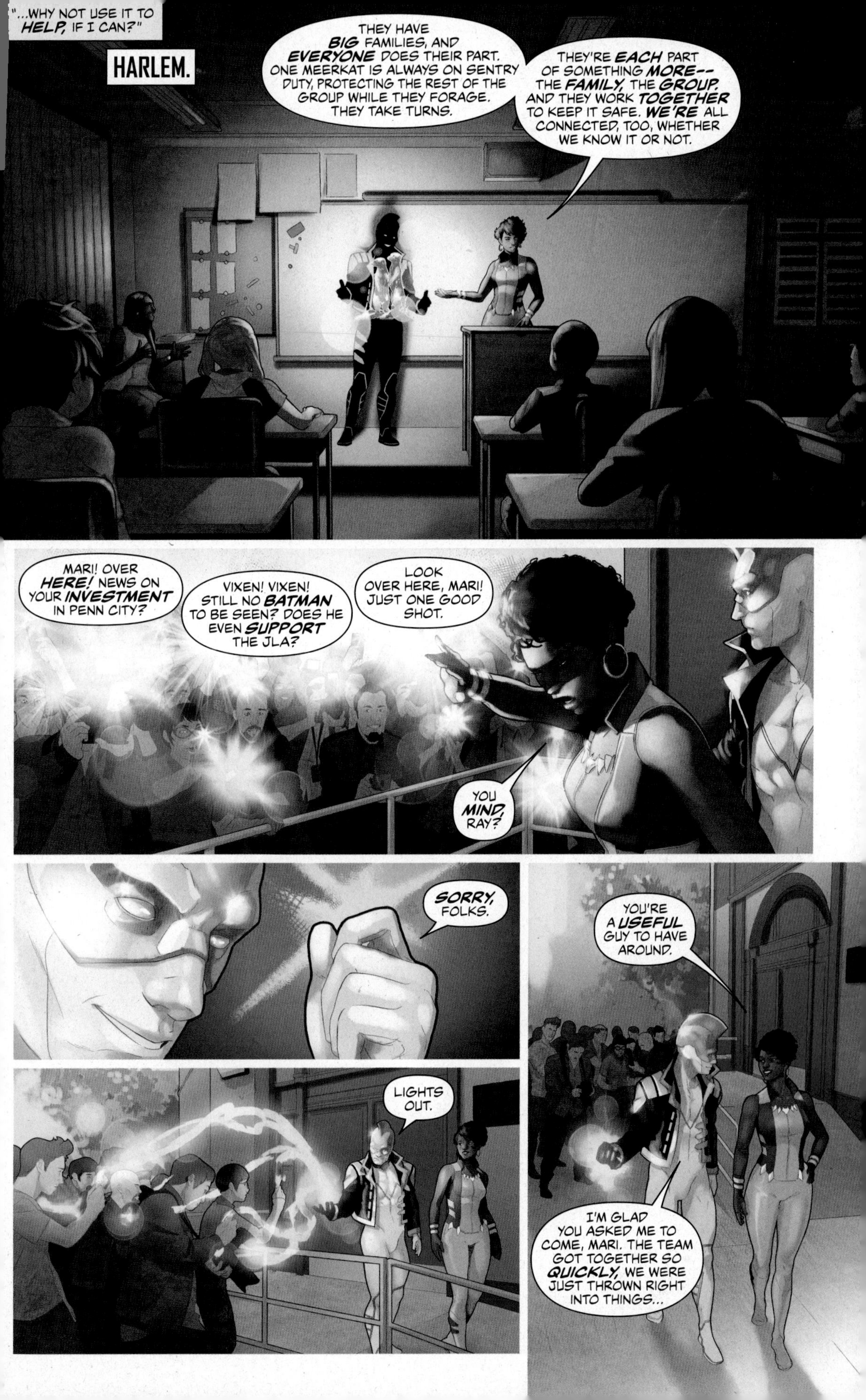
"...WHY NOT USE IT TO HELP, IF I CAN?"
HARLEM.
THEY HAVE BIG FAMILIES, AND EVERYONE DOES THEIR PART. ONE MEERKAT IS ALWAYS ON SENTRY DUTY, PROTECTING THE REST OF THE GROUP WHILE THEY FORAGE. THEY TAKE TURNS.
THEY'RE EACH PART OF SOMETHING MORE-- THE FAMILY, THE GROUP, AND THEY WORK TOGETHER TO KEEP IT SAFE. WE'RE ALL CONNECTED, TOO, WHETHER WE KNOW IT OR NOT.
MARI! OVER HERE! NEWS ON YOUR INVESTMENT IN PENN CITY?
VIXEN! VIXEN! STILL NO BATMAN TO BE SEEN? DOES HE EVEN SUPPORT THE JLA?
LOOK OVER HERE, MARI! JUST ONE GOOD SHOT.
YOU MIND, RAY?
SORRY, FOLKS.
LIGHTS OUT.
YOU'RE A USEFUL GUY TO HAVE AROUND.
I'M GLAD YOU ASKED ME TO COME, MARI. THE TEAM GOT TOGETHER SO QUICKLY, WE WERE JUST THROWN RIGHT INTO THINGS...

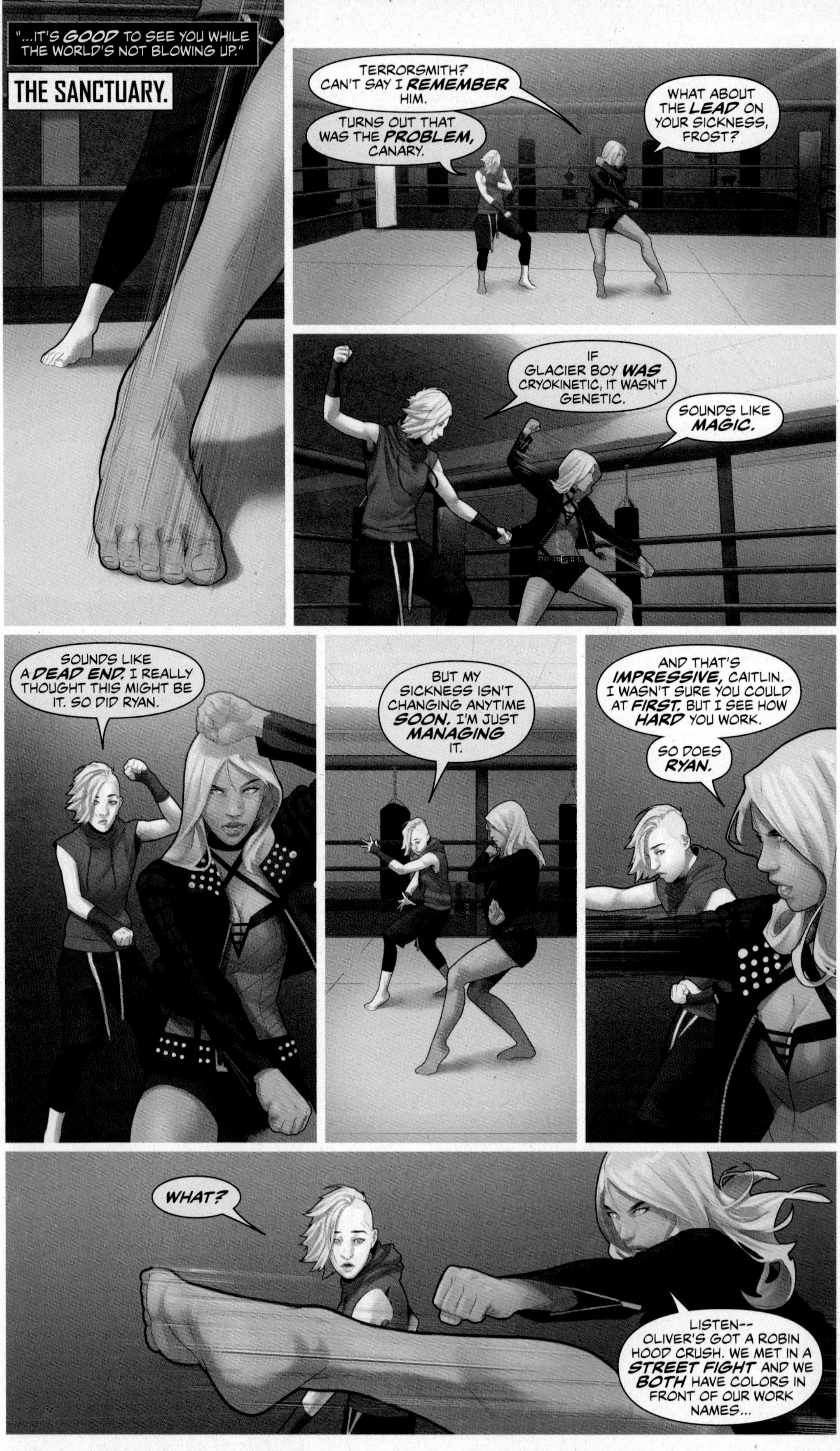
"...IT'S GOOD TO SEE YOU WHILE THE WORLD'S NOT BLOWING UP."
THE SANCTUARY.
TERRORSMITH? CAN'T SAY I REMEMBER HIM.
TURNS OUT THAT WAS THE PROBLEM, CANARY.
WHAT ABOUT THE LEAD ON YOUR SICKNESS, FROST?
IF GLACIER BOY WAS CRYOKINETIC, IT WASN'T GENETIC.
SOUNDS LIKE MAGIC.
SOUNDS LIKE A DEAD END. I REALLY THOUGHT THIS MIGHT BE IT. SO DID RYAN.
BUT MY SICKNESS ISN'T CHANGING ANYTIME SOON. I'M JUST MANAGING IT.
AND THAT'S IMPRESSIVE, CAITLIN. I WASN'T SURE YOU COULD AT FIRST. BUT I SEE HOW HARD YOU WORK.
SO DOES RYAN.
WHAT?
LISTEN-- OLIVER'S GOT A ROBIN HOOD CRUSH. WE MET IN A STREET FIGHT AND WE BOTH HAVE COLORS IN FRONT OF OUR WORK NAMES...

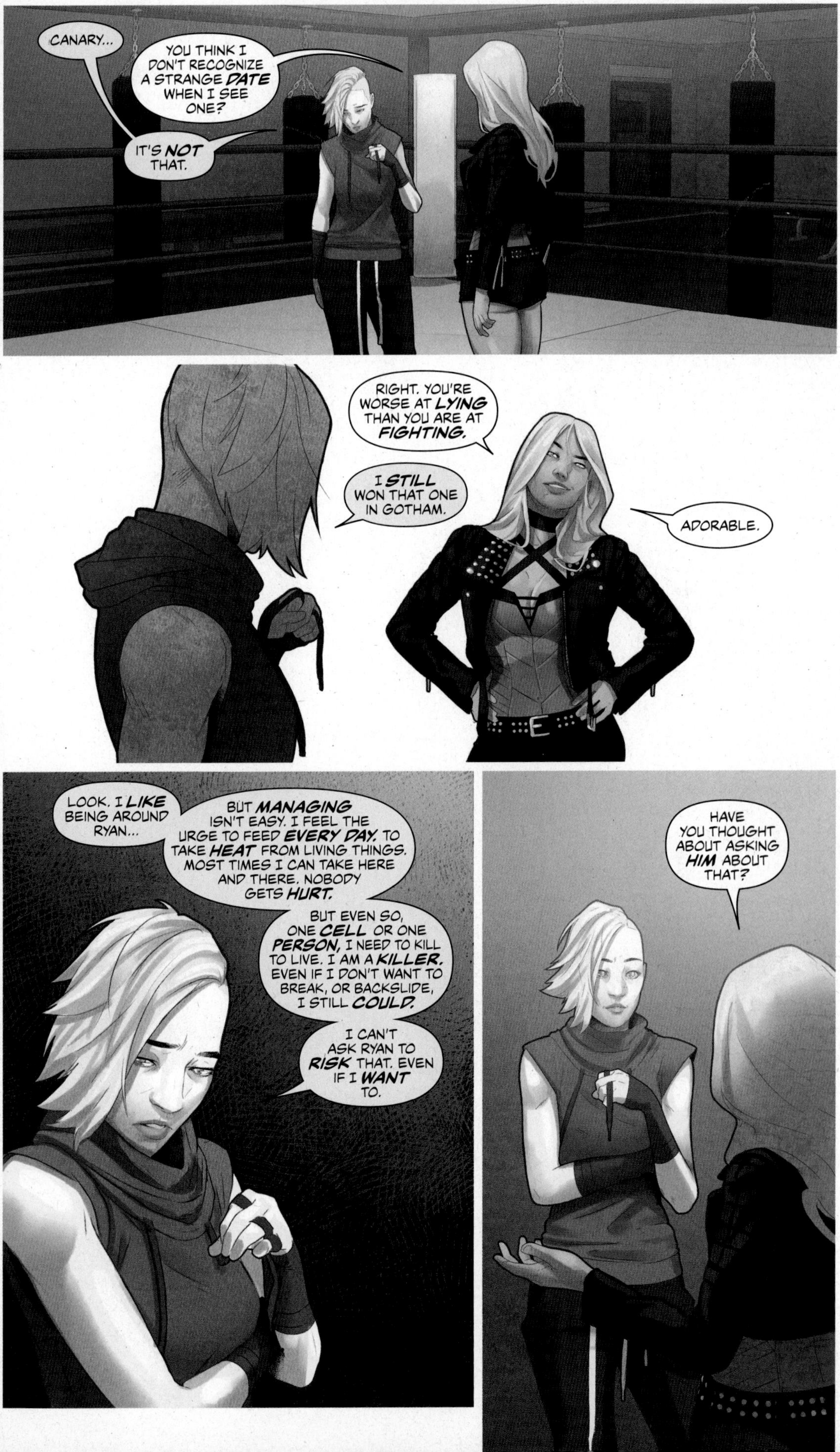

CANARY...
YOU THINK I DON'T RECOGNIZE A STRANGE DATE WHEN I SEE ONE?
IT'S NOT THAT.
RIGHT. YOU'RE WORSE AT LYING THAN YOU ARE AT FIGHTING.
I STILL WON THAT ONE IN GOTHAM.
ADORABLE.
LOOK. I LIKE BEING AROUND RYAN...
BUT MANAGING ISN'T EASY. I FEEL THE URGE TO FEED EVERY DAY. TO TAKE HEAT FROM LIVING THINGS. MOST TIMES I CAN TAKE HERE AND THERE. NOBODY GETS HURT.
BUT EVEN SO, ONE CELL OR ONE PERSON, I NEED TO KILL TO LIVE. I AM A KILLER. EVEN IF I DON'T WANT TO BREAK, OR BACKSLIDE, I STILL COULD.
I CAN'T ASK RYAN TO RISK THAT. EVEN IF I WANT TO.
HAVE YOU THOUGHT ABOUT ASKING HIM ABOUT THAT?

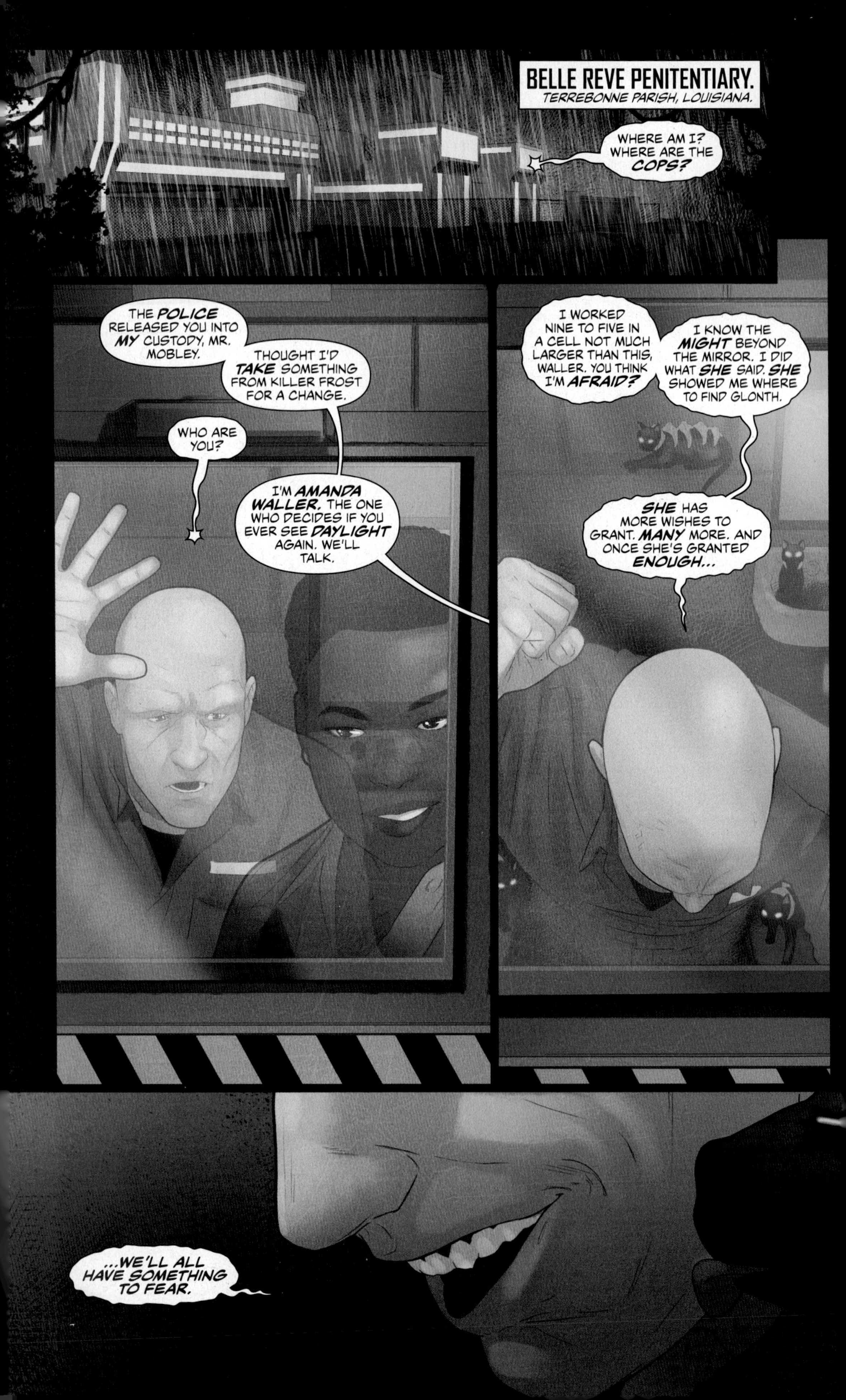
BELLE REVE PENITENTIARY.
TERREBONNE PARISH, LOUISIANA.
WHERE AM I? WHERE ARE THE COPS?
THE POLICE RELEASED YOU INTO MY CUSTODY, MR. MOBLEY.
THOUGHT I'D TAKE SOMETHING FROM KILLER FROST FOR A CHANGE.
WHO ARE YOU?
I'M AMANDA WALLER. THE ONE WHO DECIDES IF YOU EVER SEE DAYLIGHT AGAIN. WE'LL TALK.
I WORKED NINE TO FIVE IN A CELL NOT MUCH LARGER THAN THIS, WALLER. YOU THINK I'M AFRAID?
I KNOW THE MIGHT BEYOND THE MIRROR. I DID WHAT SHE SAID. SHE SHOWED ME WHERE TO FIND GLONTH.
SHE HAS MORE WISHES TO GRANT. MANY MORE. AND ONCE SHE'S GRANTED ENOUGH...
...WE'LL ALL HAVE SOMETHING TO FEAR.

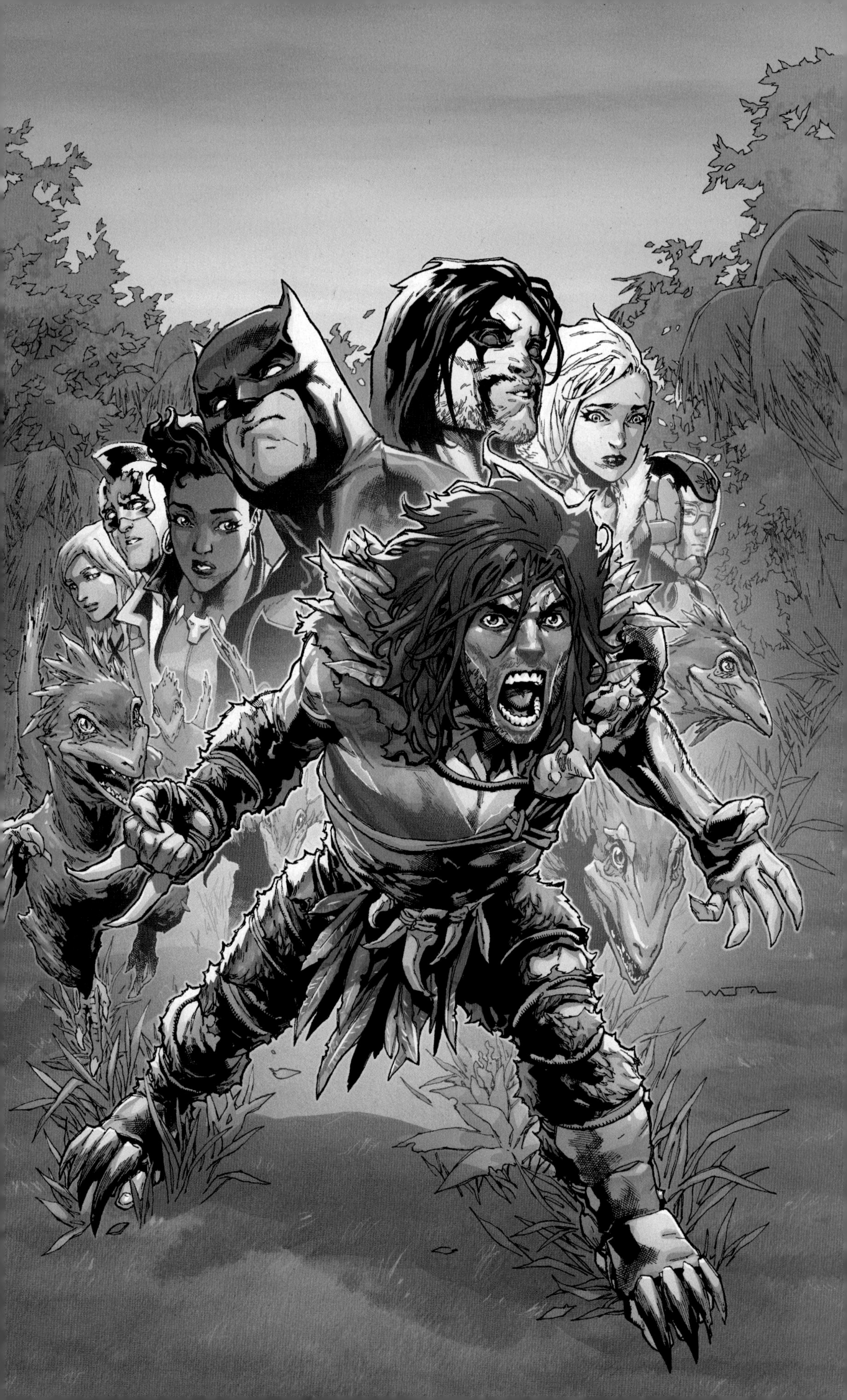

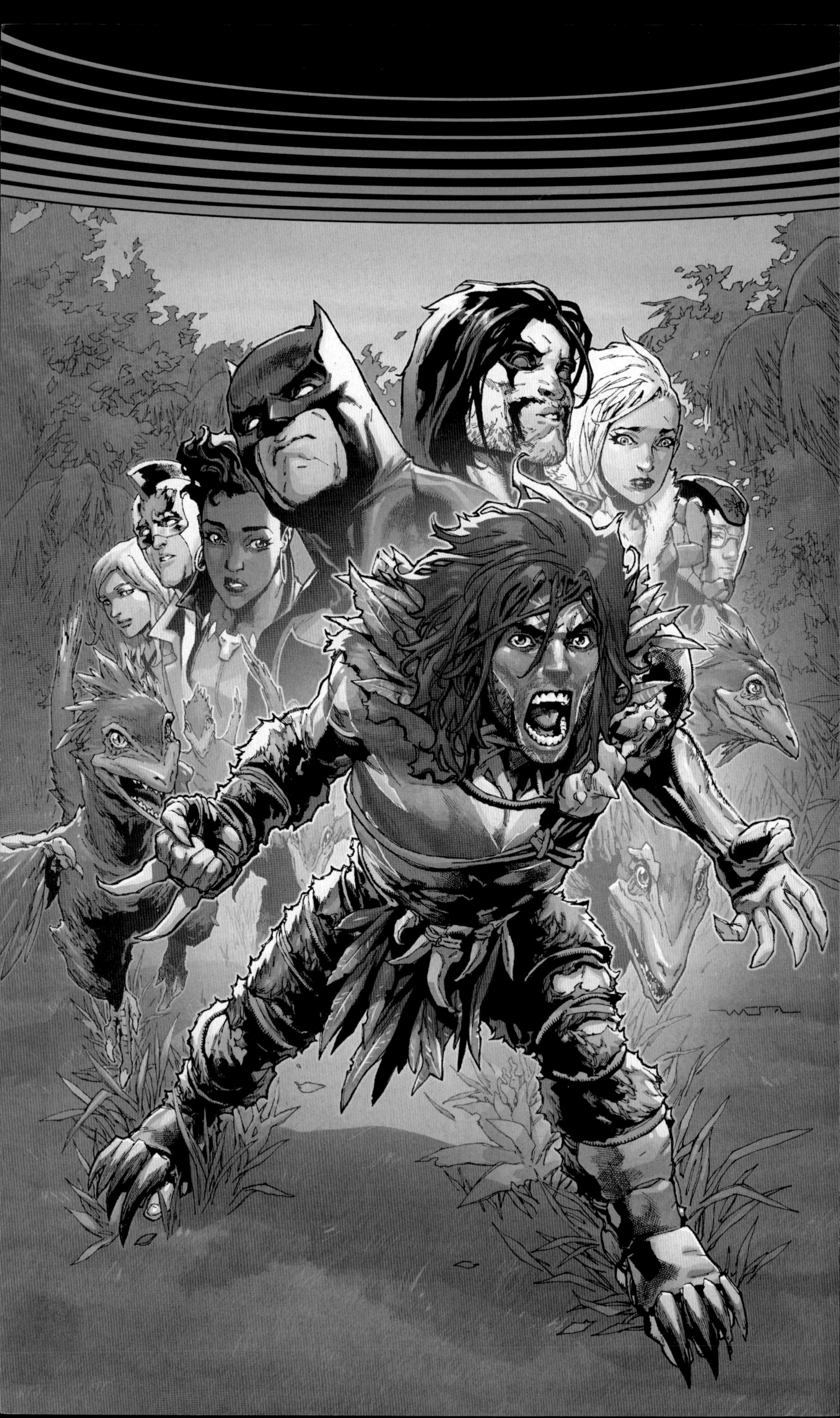

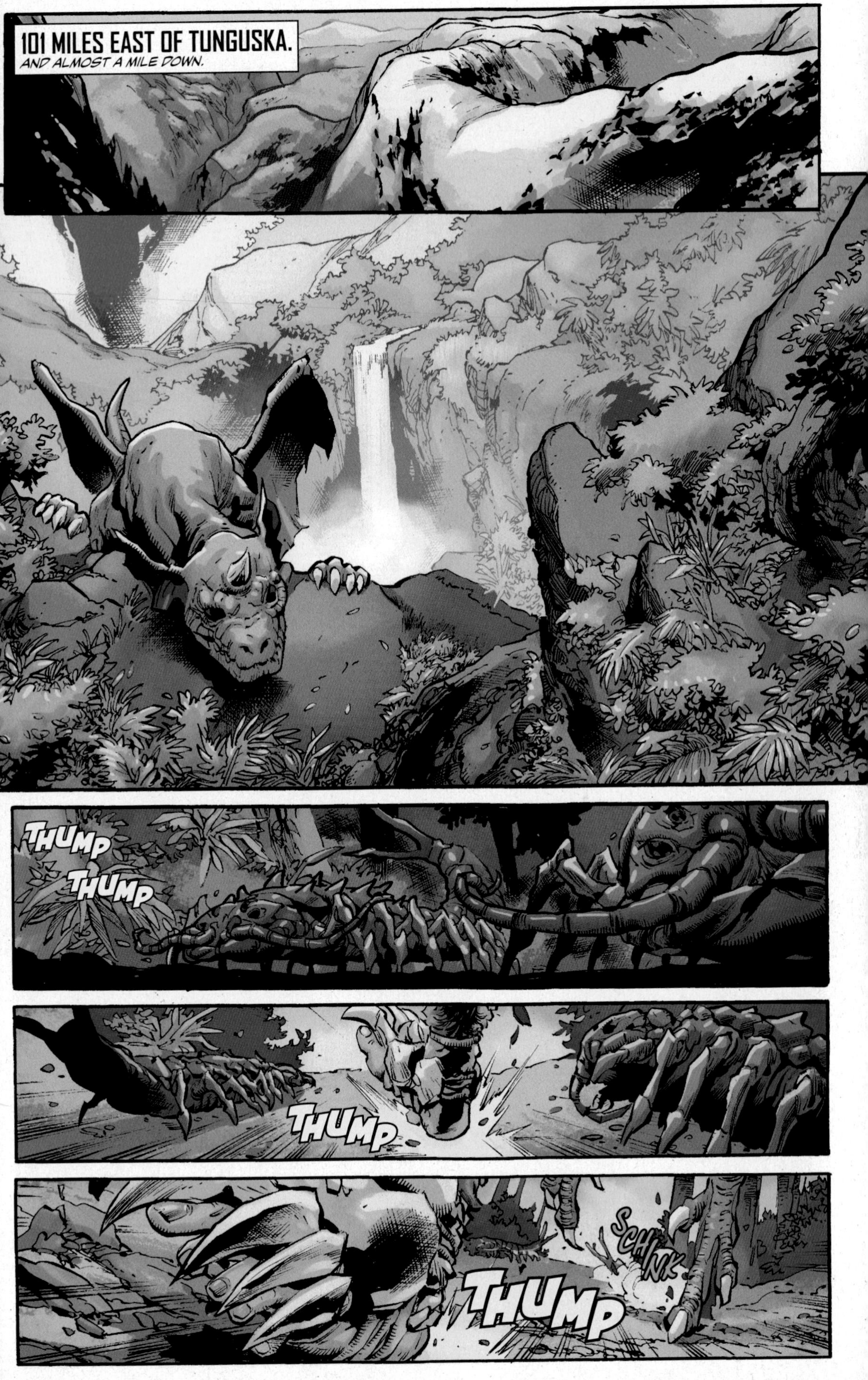
101 MILES EAST OF TUNGUSKA.
AND ALMOST A MILE DOWN.
THUMP
THUMP
THUMP
SCHINK
THUMP

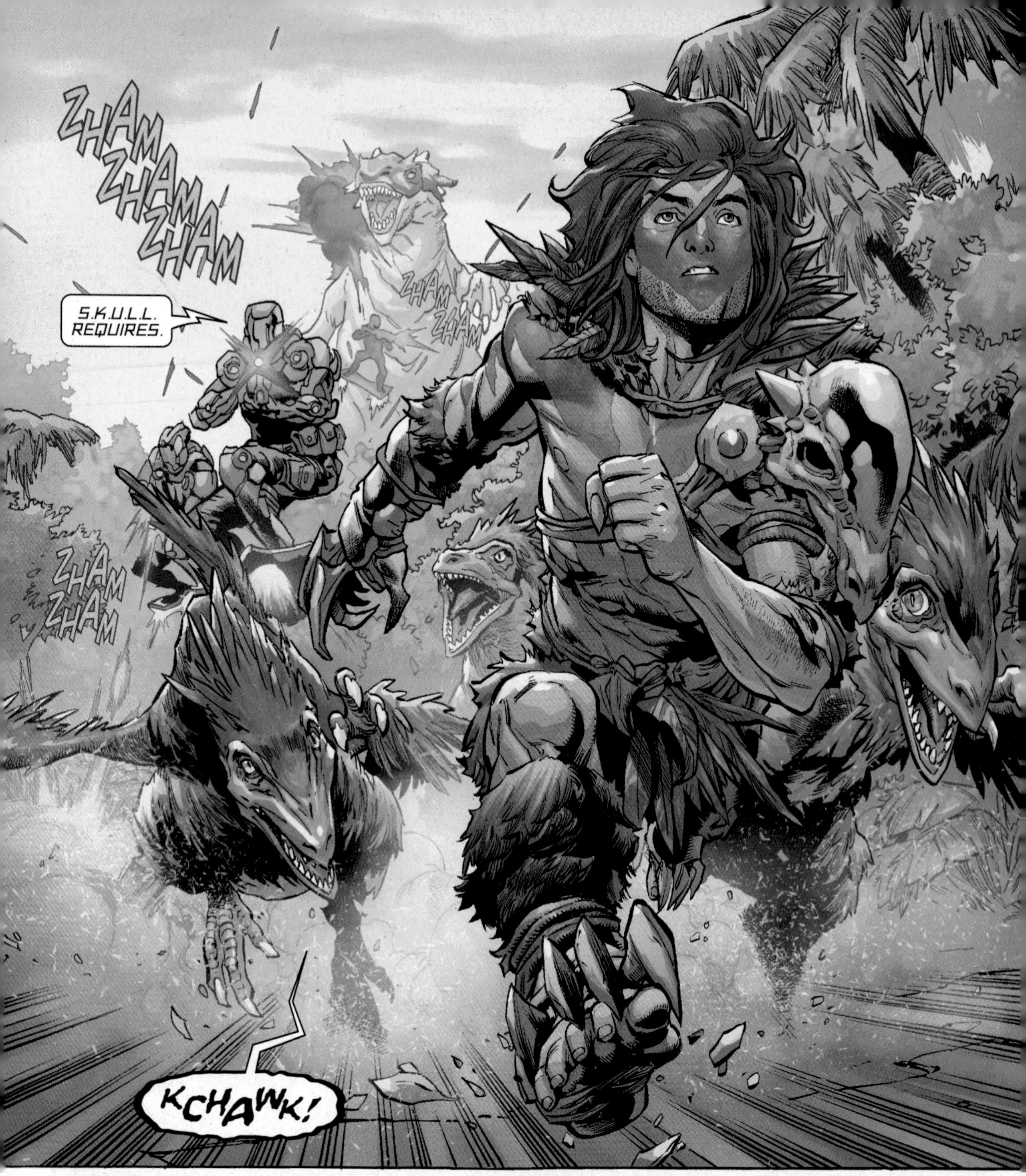
ZHAM
ZHAMAM
ZHAMAM
ZHAM
S.K.U.L.L. REQUIRES.
ZHAM
ZHAM
ZHAM
ZHAM
KCHAWK!

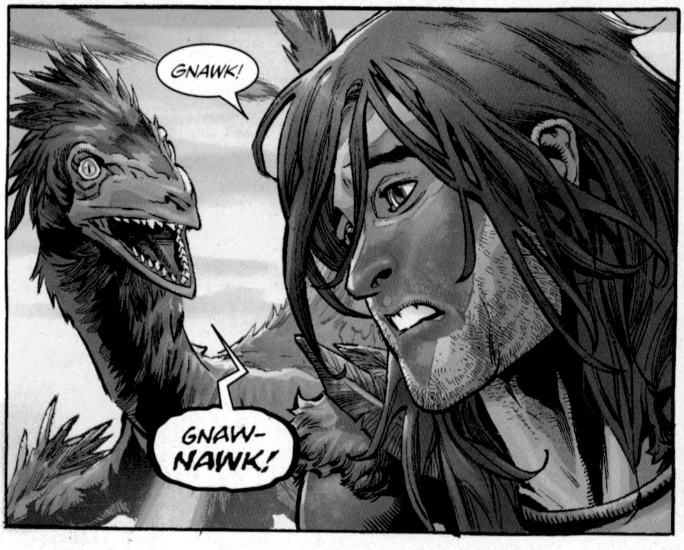
GNAWK!
GNAW-
NAWK!

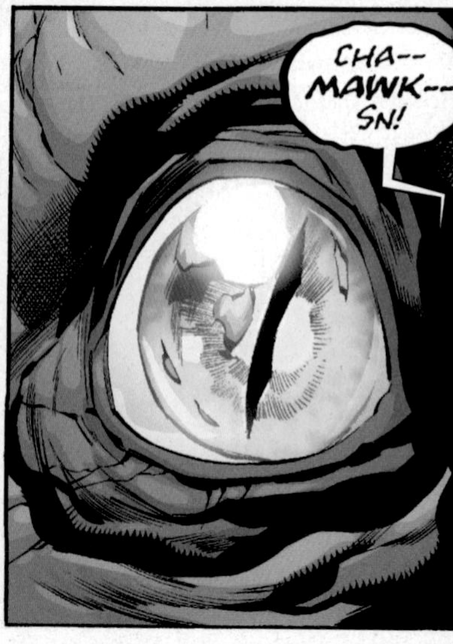
CHA--
MAWK--
SN!

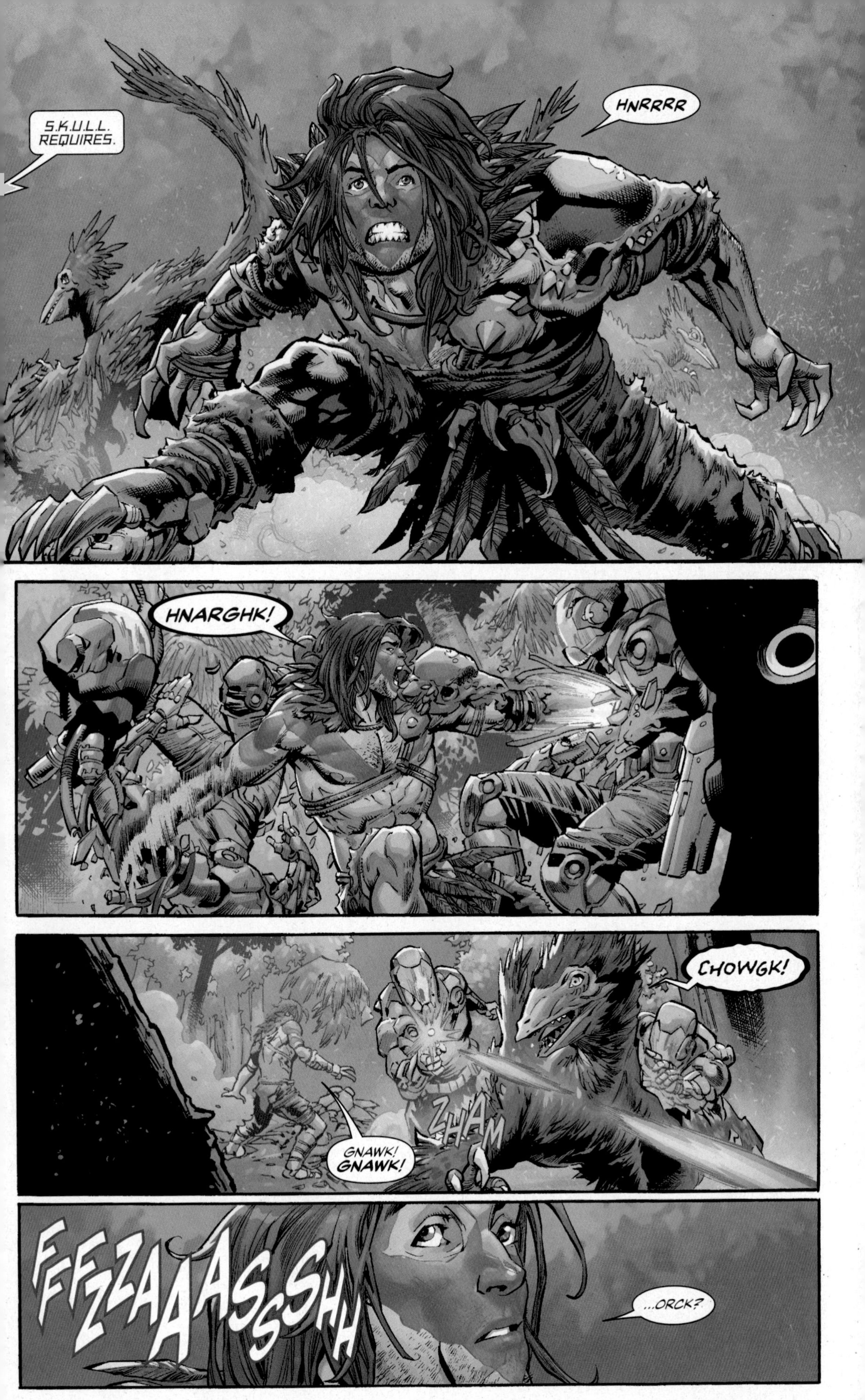
S.K.U.L.L. REQUIRES.
HNRRRR
HNARGHK!
CHOWGK!
ZHAM
GNAWK! GNAWK!
FFZZAAAASSSHH
...ORCK?

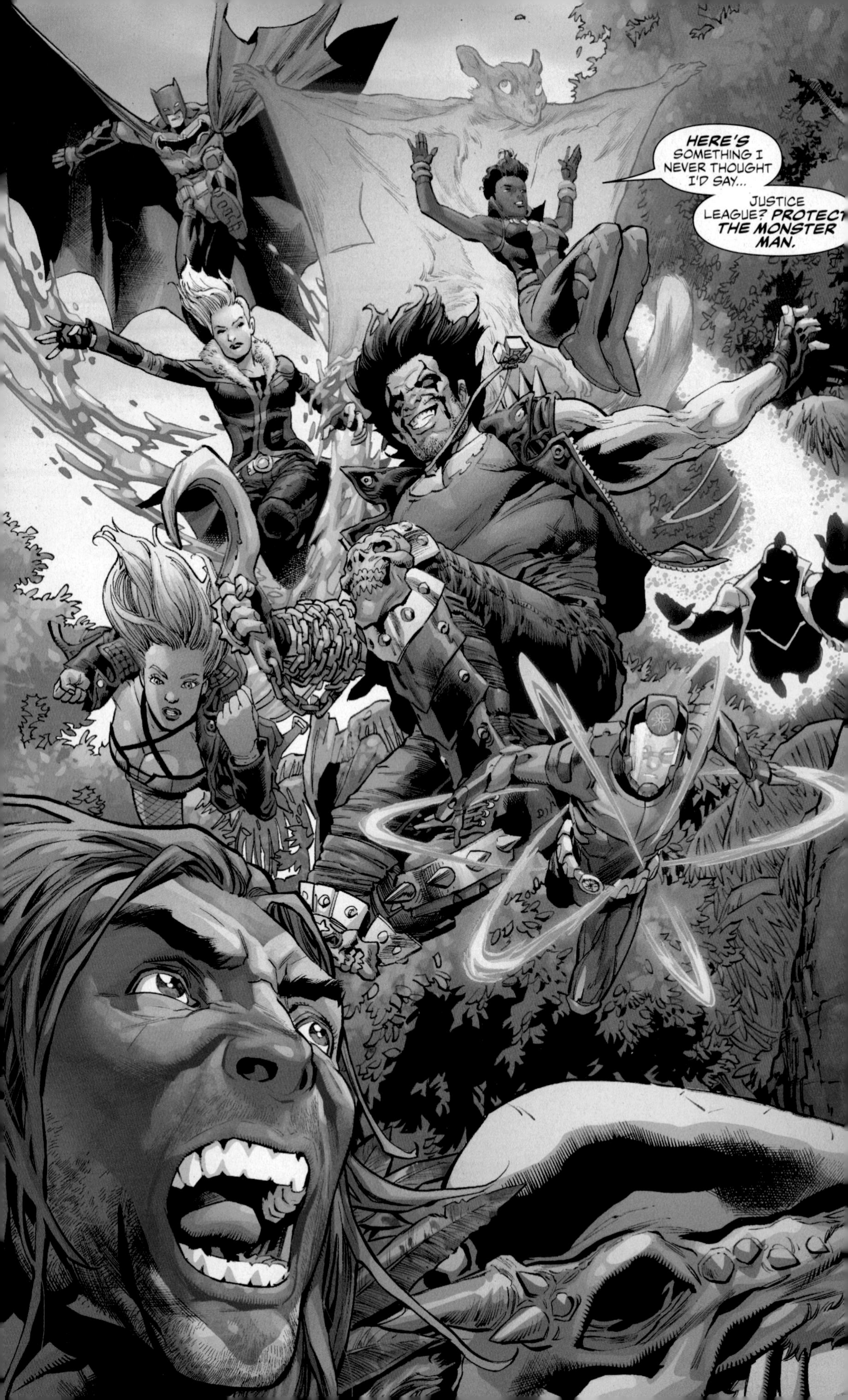
HERE'S SOMETHING I NEVER THOUGHT I'D SAY...
JUSTICE LEAGUE? PROTECT THE MONSTER MAN.

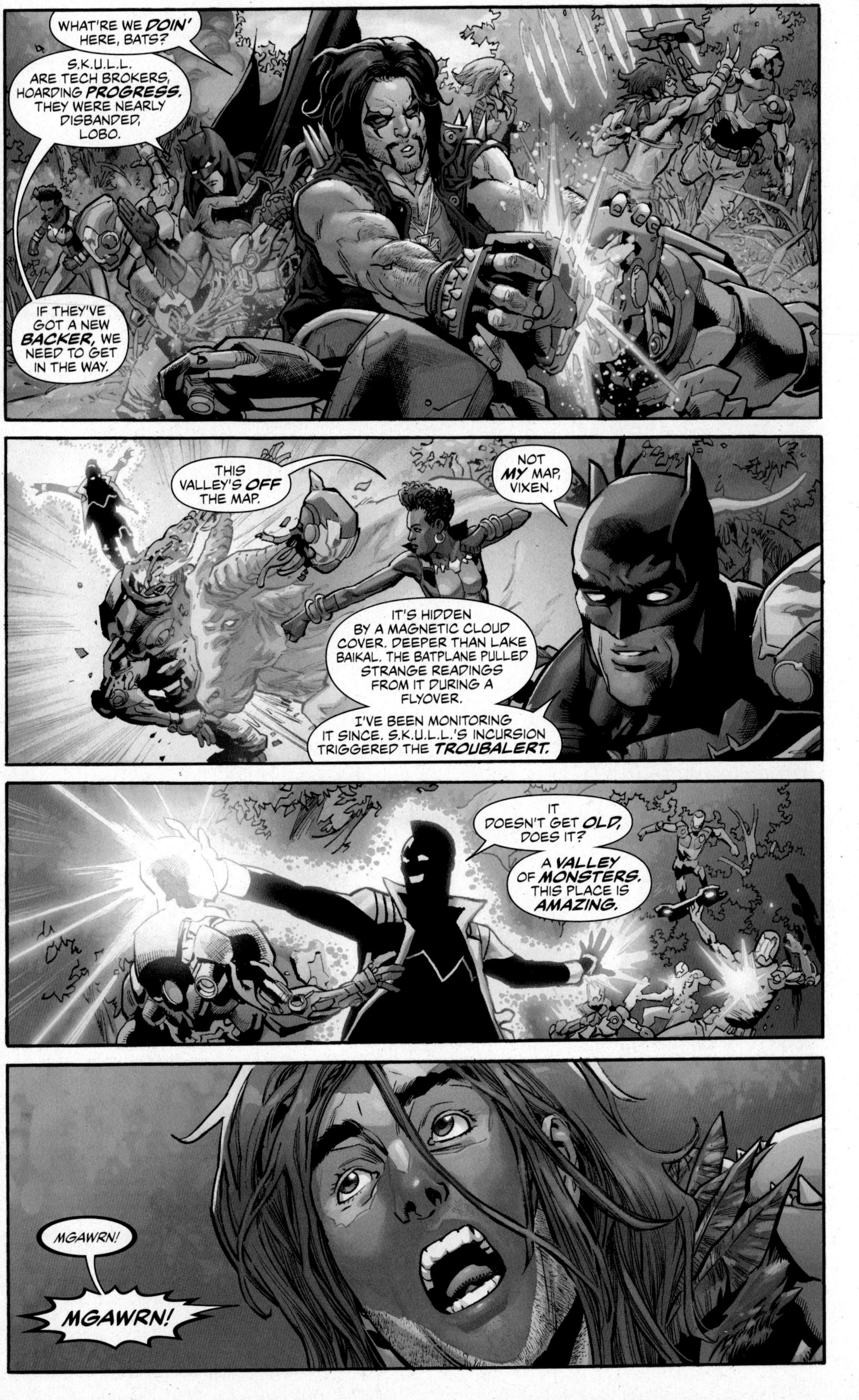
WHAT'RE WE DOIN' HERE, BATS?
S.K.U.L.L. ARE TECH BROKERS, HOARDING PROGRESS. THEY WERE NEARLY DISBANDED, LOBO.
IF THEY'VE GOT A NEW BACKER, WE NEED TO GET IN THE WAY.
THIS VALLEY'S OFF THE MAP.
NOT MY MAP, VIXEN.
IT'S HIDDEN BY A MAGNETIC CLOUD COVER. DEEPER THAN LAKE BAIKAL. THE BATPLANE PULLED STRANGE READINGS FROM IT DURING A FLYOVER.
I'VE BEEN MONITORING IT SINCE. S.K.U.L.L.'S INCURSION TRIGGERED THE TROUBALERT.
IT DOESN'T GET OLD, DOES IT?
A VALLEY OF MONSTERS. THIS PLACE IS AMAZING.
MGAWRN!
MGAWRN!

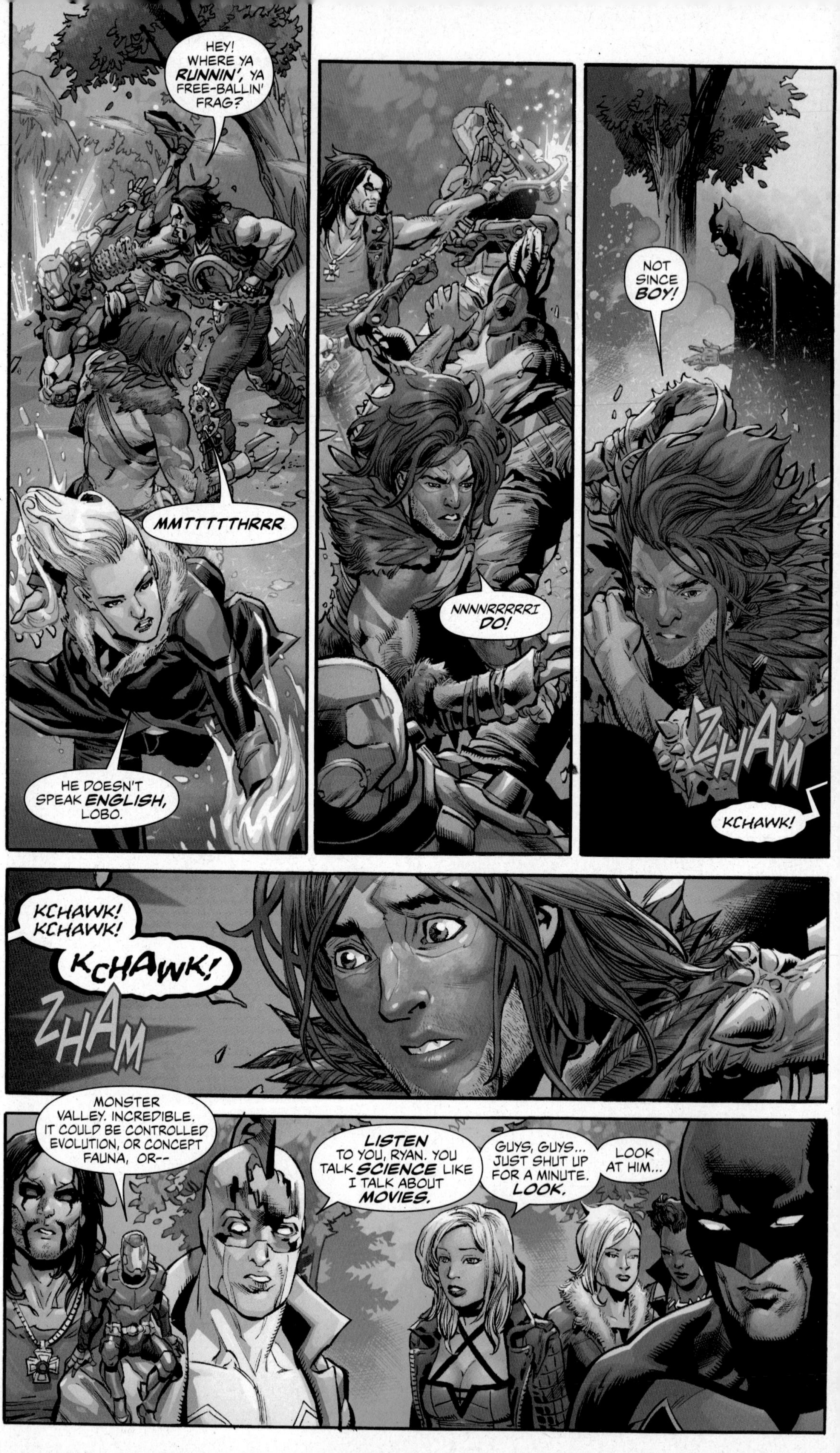
HEY! WHERE YA RUNNIN', YA FREE-BALLIN' FRAG?
MMTTTTTHRRR
HE DOESN'T SPEAK ENGLISH, LOBO.
NNNNRRRRRI DO!
NOT SINCE BOY!
ZHAM
KCHAWK!
KCHAWK! KCHAWK!
KCHAWK!
ZHAM
MONSTER VALLEY. INCREDIBLE. IT COULD BE CONTROLLED EVOLUTION, OR CONCEPT FAUNA, OR--
LISTEN TO YOU, RYAN. YOU TALK SCIENCE LIKE I TALK ABOUT MOVIES.
GUYS, GUYS... JUST SHUT UP FOR A MINUTE. LOOK.
LOOK AT HIM...

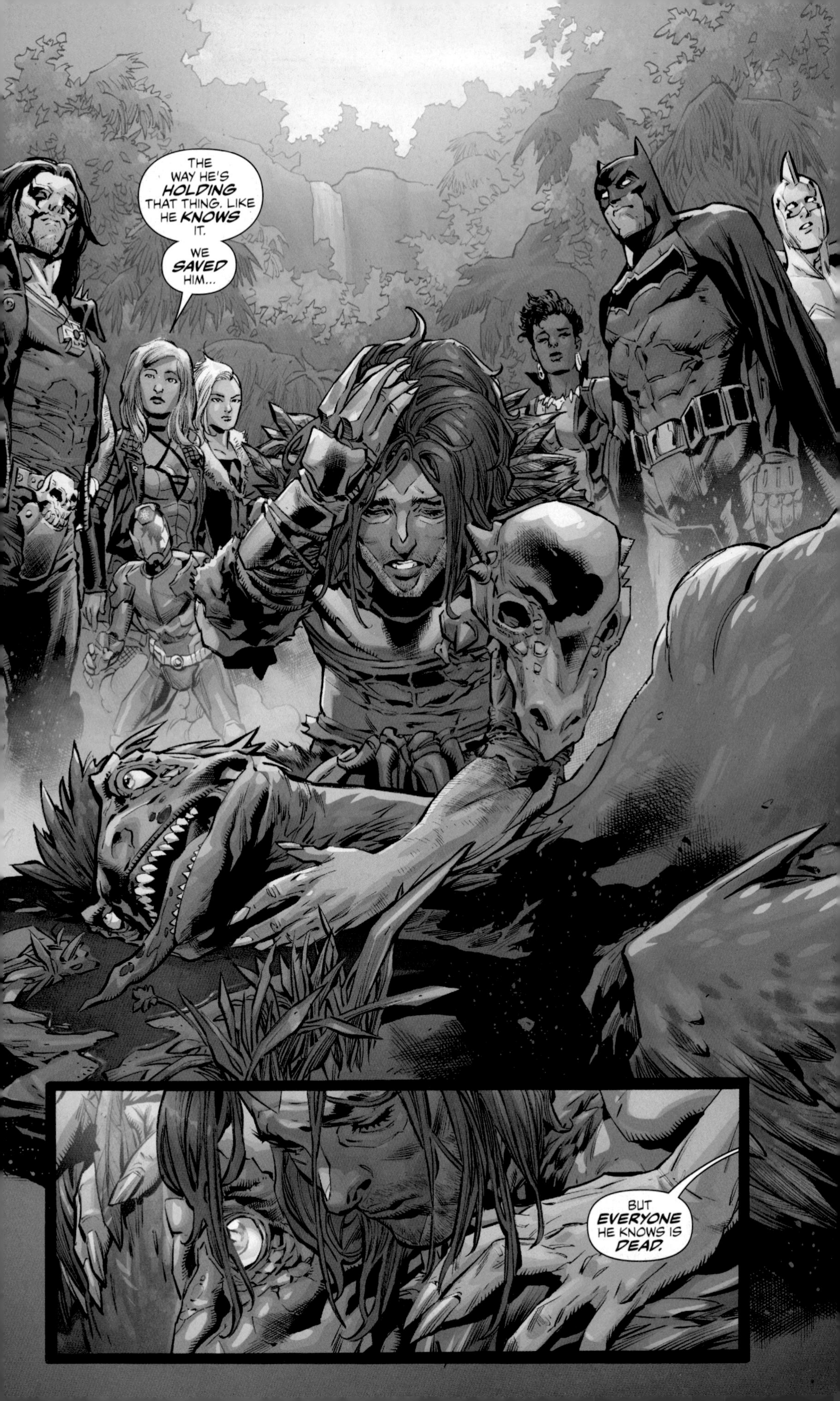
THE WAY HE'S HOLDING THAT THING. LIKE HE KNOWS IT.
WE SAVED HIM...
BUT EVERYONE HE KNOWS IS DEAD.

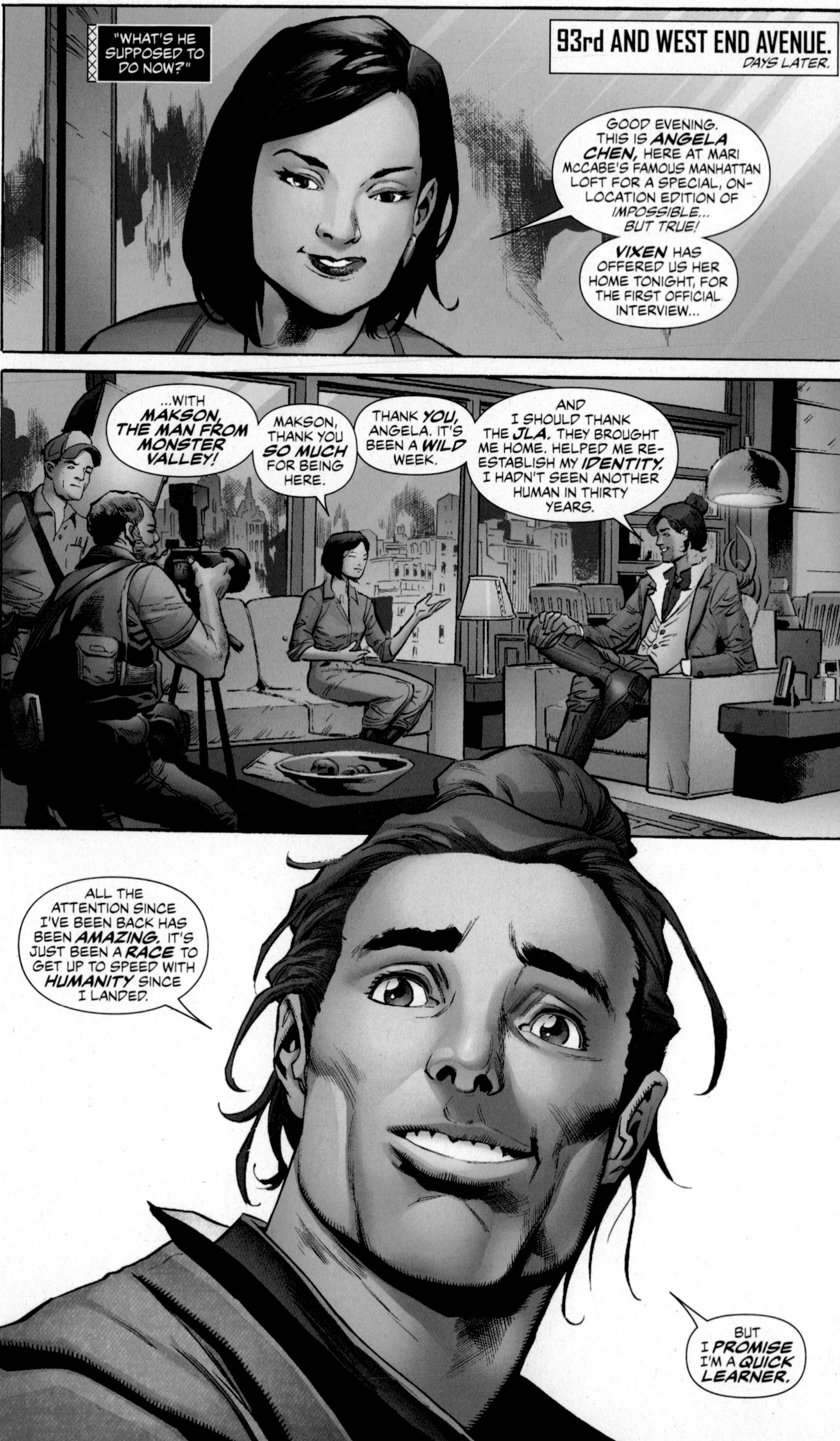
"WHAT'S HE SUPPOSED TO DO NOW?"
93rd AND WEST END AVENUE. DAYS LATER.
GOOD EVENING. THIS IS ANGELA CHEN, HERE AT MARI McCABE'S FAMOUS MANHATTAN LOFT FOR A SPECIAL, ON-LOCATION EDITION OF IMPOSSIBLE... BUT TRUE!
VIXEN HAS OFFERED US HER HOME TONIGHT, FOR THE FIRST OFFICIAL INTERVIEW...
...WITH MAKSON, THE MAN FROM MONSTER VALLEY!
MAKSON, THANK YOU SO MUCH FOR BEING HERE.
THANK YOU, ANGELA. IT'S BEEN A WILD WEEK.
AND I SHOULD THANK THE JLA. THEY BROUGHT ME HOME. HELPED ME RE-ESTABLISH MY IDENTITY. I HADN'T SEEN ANOTHER HUMAN IN THIRTY YEARS.
ALL THE ATTENTION SINCE I'VE BEEN BACK HAS BEEN AMAZING. IT'S JUST BEEN A RACE TO GET UP TO SPEED WITH HUMANITY SINCE I LANDED.
BUT I PROMISE I'M A QUICK LEARNER.

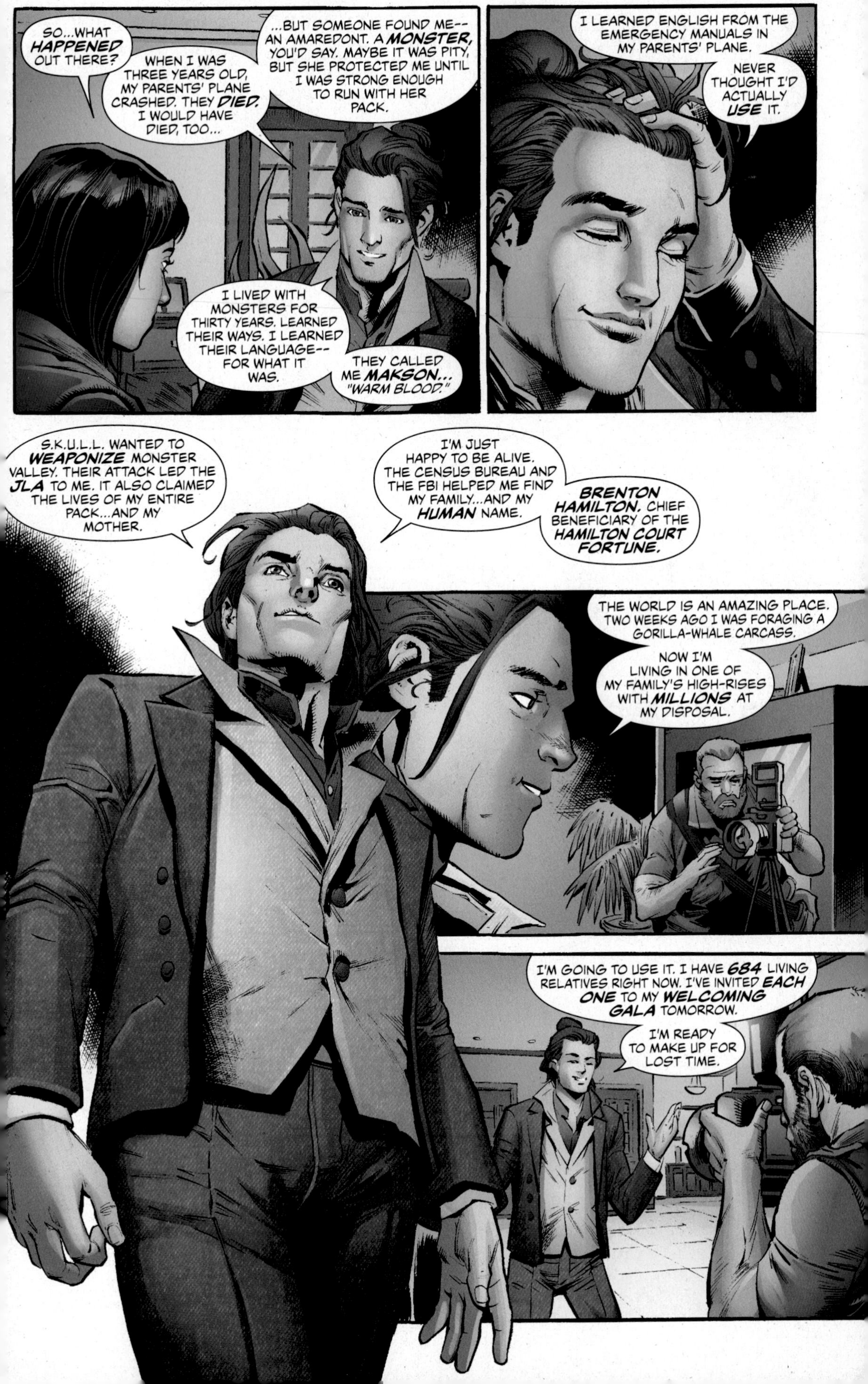
SO...WHAT HAPPENED OUT THERE?
WHEN I WAS THREE YEARS OLD, MY PARENTS' PLANE CRASHED. THEY DIED. I WOULD HAVE DIED, TOO...
...BUT SOMEONE FOUND ME-- AN AMAREDONT. A MONSTER, YOU'D SAY. MAYBE IT WAS PITY, BUT SHE PROTECTED ME UNTIL I WAS STRONG ENOUGH TO RUN WITH HER PACK.
I LIVED WITH MONSTERS FOR THIRTY YEARS. LEARNED THEIR WAYS. I LEARNED THEIR LANGUAGE-- FOR WHAT IT WAS.
THEY CALLED ME MAKSON... "WARM BLOOD."
I LEARNED ENGLISH FROM THE EMERGENCY MANUALS IN MY PARENTS' PLANE.
NEVER THOUGHT I'D ACTUALLY USE IT.
S.K.U.L.L. WANTED TO WEAPONIZE MONSTER VALLEY. THEIR ATTACK LED THE JLA TO ME. IT ALSO CLAIMED THE LIVES OF MY ENTIRE PACK...AND MY MOTHER.
I'M JUST HAPPY TO BE ALIVE. THE CENSUS BUREAU AND THE FBI HELPED ME FIND MY FAMILY...AND MY HUMAN NAME.
BRENTON HAMILTON. CHIEF BENEFICIARY OF THE HAMILTON COURT FORTUNE.
THE WORLD IS AN AMAZING PLACE. TWO WEEKS AGO I WAS FORAGING A GORILLA-WHALE CARCASS.
NOW I'M LIVING IN ONE OF MY FAMILY'S HIGH-RISES WITH MILLIONS AT MY DISPOSAL.
I'M GOING TO USE IT. I HAVE 684 LIVING RELATIVES RIGHT NOW. I'VE INVITED EACH ONE TO MY WELCOMING GALA TOMORROW.
I'M READY TO MAKE UP FOR LOST TIME.

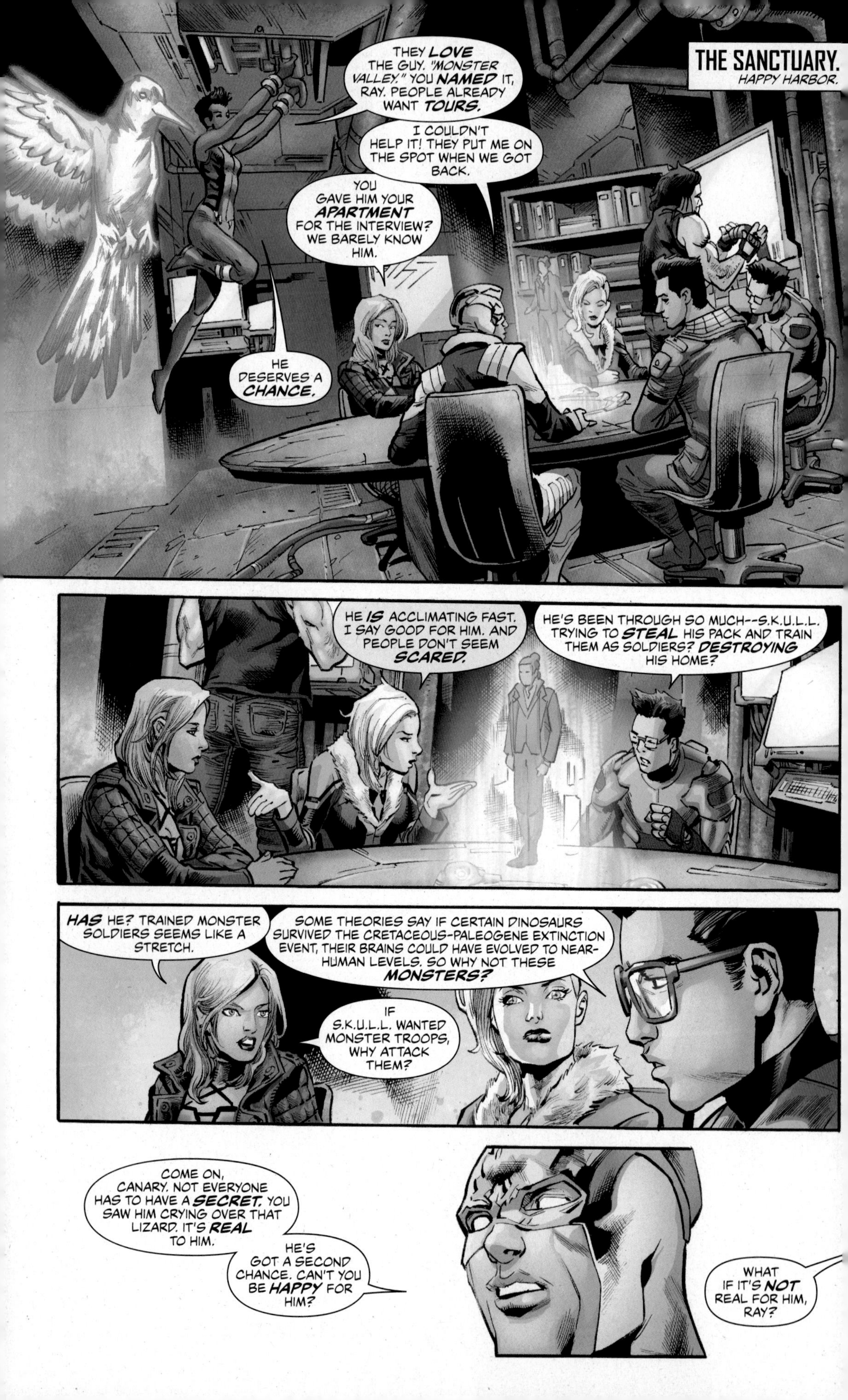
THE SANCTUARY.
HAPPY HARBOR.
THEY LOVE THE GUY. "MONSTER VALLEY." YOU NAMED IT, RAY. PEOPLE ALREADY WANT TOURS.
I COULDN'T HELP IT! THEY PUT ME ON THE SPOT WHEN WE GOT BACK.
YOU GAVE HIM YOUR APARTMENT FOR THE INTERVIEW? WE BARELY KNOW HIM.
HE DESERVES A CHANCE.
HE IS ACCLIMATING FAST. I SAY GOOD FOR HIM. AND PEOPLE DON'T SEEM SCARED.
HE'S BEEN THROUGH SO MUCH--S.K.U.L.L. TRYING TO STEAL HIS PACK AND TRAIN THEM AS SOLDIERS? DESTROYING HIS HOME?
HAS HE? TRAINED MONSTER SOLDIERS SEEMS LIKE A STRETCH.
SOME THEORIES SAY IF CERTAIN DINOSAURS SURVIVED THE CRETACEOUS-PALEOGENE EXTINCTION EVENT, THEIR BRAINS COULD HAVE EVOLVED TO NEAR-HUMAN LEVELS. SO WHY NOT THESE MONSTERS?
IF S.K.U.L.L. WANTED MONSTER TROOPS, WHY ATTACK THEM?
COME ON, CANARY. NOT EVERYONE HAS TO HAVE A SECRET. YOU SAW HIM CRYING OVER THAT LIZARD. IT'S REAL TO HIM.
HE'S GOT A SECOND CHANCE. CAN'T YOU BE HAPPY FOR HIM?
WHAT IF IT'S NOT REAL FOR HIM, RAY?

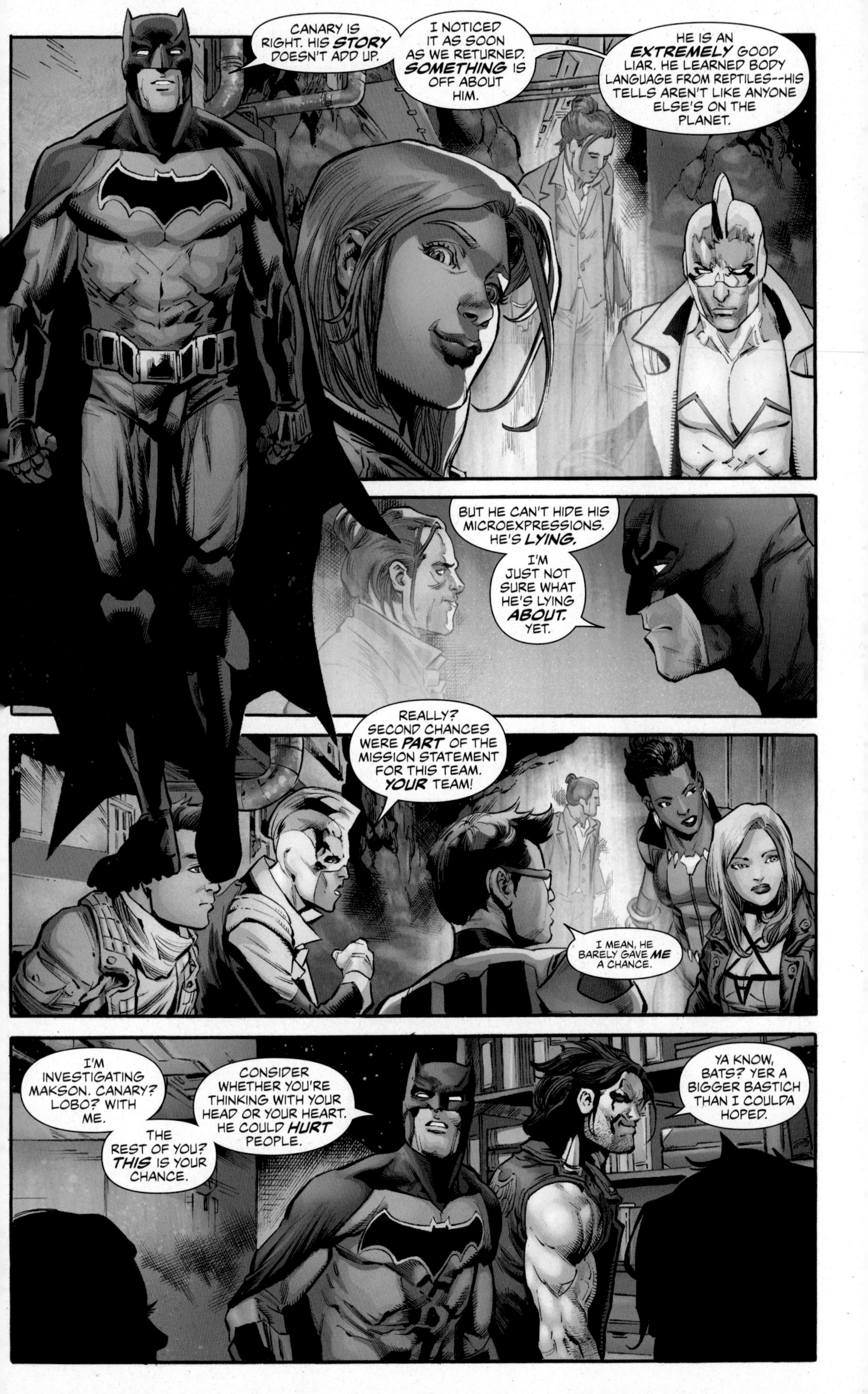
CANARY IS RIGHT. HIS STORY DOESN'T ADD UP.
I NOTICED IT AS SOON AS WE RETURNED. SOMETHING IS OFF ABOUT HIM.
HE IS AN EXTREMELY GOOD LIAR. HE LEARNED BODY LANGUAGE FROM REPTILES--HIS TELLS AREN'T LIKE ANYONE ELSE'S ON THE PLANET.
BUT HE CAN'T HIDE HIS MICROEXPRESSIONS. HE'S LYING.
I'M JUST NOT SURE WHAT HE'S LYING ABOUT. YET.
REALLY? SECOND CHANCES WERE PART OF THE MISSION STATEMENT FOR THIS TEAM. YOUR TEAM!
I MEAN, HE BARELY GAVE ME A CHANCE.
I'M INVESTIGATING MAKSON. CANARY? LOBO? WITH ME.
THE REST OF YOU? THIS IS YOUR CHANCE.
CONSIDER WHETHER YOU'RE THINKING WITH YOUR HEAD OR YOUR HEART. HE COULD HURT PEOPLE.
YA KNOW, BATS? YER A BIGGER BASTICH THAN I COULDA HOPED.

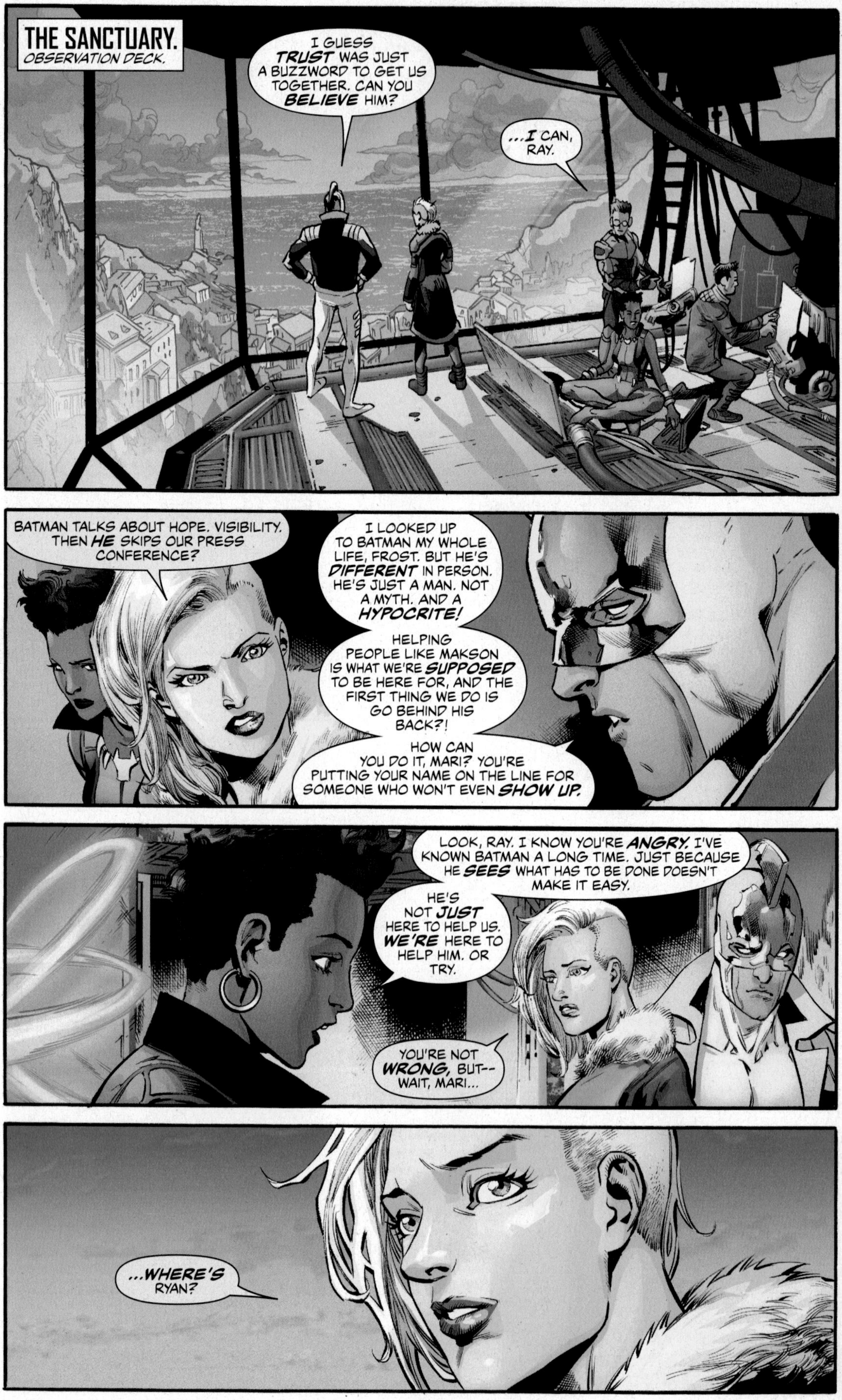
THE SANCTUARY.
OBSERVATION DECK.
I GUESS TRUST WAS JUST A BUZZWORD TO GET US TOGETHER. CAN YOU BELIEVE HIM?
...I CAN, RAY.
BATMAN TALKS ABOUT HOPE. VISIBILITY. THEN HE SKIPS OUR PRESS CONFERENCE?
I LOOKED UP TO BATMAN MY WHOLE LIFE, FROST. BUT HE'S DIFFERENT IN PERSON. HE'S JUST A MAN. NOT A MYTH. AND A HYPOCRITE!
HELPING PEOPLE LIKE MAKSON IS WHAT WE'RE SUPPOSED TO BE HERE FOR, AND THE FIRST THING WE DO IS GO BEHIND HIS BACK?!
HOW CAN YOU DO IT, MARI? YOU'RE PUTTING YOUR NAME ON THE LINE FOR SOMEONE WHO WON'T EVEN SHOW UP.
LOOK, RAY. I KNOW YOU'RE ANGRY. I'VE KNOWN BATMAN A LONG TIME. JUST BECAUSE HE SEES WHAT HAS TO BE DONE DOESN'T MAKE IT EASY.
HE'S NOT JUST HERE TO HELP US. WE'RE HERE TO HELP HIM. OR TRY.
YOU'RE NOT WRONG, BUT-- WAIT, MARI...
...WHERE'S RYAN?

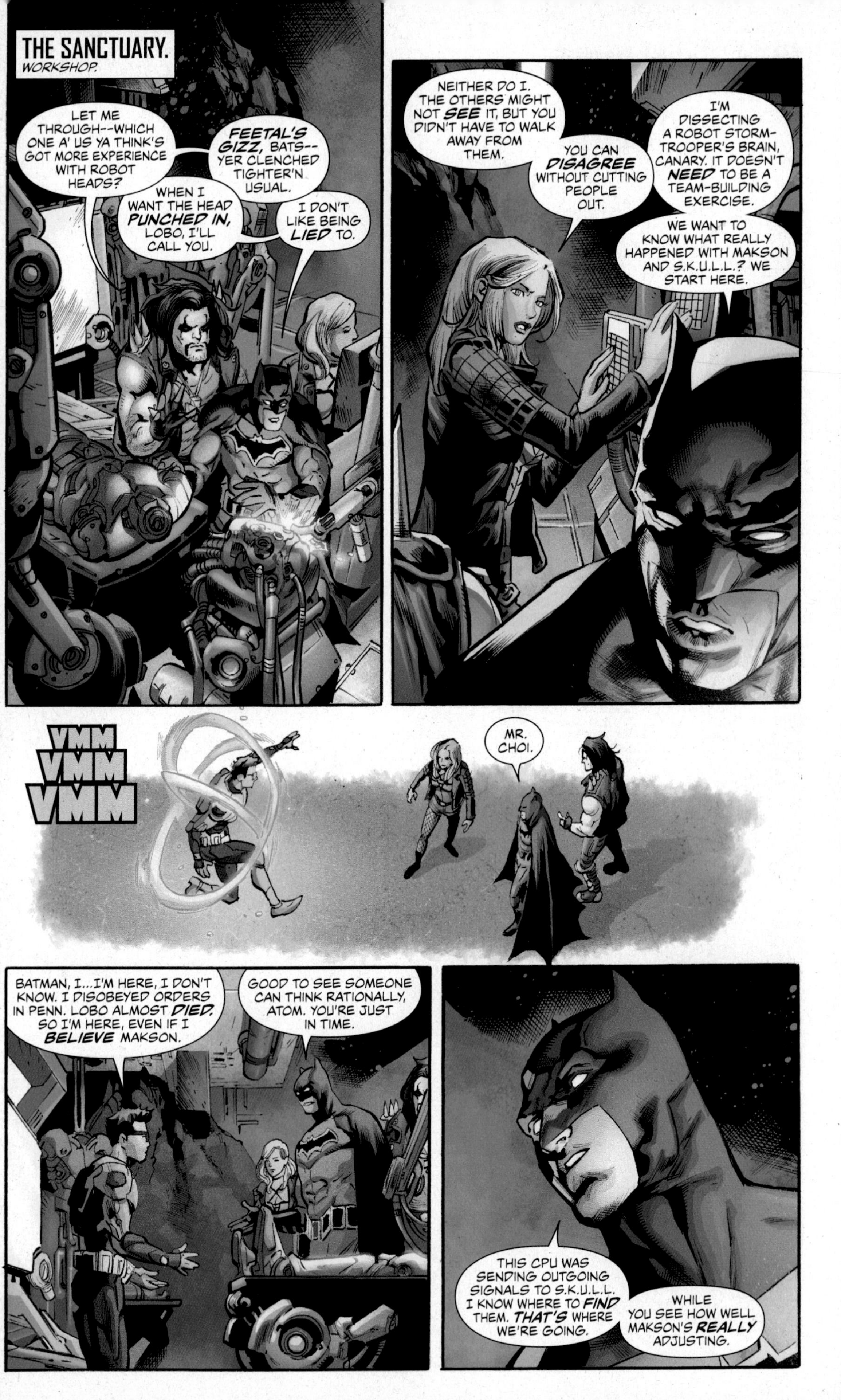
THE SANCTUARY.
WORKSHOP.
LET ME THROUGH--WHICH ONE A' US YA THINK'S GOT MORE EXPERIENCE WITH ROBOT HEADS?
FEETAL'S GIZZ, BATS--YER CLENCHED TIGHTER'N USUAL.
WHEN I WANT THE HEAD PUNCHED IN, LOBO, I'LL CALL YOU.
I DON'T LIKE BEING LIED TO.
NEITHER DO I. THE OTHERS MIGHT NOT SEE IT, BUT YOU DIDN'T HAVE TO WALK AWAY FROM THEM.
YOU CAN DISAGREE WITHOUT CUTTING PEOPLE OUT.
I'M DISSECTING A ROBOT STORM-TROOPER'S BRAIN, CANARY. IT DOESN'T NEED TO BE A TEAM-BUILDING EXERCISE.
WE WANT TO KNOW WHAT REALLY HAPPENED WITH MAKSON AND S.K.U.L.L.? WE START HERE.
VMM VMM VMM
MR. CHOI.
BATMAN, I...I'M HERE, I DON'T KNOW. I DISOBEYED ORDERS IN PENN. LOBO ALMOST DIED. SO I'M HERE, EVEN IF I BELIEVE MAKSON.
GOOD TO SEE SOMEONE CAN THINK RATIONALLY, ATOM. YOU'RE JUST IN TIME.
THIS CPU WAS SENDING OUTGOING SIGNALS TO S.K.U.L.L. I KNOW WHERE TO FIND THEM. THAT'S WHERE WE'RE GOING.
WHILE YOU SEE HOW WELL MAKSON'S REALLY ADJUSTING.

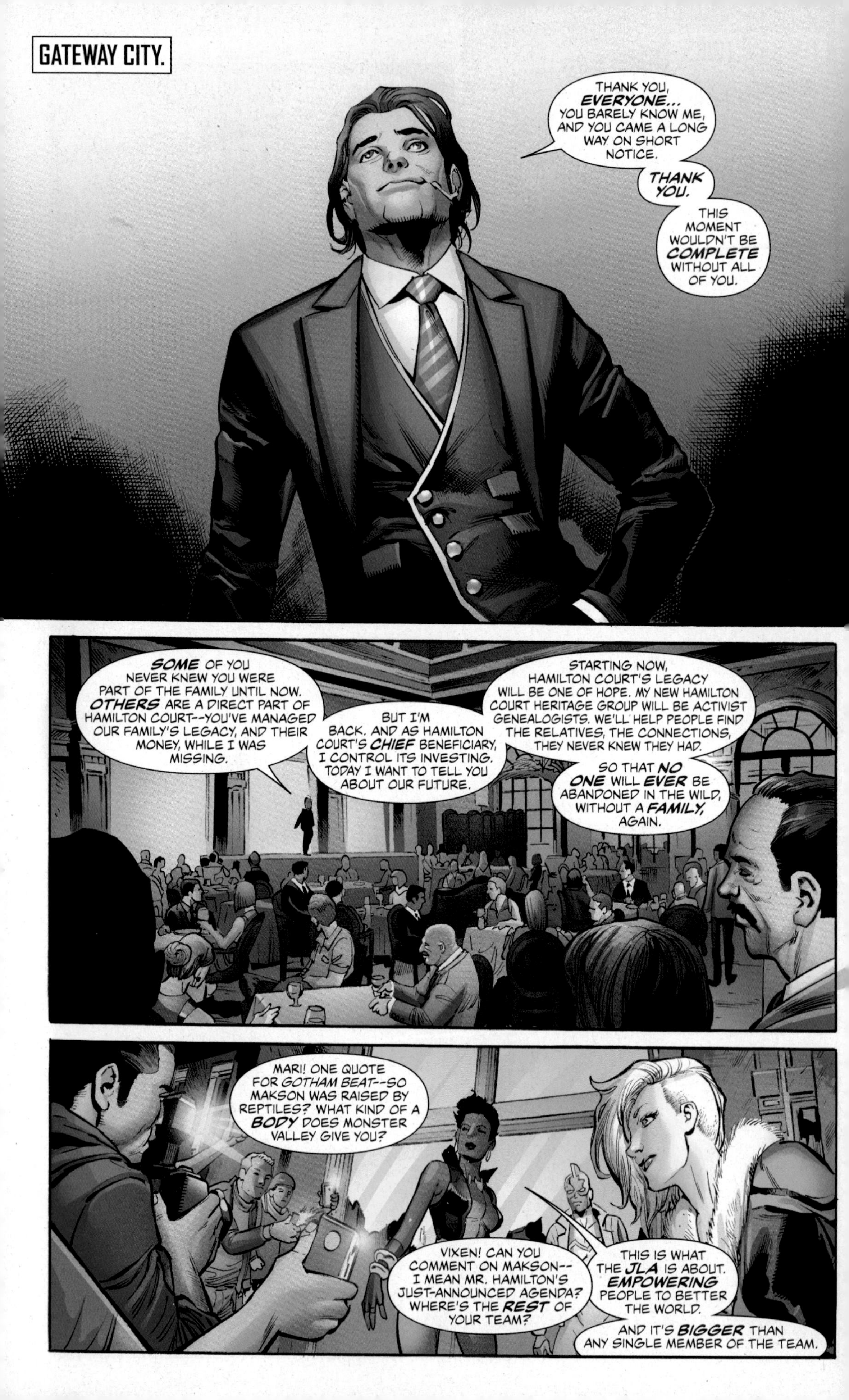

GATEWAY CITY.
THANK YOU, EVERYONE... YOU BARELY KNOW ME, AND YOU CAME A LONG WAY ON SHORT NOTICE.
THANK YOU.
THIS MOMENT WOULDN'T BE COMPLETE WITHOUT ALL OF YOU.
SOME OF YOU NEVER KNEW YOU WERE PART OF THE FAMILY UNTIL NOW. OTHERS ARE A DIRECT PART OF HAMILTON COURT--YOU'VE MANAGED OUR FAMILY'S LEGACY, AND THEIR MONEY, WHILE I WAS MISSING.
BUT I'M BACK. AND AS HAMILTON COURT'S CHIEF BENEFICIARY, I CONTROL ITS INVESTING. TODAY I WANT TO TELL YOU ABOUT OUR FUTURE.
STARTING NOW, HAMILTON COURT'S LEGACY WILL BE ONE OF HOPE. MY NEW HAMILTON COURT HERITAGE GROUP WILL BE ACTIVIST GENEALOGISTS. WE'LL HELP PEOPLE FIND THE RELATIVES, THE CONNECTIONS, THEY NEVER KNEW THEY HAD.
SO THAT NO ONE WILL EVER BE ABANDONED IN THE WILD, WITHOUT A FAMILY, AGAIN.
MARI! ONE QUOTE FOR GOTHAM BEAT--SO MAKSON WAS RAISED BY REPTILES? WHAT KIND OF A BODY DOES MONSTER VALLEY GIVE YOU?
VIXEN! CAN YOU COMMENT ON MAKSON--I MEAN MR. HAMILTON'S JUST-ANNOUNCED AGENDA? WHERE'S THE REST OF YOUR TEAM?
THIS IS WHAT THE JLA IS ABOUT. EMPOWERING PEOPLE TO BETTER THE WORLD.
AND IT'S BIGGER THAN ANY SINGLE MEMBER OF THE TEAM.

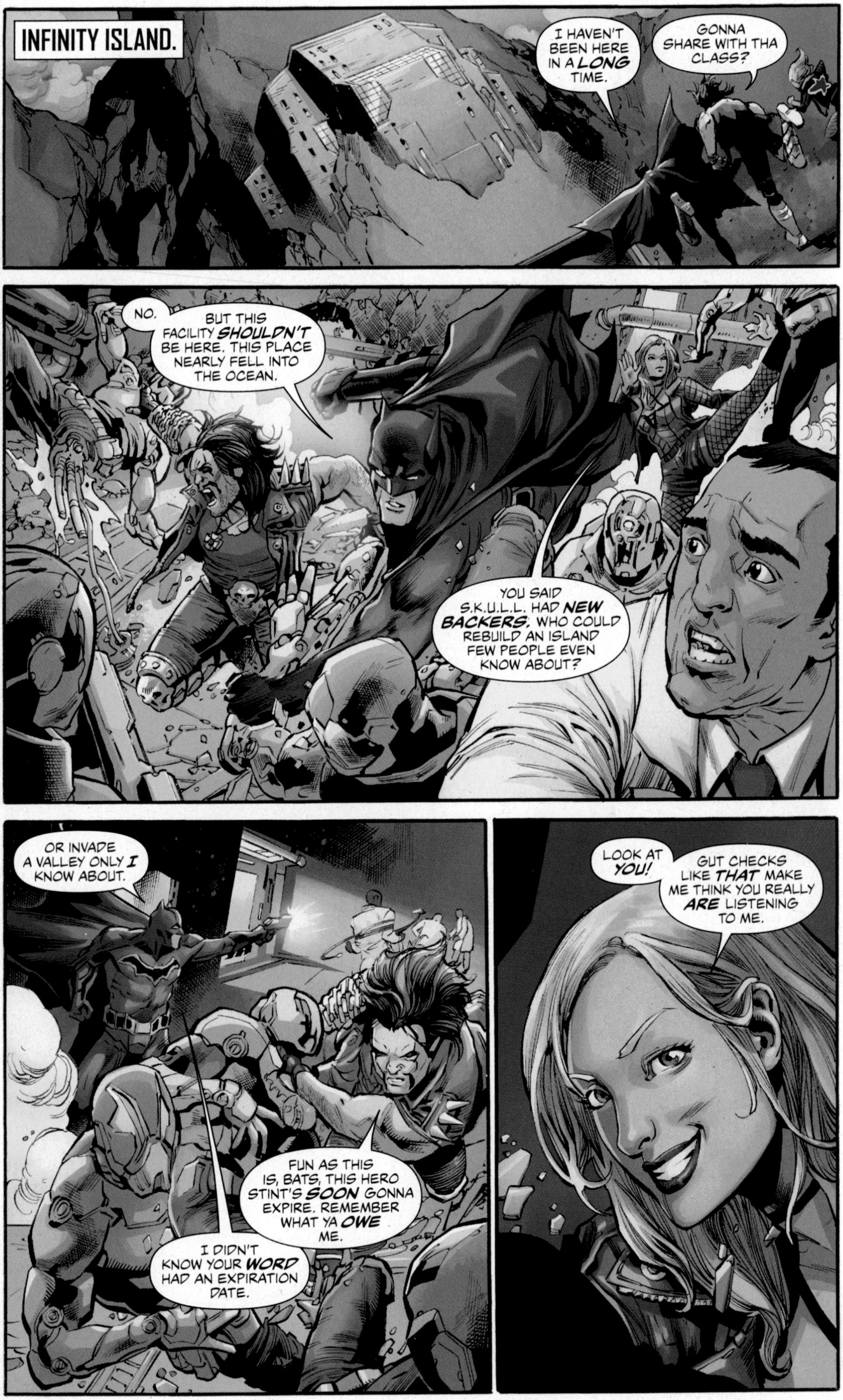
INFINITY ISLAND.
I HAVEN'T BEEN HERE IN A LONG TIME.
GONNA SHARE WITH THA CLASS?
NO.
BUT THIS FACILITY SHOULDN'T BE HERE. THIS PLACE NEARLY FELL INTO THE OCEAN.
YOU SAID S.K.U.L.L. HAD NEW BACKERS. WHO COULD REBUILD AN ISLAND FEW PEOPLE EVEN KNOW ABOUT?
OR INVADE A VALLEY ONLY I KNOW ABOUT.
FUN AS THIS IS, BATS, THIS HERO STINT'S SOON GONNA EXPIRE. REMEMBER WHAT YA OWE ME.
I DIDN'T KNOW YOUR WORD HAD AN EXPIRATION DATE.
LOOK AT YOU!
GUT CHECKS LIKE THAT MAKE ME THINK YOU REALLY ARE LISTENING TO ME.

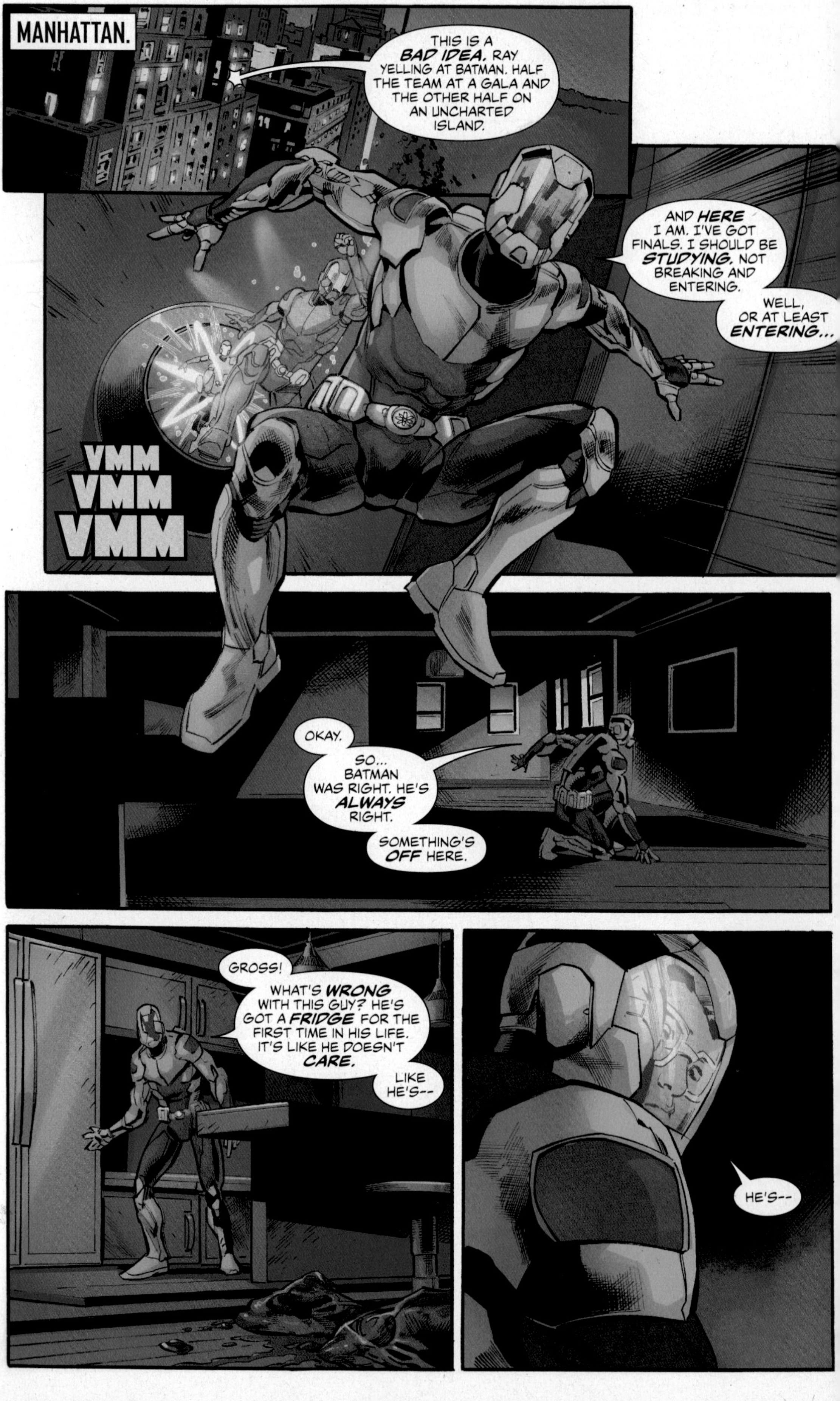
MANHATTAN.
THIS IS A BAD IDEA. RAY YELLING AT BATMAN. HALF THE TEAM AT A GALA AND THE OTHER HALF ON AN UNCHARTED ISLAND.
AND HERE I AM. I'VE GOT FINALS. I SHOULD BE STUDYING, NOT BREAKING AND ENTERING.
WELL, OR AT LEAST ENTERING...
VMM VMM VMM
OKAY.
SO... BATMAN WAS RIGHT. HE'S ALWAYS RIGHT.
SOMETHING'S OFF HERE.
GROSS!
WHAT'S WRONG WITH THIS GUY? HE'S GOT A FRIDGE FOR THE FIRST TIME IN HIS LIFE. IT'S LIKE HE DOESN'T CARE.
LIKE HE'S--
HE'S--

TAKE YER TIME, BATS!

GETTING TIRED, LOBO?

FRAG OFF! GETTIN' BORED.

OH--

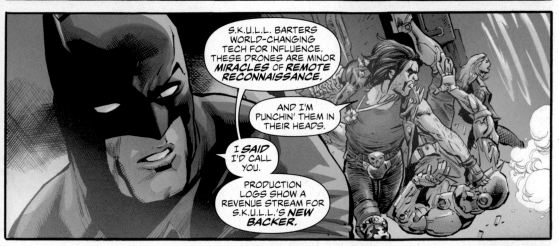

S.K.U.L.L. BARTERS WORLD-CHANGING TECH FOR INFLUENCE. THESE DRONES ARE MINOR MIRACLES OF REMOTE RECONNAISSANCE.

AND I'M PUNCHIN' THEM IN THEIR HEADS.

I SAID I'D CALL YOU.

PRODUCTION LOGS SHOW A REVENUE STREAM FOR S.K.U.L.L.'S NEW BACKER.

OH NO.

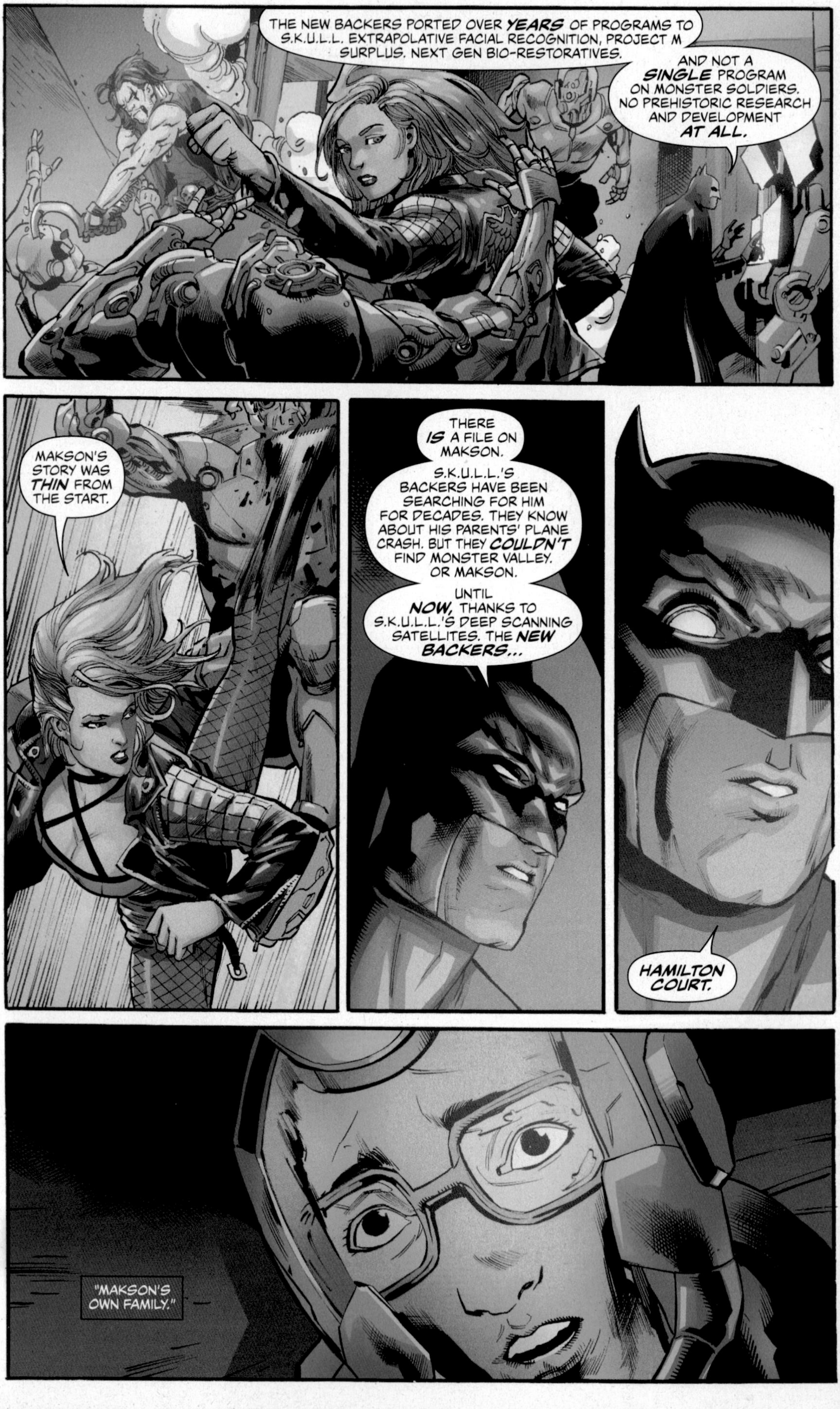
THE NEW BACKERS PORTED OVER YEARS OF PROGRAMS TO S.K.U.L.L. EXTRAPOLATIVE FACIAL RECOGNITION, PROJECT M SURPLUS. NEXT GEN BIO-RESTORATIVES.
AND NOT A SINGLE PROGRAM ON MONSTER SOLDIERS. NO PREHISTORIC RESEARCH AND DEVELOPMENT AT ALL.
MAKSON'S STORY WAS THIN FROM THE START.
THERE IS A FILE ON MAKSON.
S.K.U.L.L.'S BACKERS HAVE BEEN SEARCHING FOR HIM FOR DECADES. THEY KNOW ABOUT HIS PARENTS' PLANE CRASH. BUT THEY COULDN'T FIND MONSTER VALLEY. OR MAKSON.
UNTIL NOW, THANKS TO S.K.U.L.L.'S DEEP SCANNING SATELLITES. THE NEW BACKERS...
HAMILTON COURT.
"MAKSON'S OWN FAMILY."

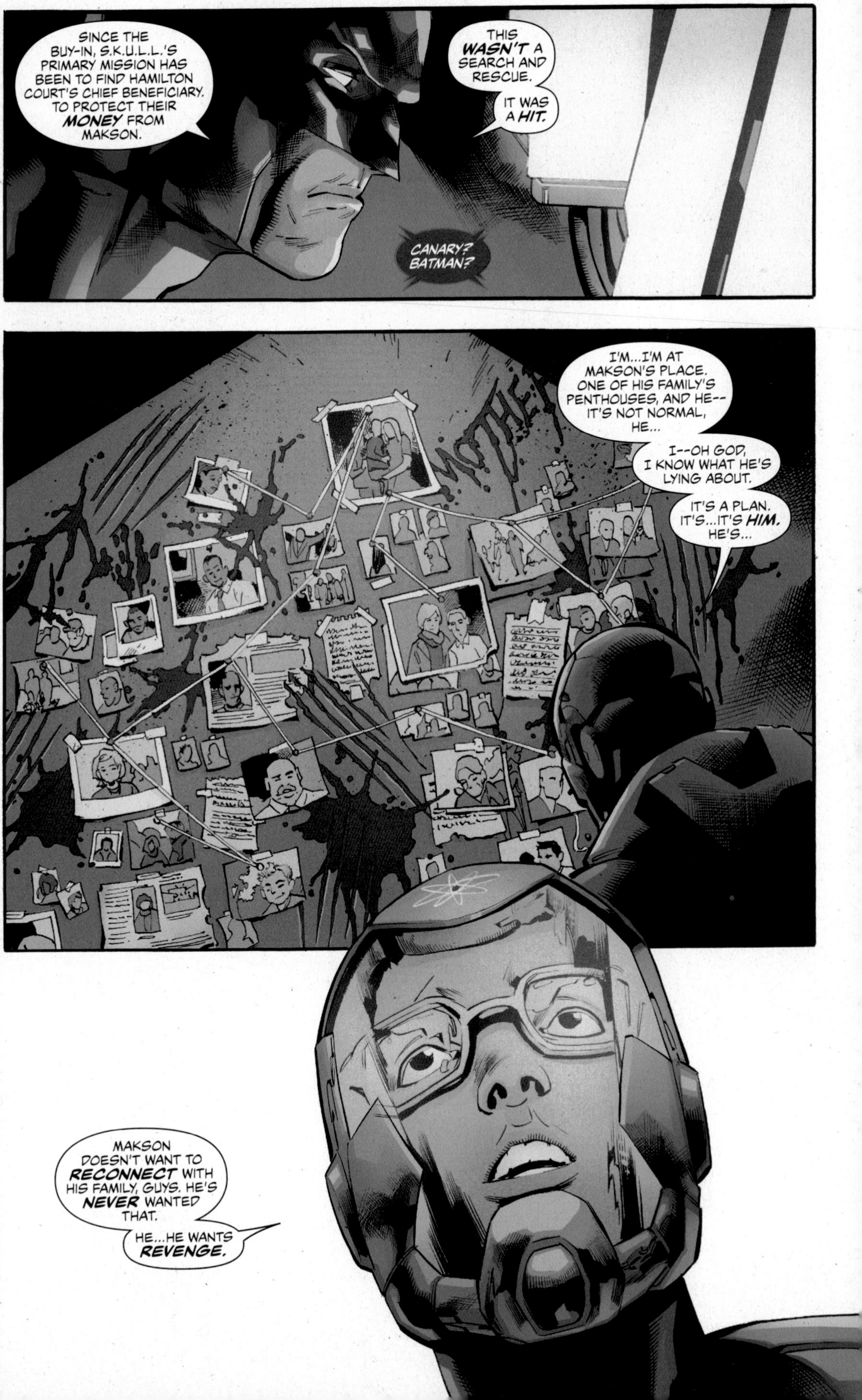

SINCE THE BUY-IN, S.K.U.L.L.'S PRIMARY MISSION HAS BEEN TO FIND HAMILTON COURT'S CHIEF BENEFICIARY. TO PROTECT THEIR MONEY FROM MAKSON.
THIS WASN'T A SEARCH AND RESCUE.
IT WAS A HIT.
CANARY? BATMAN?
I'M...I'M AT MAKSON'S PLACE. ONE OF HIS FAMILY'S PENTHOUSES, AND HE-- IT'S NOT NORMAL, HE...
I--OH GOD, I KNOW WHAT HE'S LYING ABOUT.
IT'S A PLAN. IT'S...IT'S HIM. HE'S...
MAKSON DOESN'T WANT TO RECONNECT WITH HIS FAMILY, GUYS. HE'S NEVER WANTED THAT.
HE...HE WANTS REVENGE.

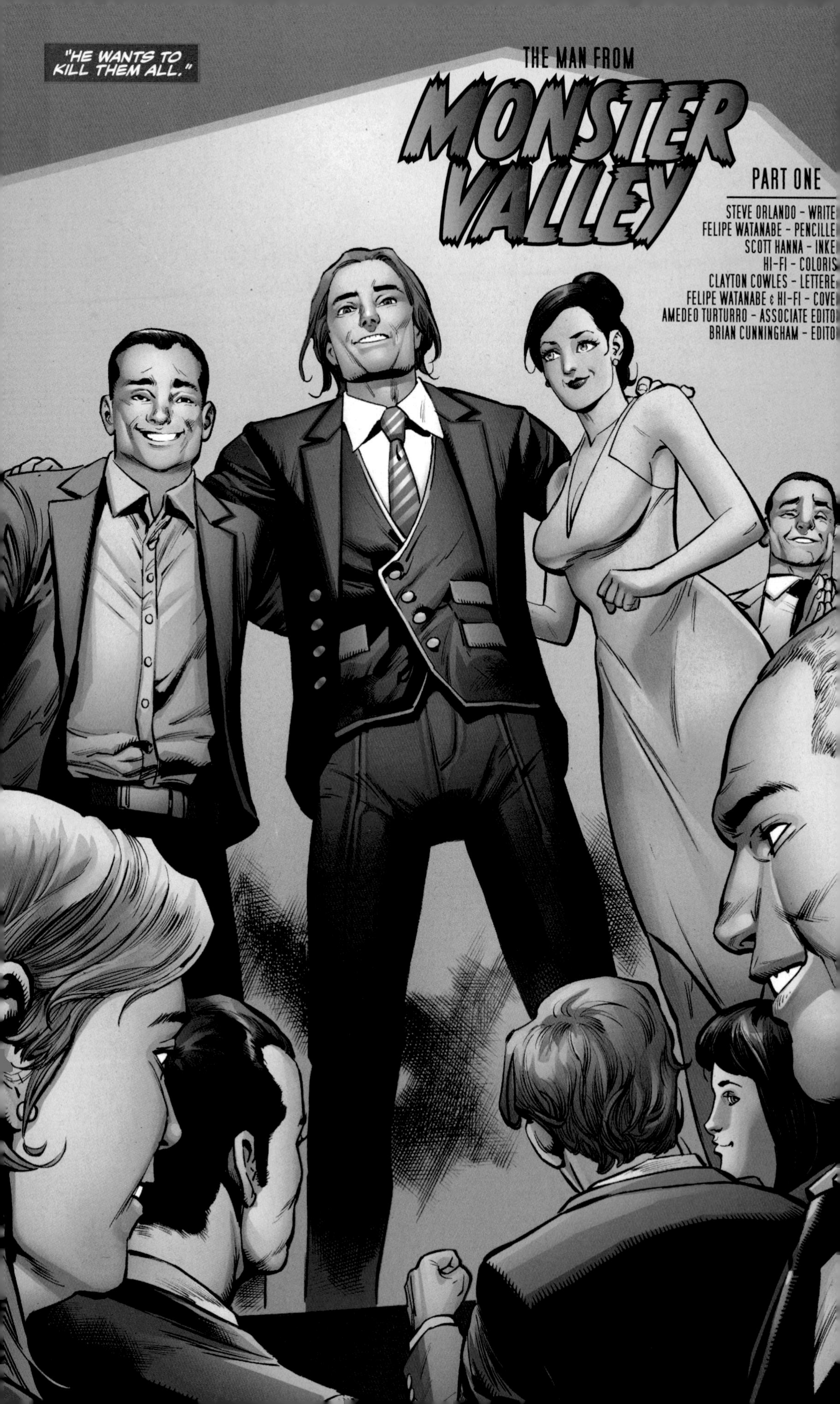
"HE WANTS TO KILL THEM ALL."
THE MAN FROM
MONSTER VALLEY
PART ONE
STEVE ORLANDO - WRITE
FELIPE WATANABE - PENCILLE
SCOTT HANNA - INKE
HI-FI - COLORIS
CLAYTON COWLES - LETTERE
FELIPE WATANABE & HI-FI - COVE
AMEDEO TURTURRO - ASSOCIATE EDITO
BRIAN CUNNINGHAM - EDITO

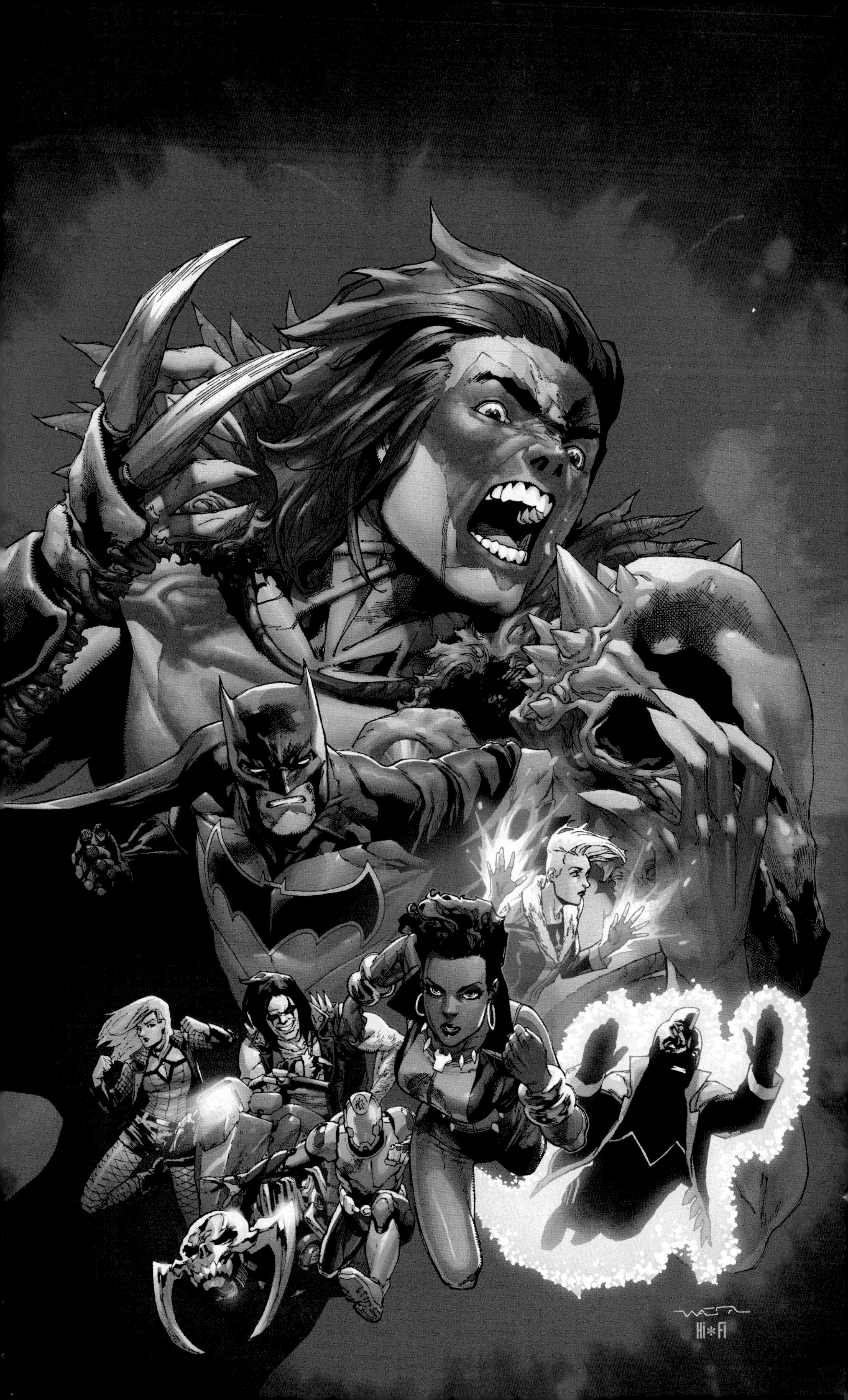

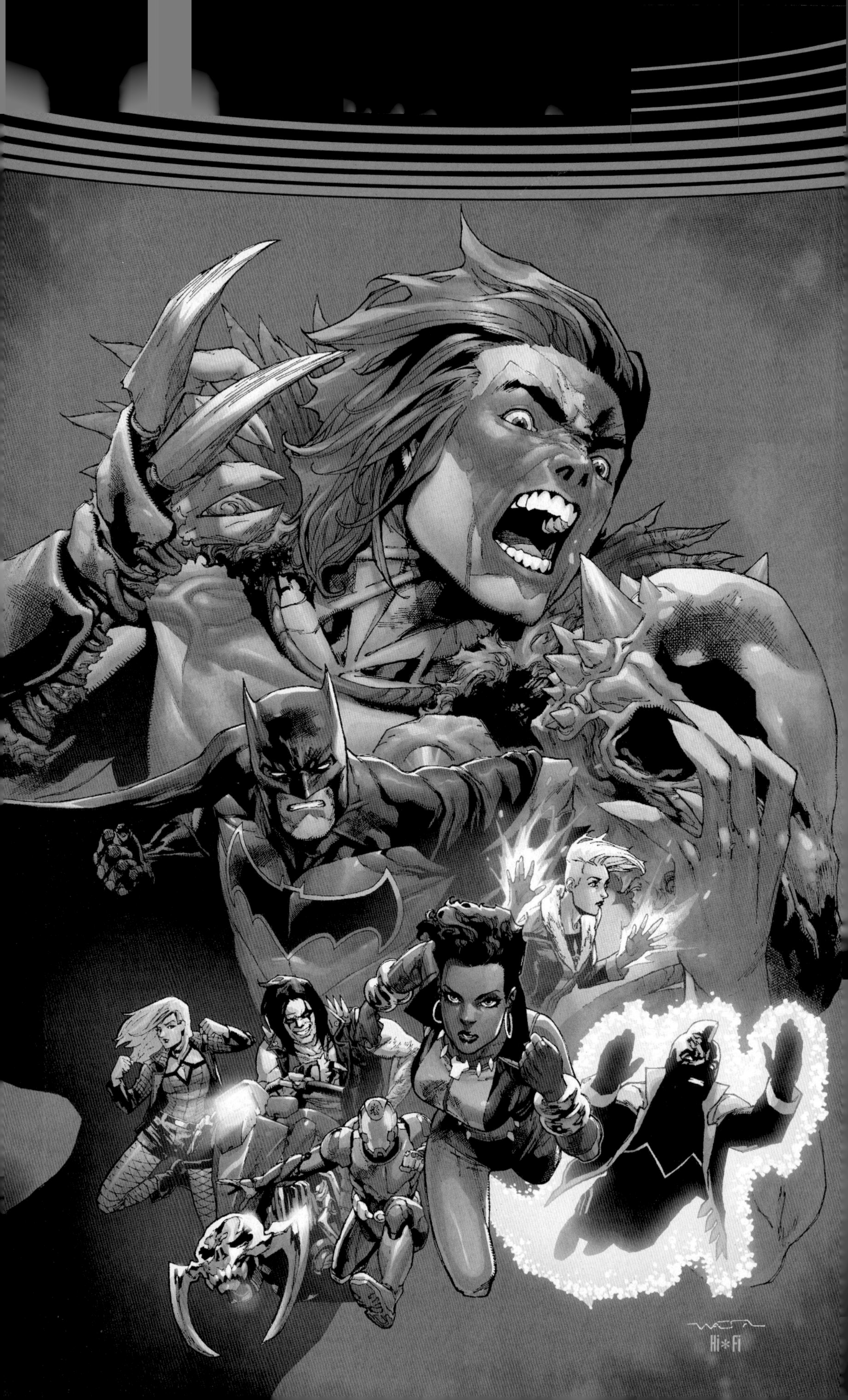
Hi*Fi

INFINITY ISLAND.

...MAKSON'S FAMILY'S **HEAVY** IN BLACK MARKET INVESTMENTS.

THEY SENT **S.K.U.L.L.** TO **KILL** HIM.

MANHATTAN.

WHAT ARE YOU SEEING IN HIS APARTMENT, ATOM? REPEAT.

HIS **PLAN,** CANARY. I--I FOUND HIS **PLAN.** I'M SCANNING IT NOW...

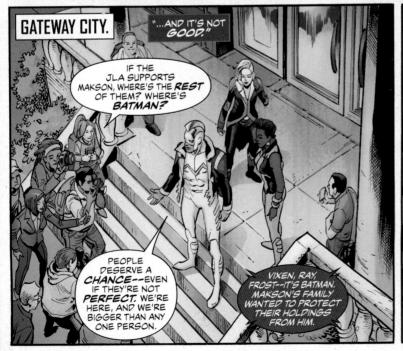

GATEWAY CITY.

"...AND IT'S NOT **GOOD.**"

IF THE JLA SUPPORTS MAKSON, WHERE'S THE **REST** OF THEM? WHERE'S **BATMAN?**

PEOPLE DESERVE A **CHANCE**--EVEN IF THEY'RE NOT **PERFECT.** WE'RE HERE, AND WE'RE BIGGER THAN ANY ONE PERSON.

VIXEN, RAY, FROST--IT'S BATMAN. MAKSON'S FAMILY WANTED TO PROTECT THEIR HOLDINGS FROM HIM.

THEY FOUND HIM. THEY KILLED HIS MOTHER IN MONSTER VALLEY-- THAT **CREATURE.** HE WANTS **REVENGE.**

GUYS, BATMAN'S RIGHT...

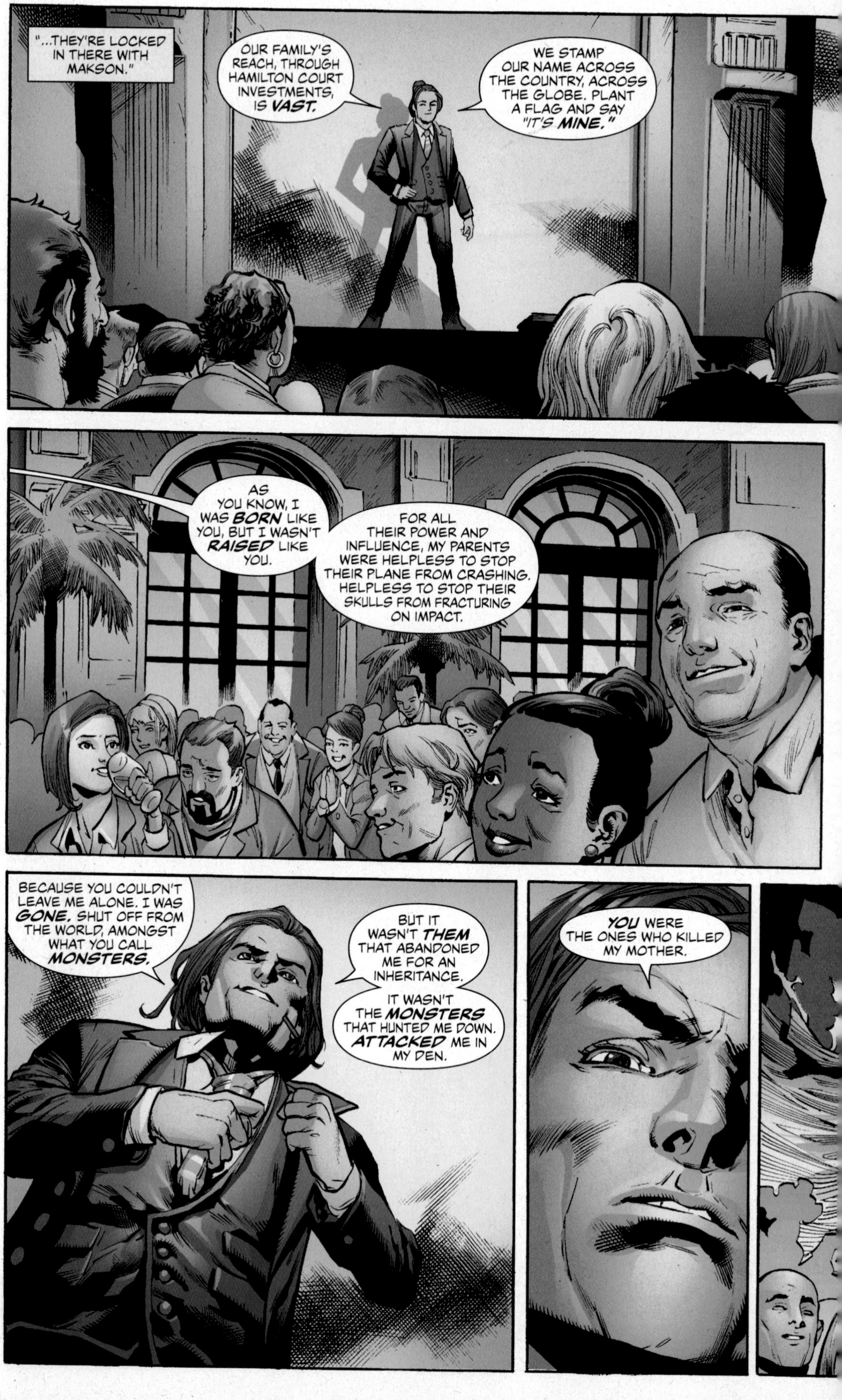
"...THEY'RE LOCKED IN THERE WITH MAKSON."
OUR FAMILY'S REACH, THROUGH HAMILTON COURT INVESTMENTS, IS *VAST.*
WE STAMP OUR NAME ACROSS THE COUNTRY, ACROSS THE GLOBE. PLANT A FLAG AND SAY "IT'S *MINE.*"
AS YOU KNOW, I WAS *BORN* LIKE YOU, BUT I WASN'T *RAISED* LIKE YOU.
FOR ALL THEIR POWER AND INFLUENCE, MY PARENTS WERE HELPLESS TO STOP THEIR PLANE FROM CRASHING. HELPLESS TO STOP THEIR SKULLS FROM FRACTURING ON IMPACT.
BECAUSE YOU COULDN'T LEAVE ME ALONE. I WAS *GONE.* SHUT OFF FROM THE WORLD, AMONGST WHAT YOU CALL *MONSTERS.*
BUT IT WASN'T *THEM* THAT ABANDONED ME FOR AN INHERITANCE.
IT WASN'T THE *MONSTERS* THAT HUNTED ME DOWN. *ATTACKED* ME IN MY DEN.
YOU WERE THE ONES WHO KILLED MY MOTHER.

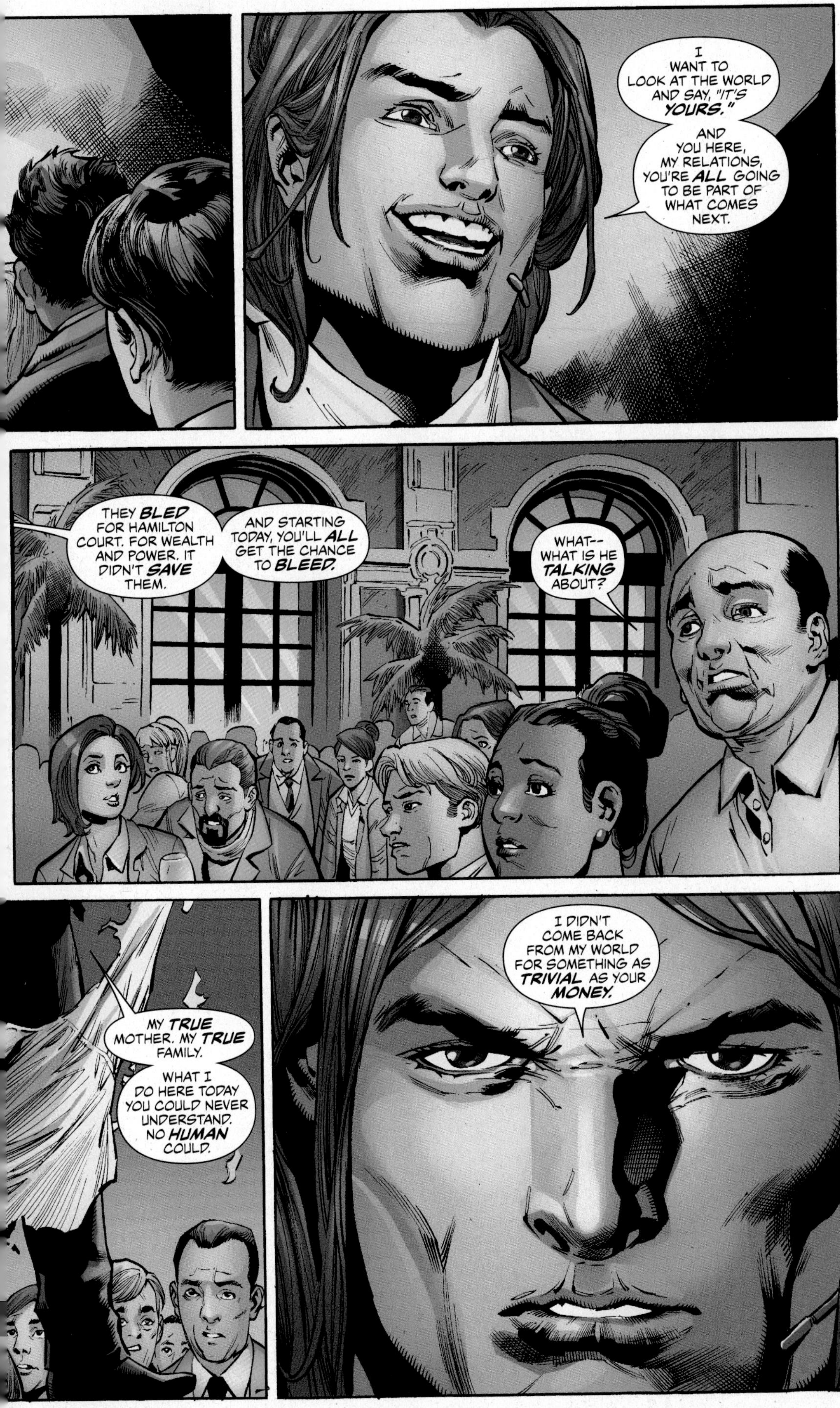
I WANT TO LOOK AT THE WORLD AND SAY, "IT'S YOURS."
AND YOU HERE, MY RELATIONS, YOU'RE ALL GOING TO BE PART OF WHAT COMES NEXT.
THEY BLED FOR HAMILTON COURT. FOR WEALTH AND POWER. IT DIDN'T SAVE THEM.
AND STARTING TODAY, YOU'LL ALL GET THE CHANCE TO BLEED.
WHAT-- WHAT IS HE TALKING ABOUT?
MY TRUE MOTHER. MY TRUE FAMILY.
WHAT I DO HERE TODAY YOU COULD NEVER UNDERSTAND. NO HUMAN COULD.
I DIDN'T COME BACK FROM MY WORLD FOR SOMETHING AS TRIVIAL AS YOUR MONEY.

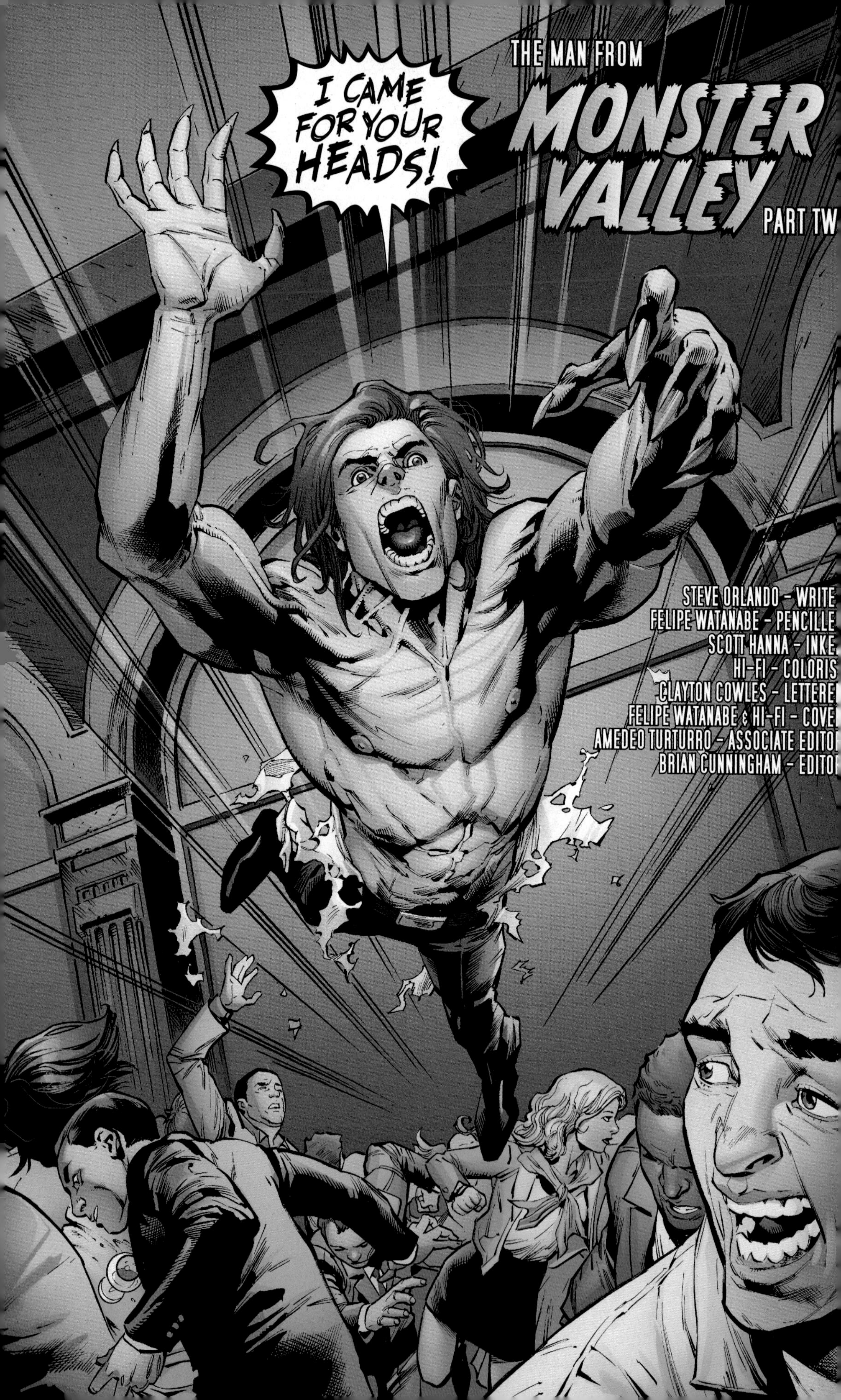
I CAME FOR YOUR HEADS!
THE MAN FROM
MONSTER VALLEY
PART TW
STEVE ORLANDO - WRITE
FELIPE WATANABE - PENCILLE
SCOTT HANNA - INKE
HI-FI - COLORIS
CLAYTON COWLES - LETTERE
FELIPE WATANABE & HI-FI - COVE
AMEDEO TURTURRO - ASSOCIATE EDITO
BRIAN CUNNINGHAM - EDITO

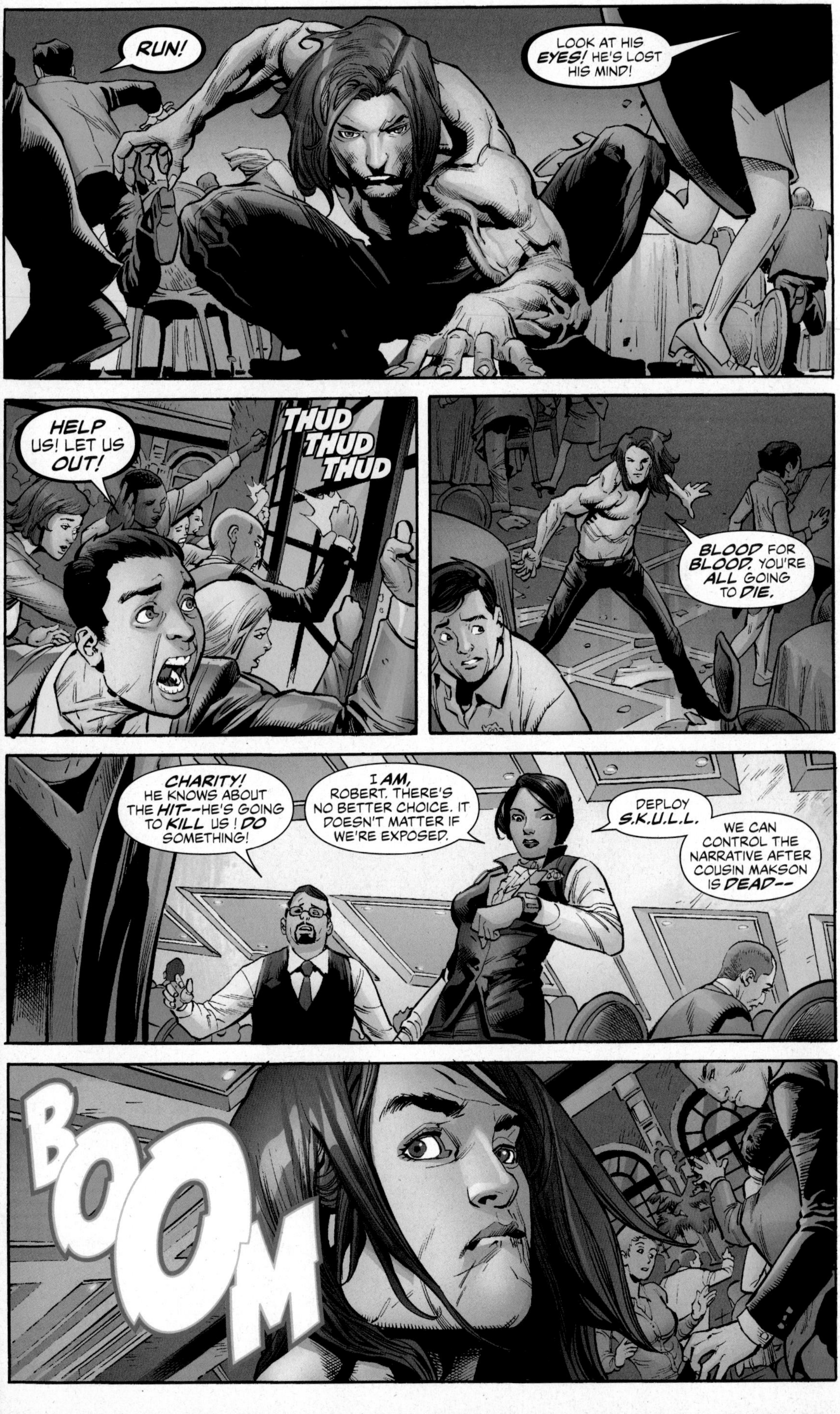
RUN!
LOOK AT HIS EYES! HE'S LOST HIS MIND!
HELP US! LET US OUT!
THUD THUD THUD
BLOOD FOR BLOOD. YOU'RE ALL GOING TO DIE.
CHARITY! HE KNOWS ABOUT THE HIT--HE'S GOING TO KILL US! DO SOMETHING!
I AM, ROBERT. THERE'S NO BETTER CHOICE. IT DOESN'T MATTER IF WE'RE EXPOSED.
DEPLOY S.K.U.L.L.
WE CAN CONTROL THE NARRATIVE AFTER COUSIN MAKSON IS DEAD--
BOOOM

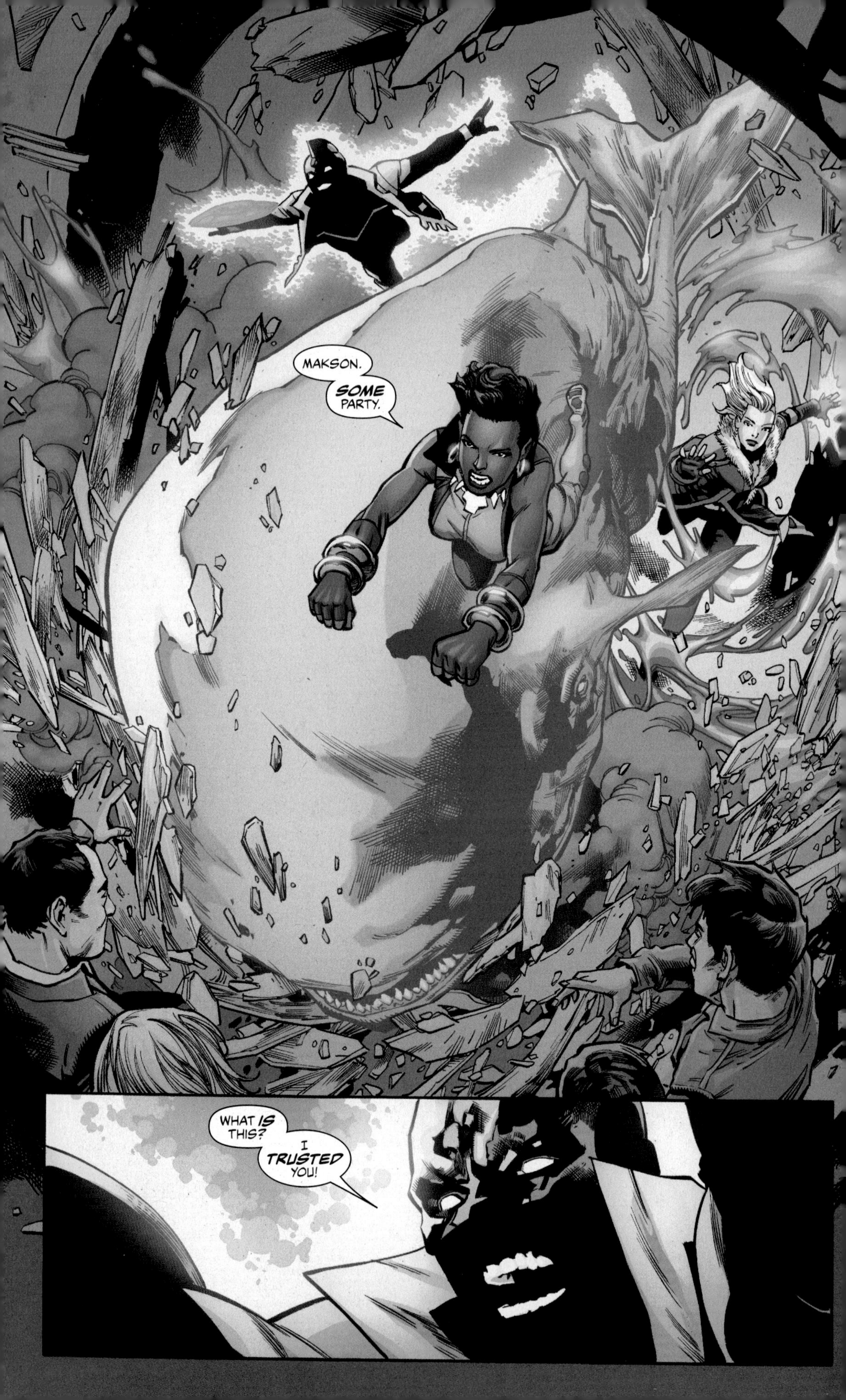
MAKSON.
SOME PARTY.
WHAT IS THIS?
I TRUSTED YOU!

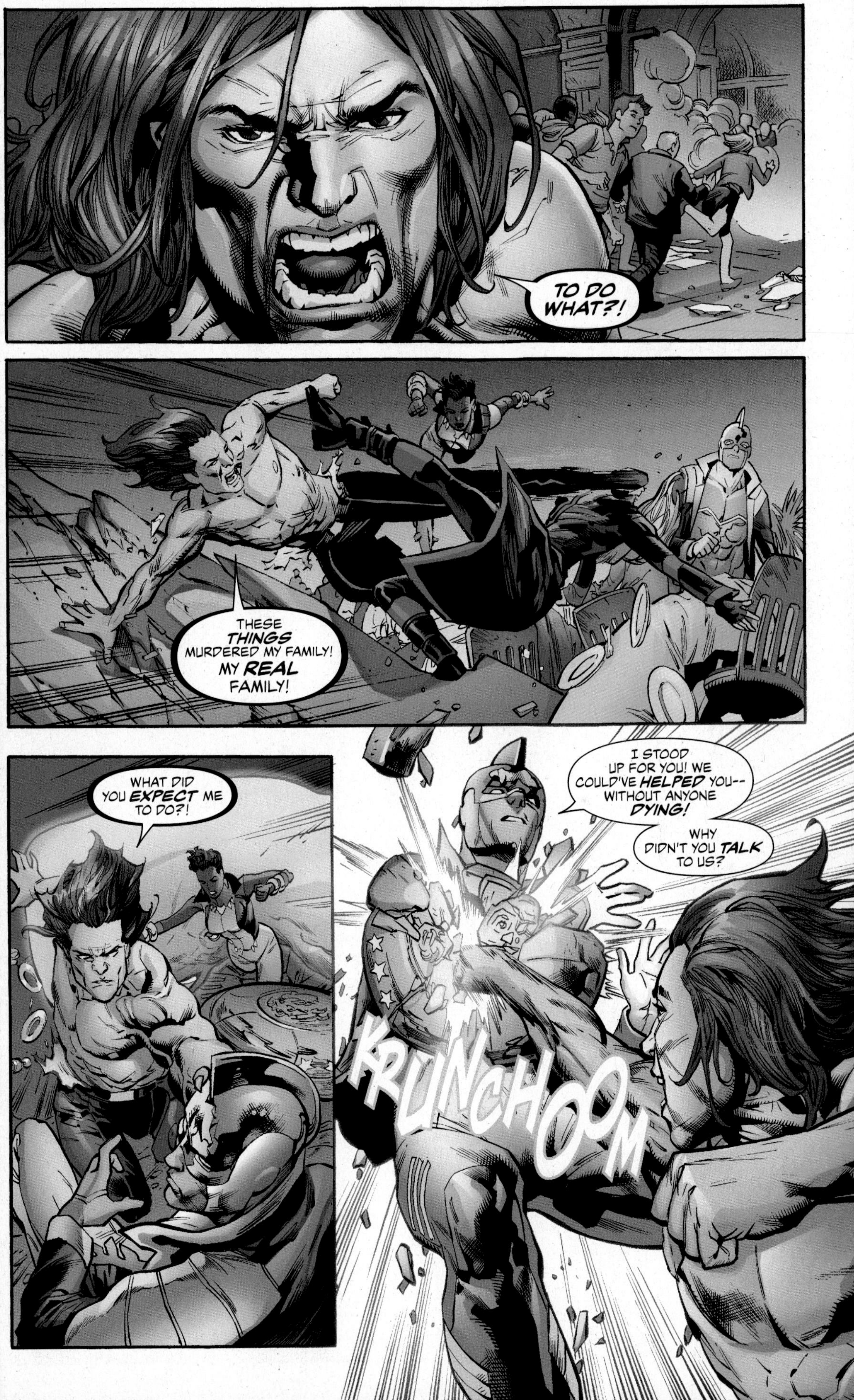
TO DO WHAT?!
THESE THINGS MURDERED MY FAMILY! MY REAL FAMILY!
WHAT DID YOU EXPECT ME TO DO?!
I STOOD UP FOR YOU! WE COULD'VE HELPED YOU-- WITHOUT ANYONE DYING!
WHY DIDN'T YOU TALK TO US?
KRUNCHOOM

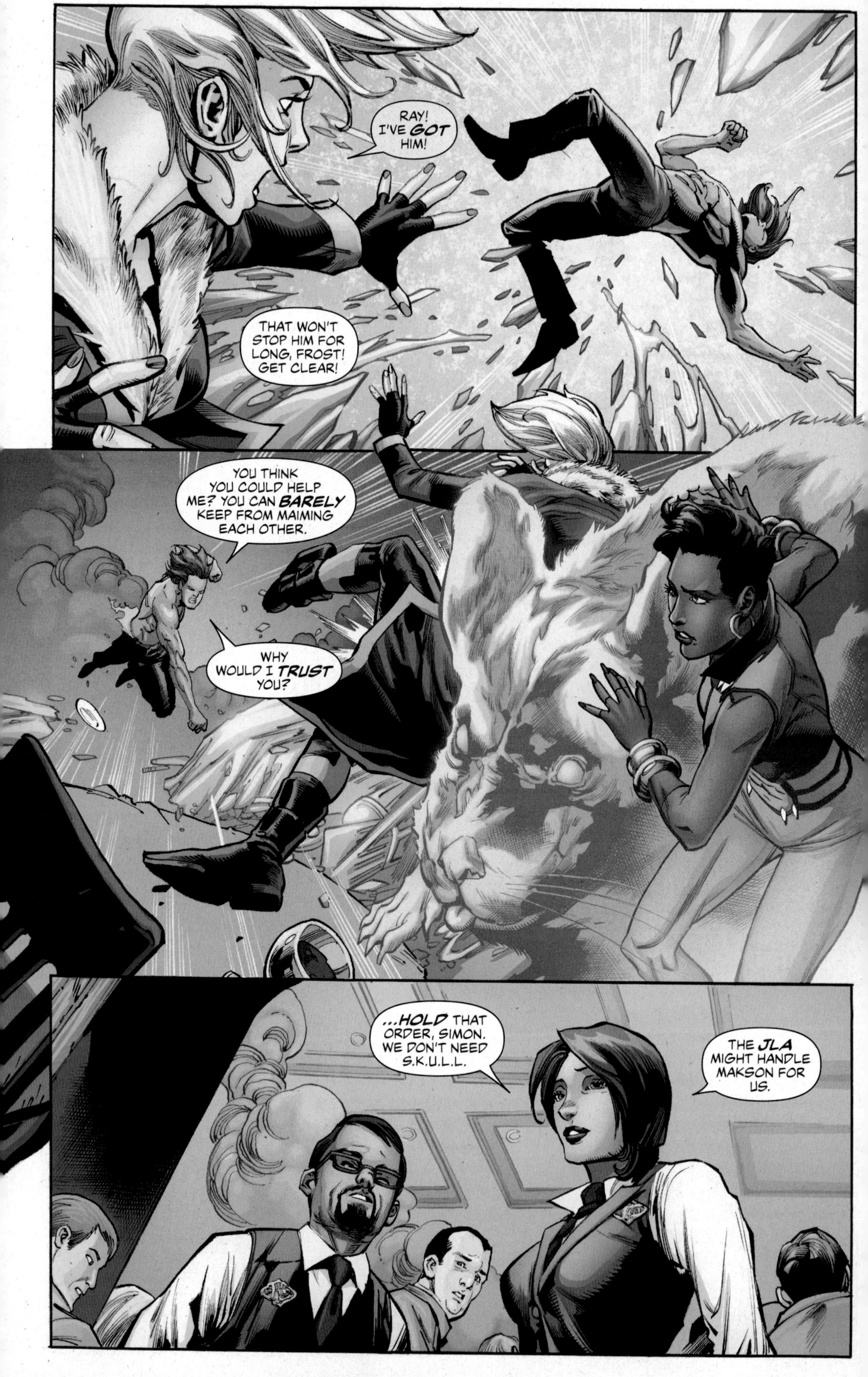
RAY! I'VE GOT HIM!
THAT WON'T STOP HIM FOR LONG, FROST! GET CLEAR!
YOU THINK YOU COULD HELP ME? YOU CAN BARELY KEEP FROM MAIMING EACH OTHER.
WHY WOULD I TRUST YOU?
...HOLD THAT ORDER, SIMON. WE DON'T NEED S.K.U.L.L.
THE JLA MIGHT HANDLE MAKSON FOR US.

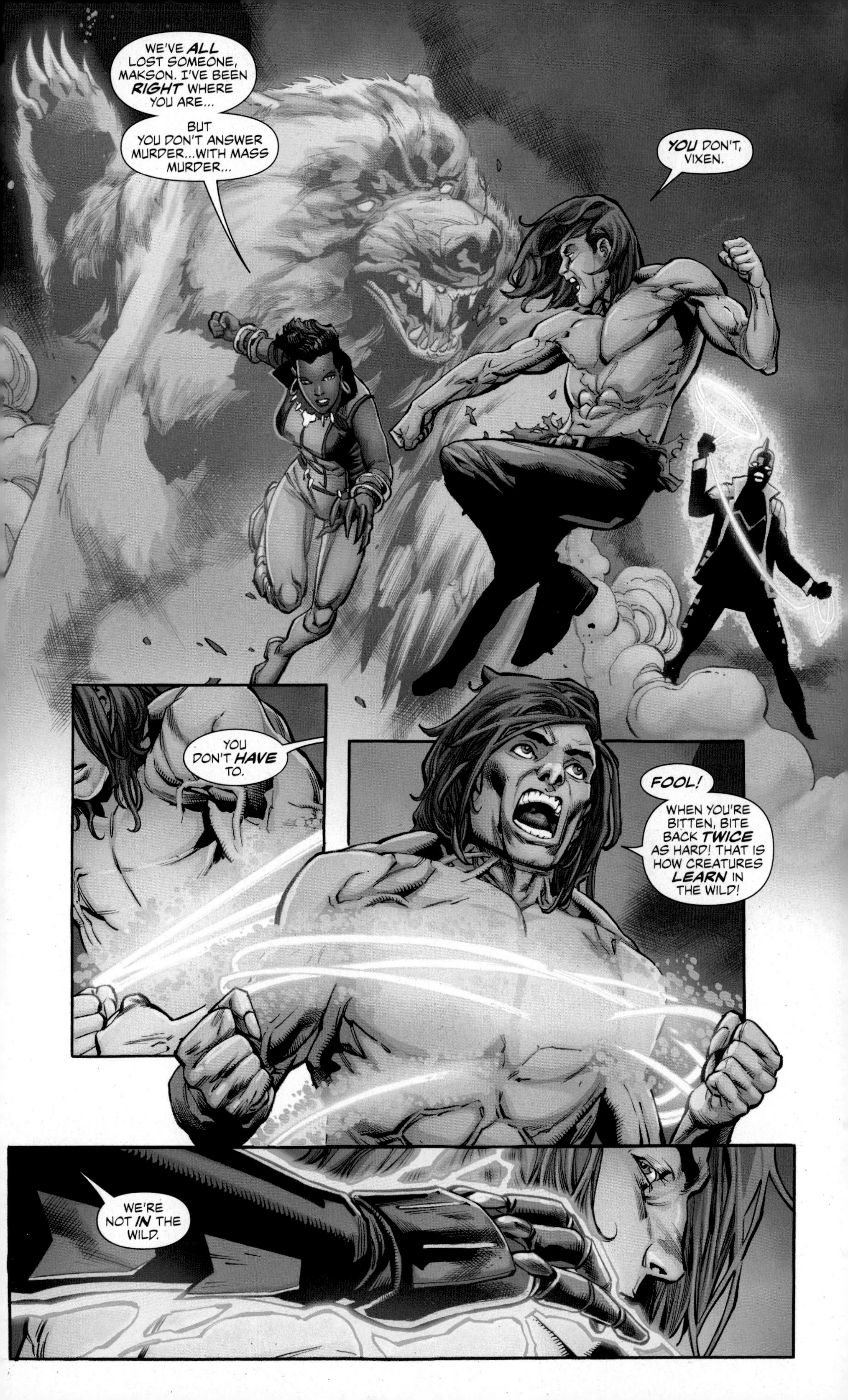
WE'VE ALL LOST SOMEONE, MAKSON. I'VE BEEN RIGHT WHERE YOU ARE...
BUT YOU DON'T ANSWER MURDER...WITH MASS MURDER...
YOU DON'T, VIXEN.
YOU DON'T HAVE TO.
FOOL!
WHEN YOU'RE BITTEN, BITE BACK TWICE AS HARD! THAT IS HOW CREATURES LEARN IN THE WILD!
WE'RE NOT IN THE WILD.

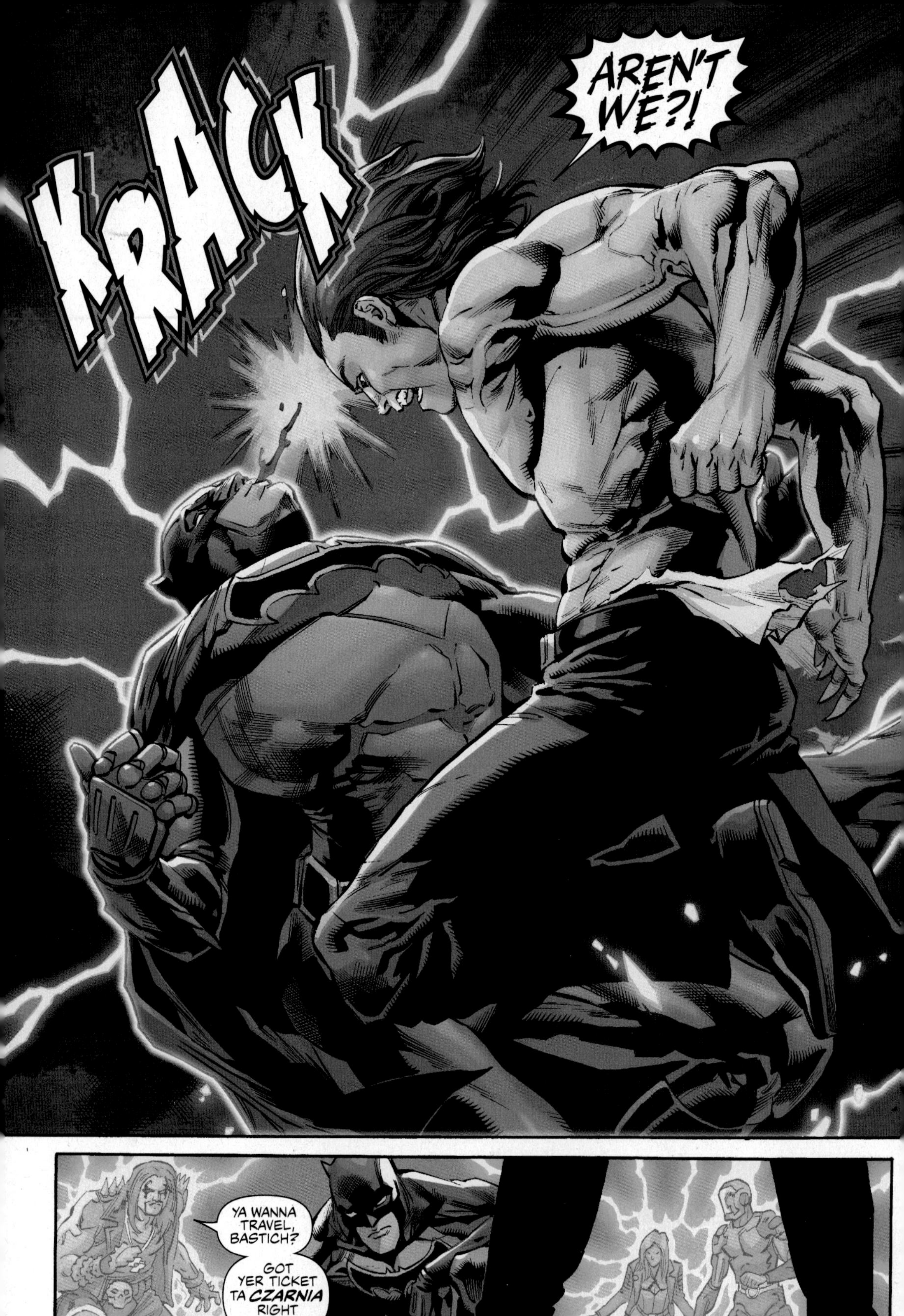
KRACK
AREN'T WE?!

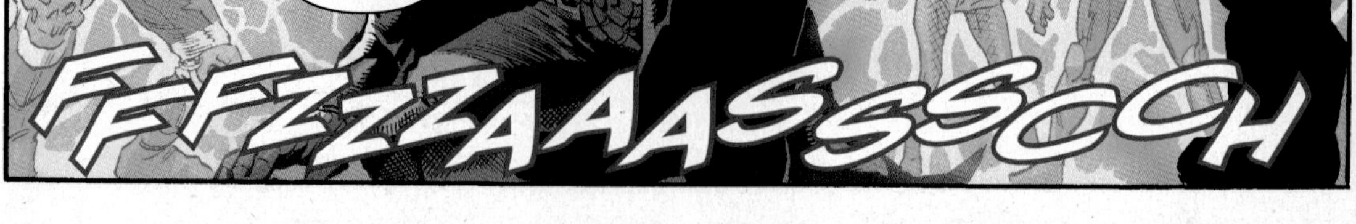
YA WANNA TRAVEL, BASTICH?
GOT YER TICKET TA CZARNIA RIGHT HERE.
FFFZZZAAASSSCCH

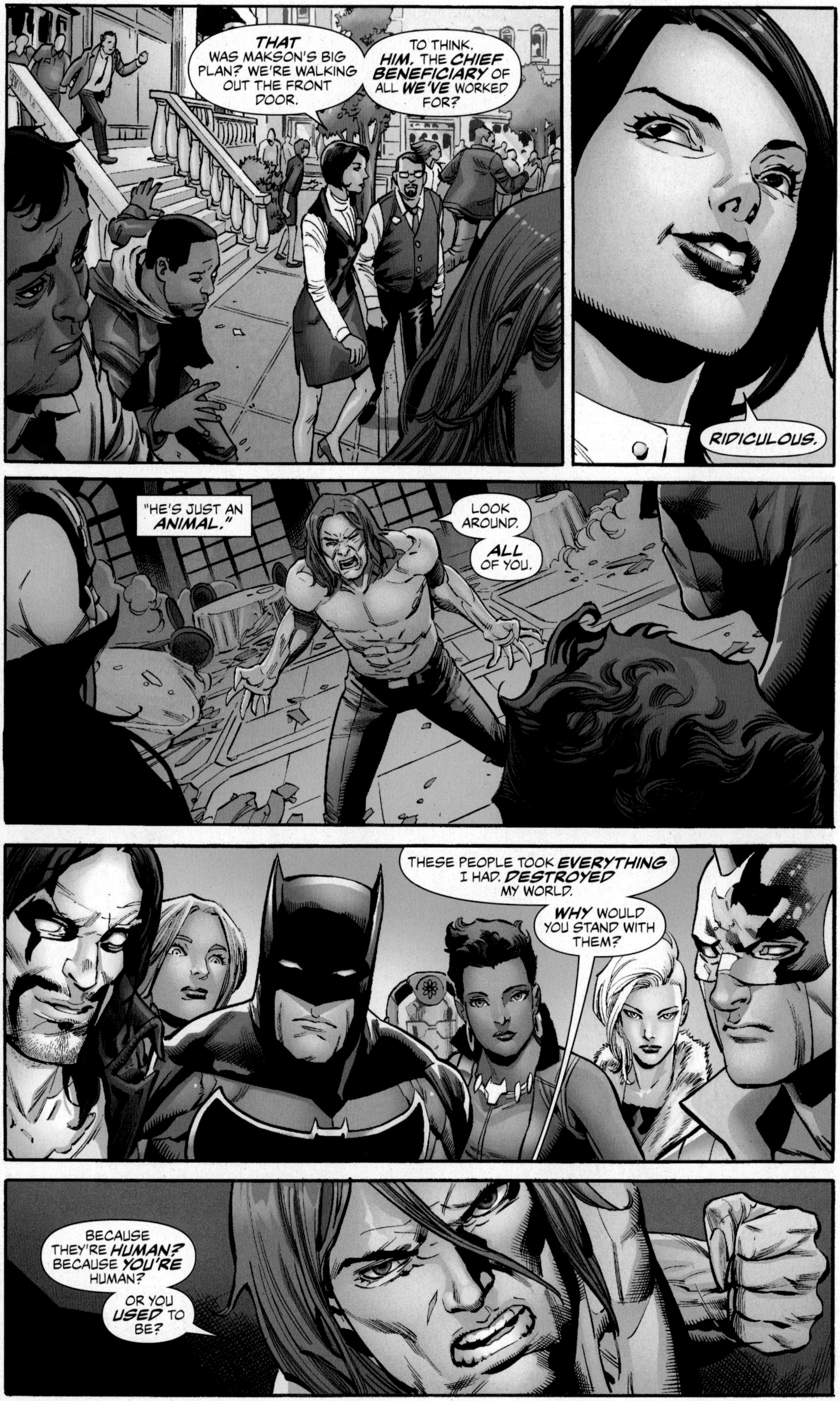
THAT WAS MAKSON'S BIG PLAN? WE'RE WALKING OUT THE FRONT DOOR.
TO THINK. HIM, THE CHIEF BENEFICIARY OF ALL WE'VE WORKED FOR?
RIDICULOUS.
"HE'S JUST AN ANIMAL."
LOOK AROUND.
ALL OF YOU.
THESE PEOPLE TOOK EVERYTHING I HAD. DESTROYED MY WORLD.
WHY WOULD YOU STAND WITH THEM?
BECAUSE THEY'RE HUMAN? BECAUSE YOU'RE HUMAN?
OR YOU USED TO BE?

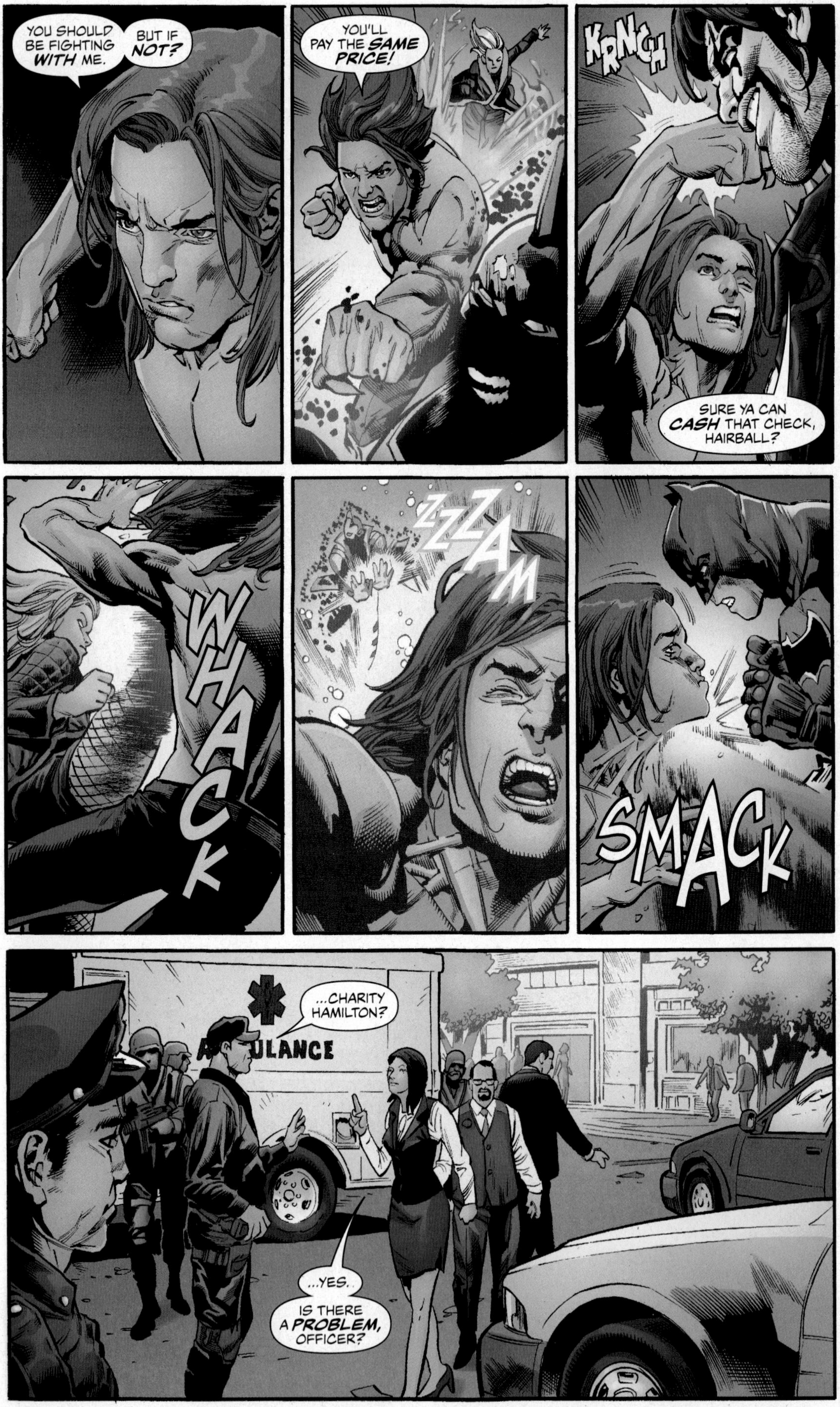

YOU SHOULD BE FIGHTING WITH ME.
BUT IF NOT?
YOU'LL PAY THE SAME PRICE!
KRNCH
SURE YA CAN CASH THAT CHECK, HAIRBALL?
WHACK
ZZZZAM
SMACK
...CHARITY HAMILTON?
AMBULANCE
...YES.
IS THERE A PROBLEM, OFFICER?

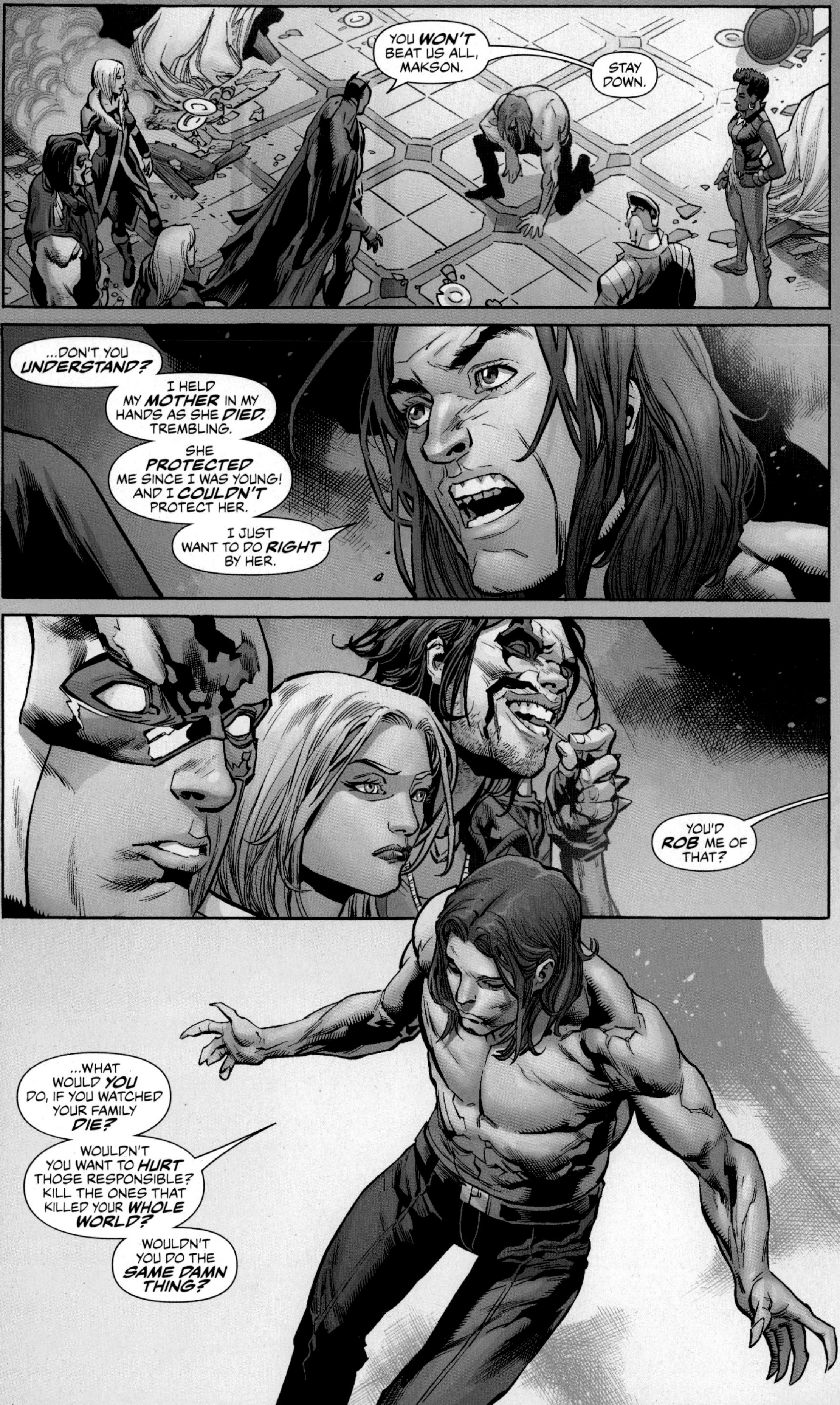
YOU WON'T BEAT US ALL, MAKSON.
STAY DOWN.
...DON'T YOU UNDERSTAND?
I HELD MY MOTHER IN MY HANDS AS SHE DIED. TREMBLING.
SHE PROTECTED ME SINCE I WAS YOUNG! AND I COULDN'T PROTECT HER.
I JUST WANT TO DO RIGHT BY HER.
YOU'D ROB ME OF THAT?
...WHAT WOULD YOU DO, IF YOU WATCHED YOUR FAMILY DIE?
WOULDN'T YOU WANT TO HURT THOSE RESPONSIBLE? KILL THE ONES THAT KILLED YOUR WHOLE WORLD?
WOULDN'T YOU DO THE SAME DAMN THING?

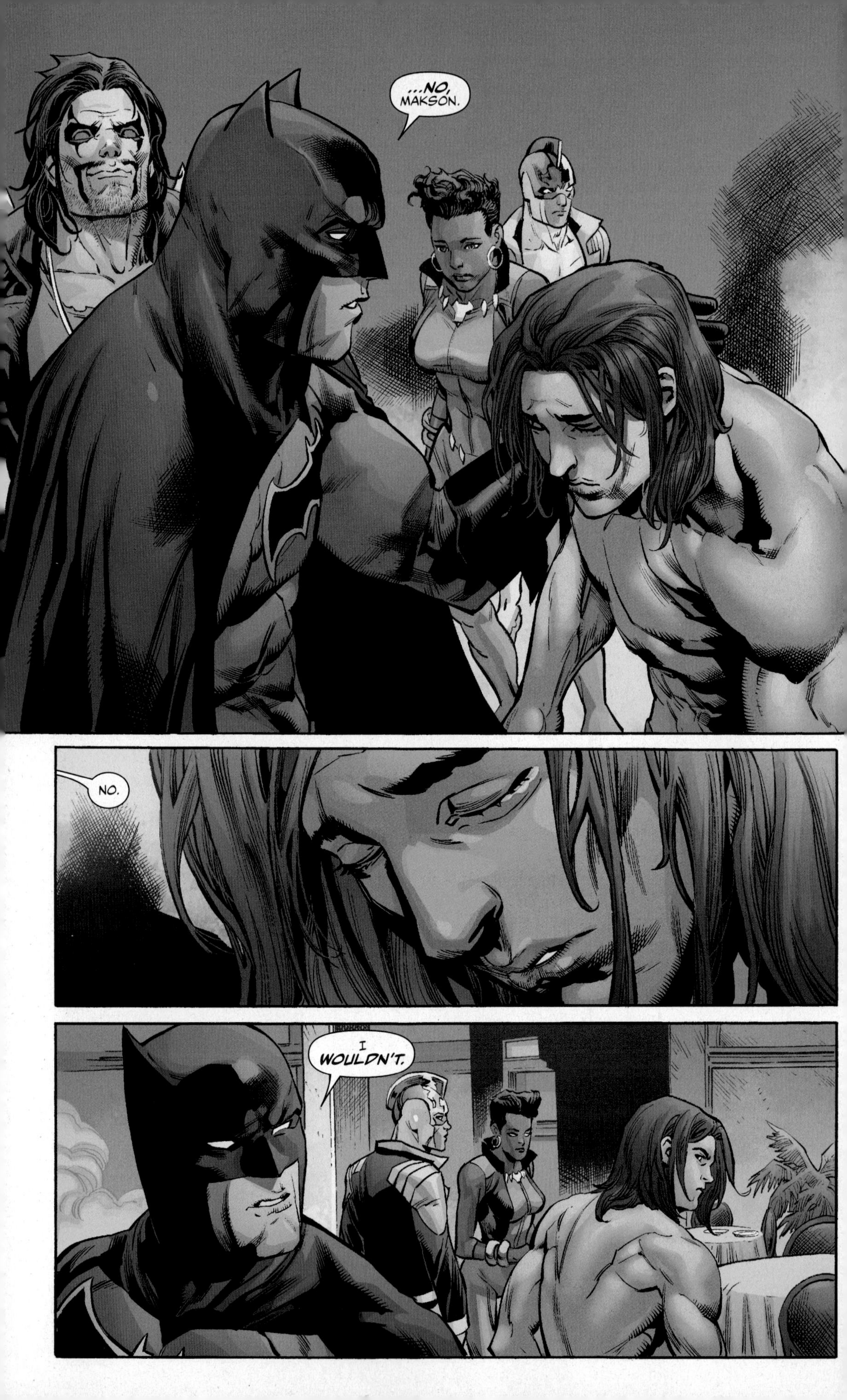
...NO, MAKSON.
NO.
I WOULDN'T.

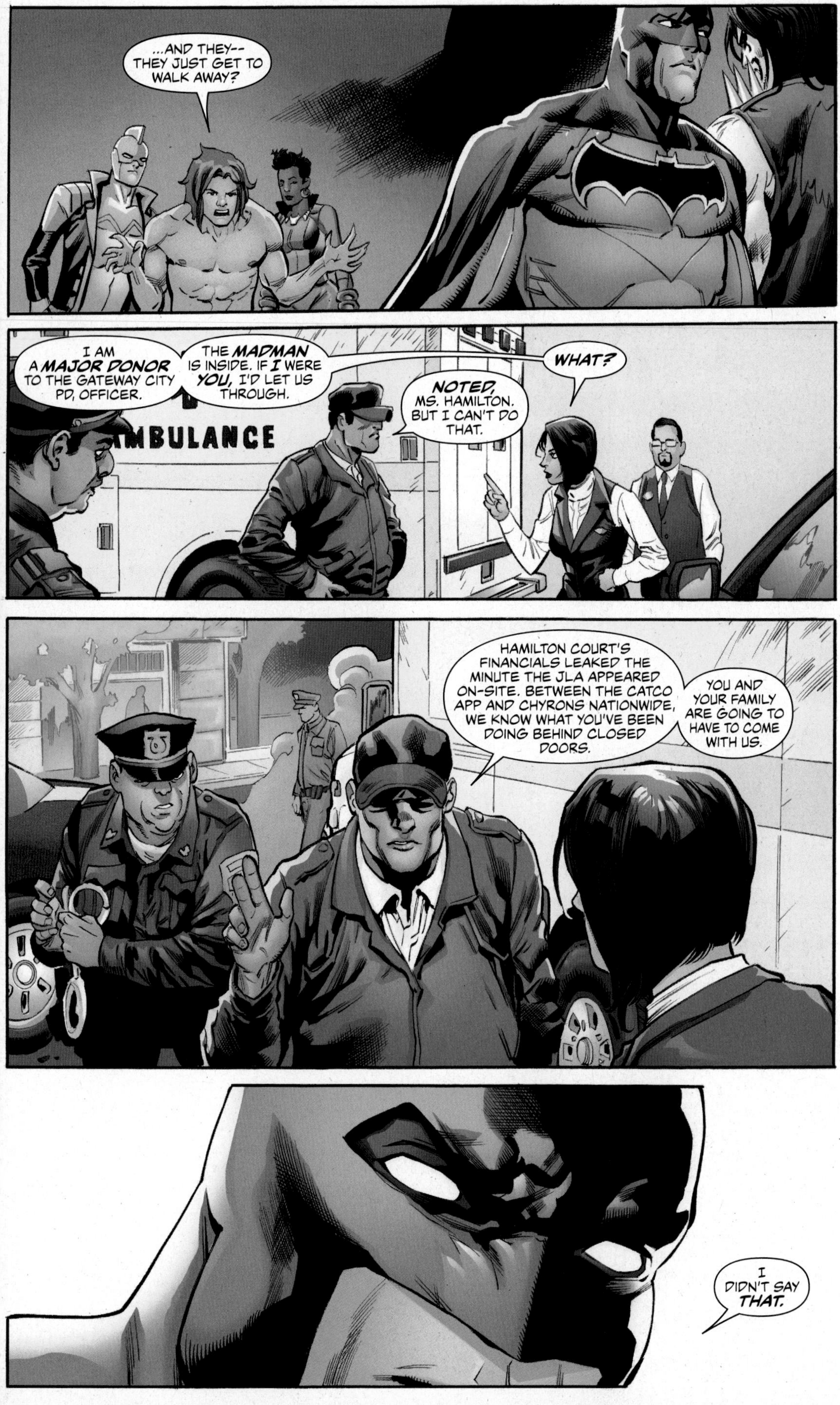
...AND THEY-- THEY JUST GET TO WALK AWAY?
I AM A MAJOR DONOR TO THE GATEWAY CITY PD, OFFICER.
THE MADMAN IS INSIDE. IF I WERE YOU, I'D LET US THROUGH.
NOTED, MS. HAMILTON. BUT I CAN'T DO THAT.
WHAT?
AMBULANCE
HAMILTON COURT'S FINANCIALS LEAKED THE MINUTE THE JLA APPEARED ON-SITE. BETWEEN THE CATCO APP AND CHYRONS NATIONWIDE, WE KNOW WHAT YOU'VE BEEN DOING BEHIND CLOSED DOORS.
YOU AND YOUR FAMILY ARE GOING TO HAVE TO COME WITH US.
I DIDN'T SAY THAT.

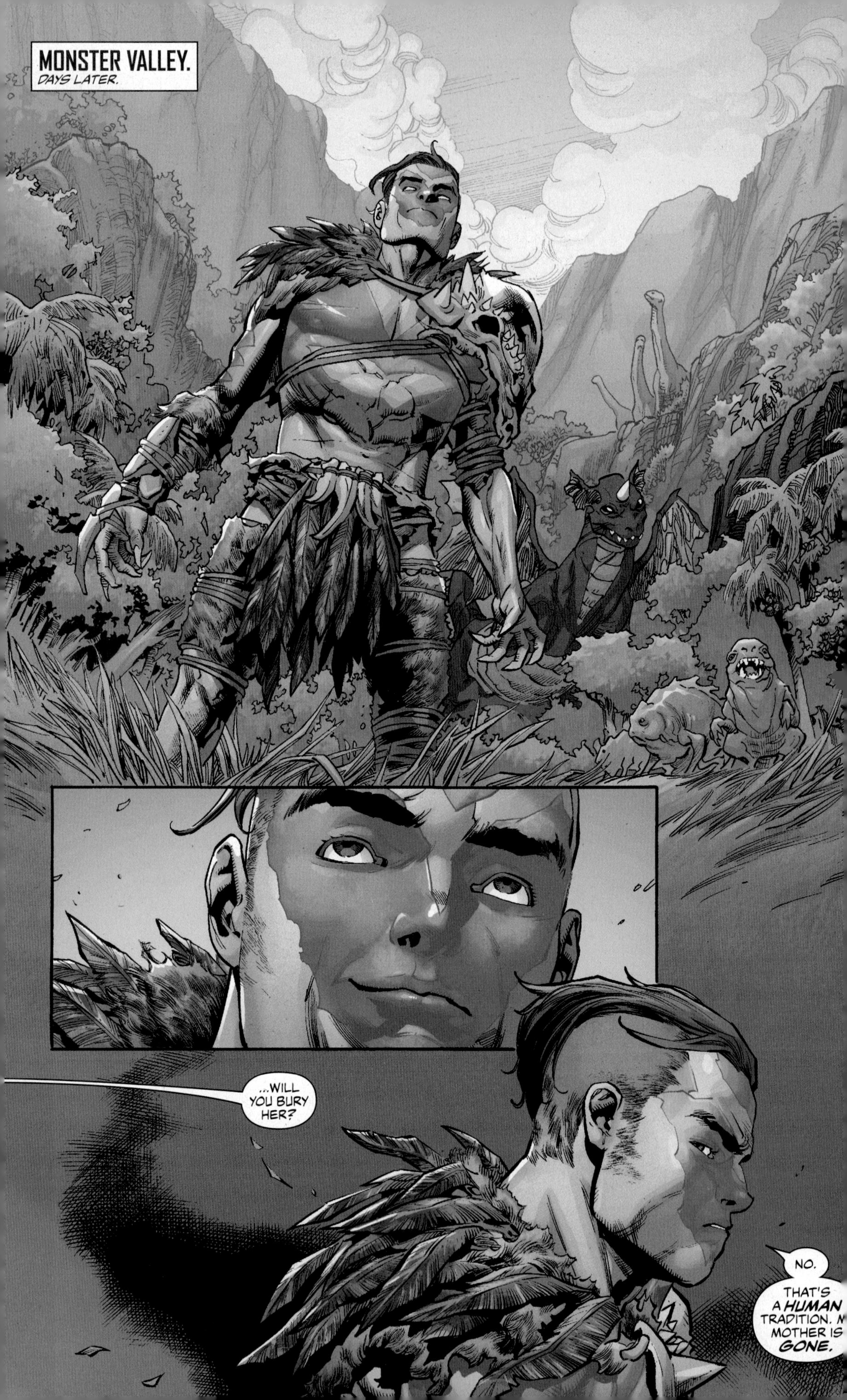
MONSTER VALLEY.
DAYS LATER.
...WILL YOU BURY HER?
NO.
THAT'S A HUMAN TRADITION.
MOTHER IS GONE.

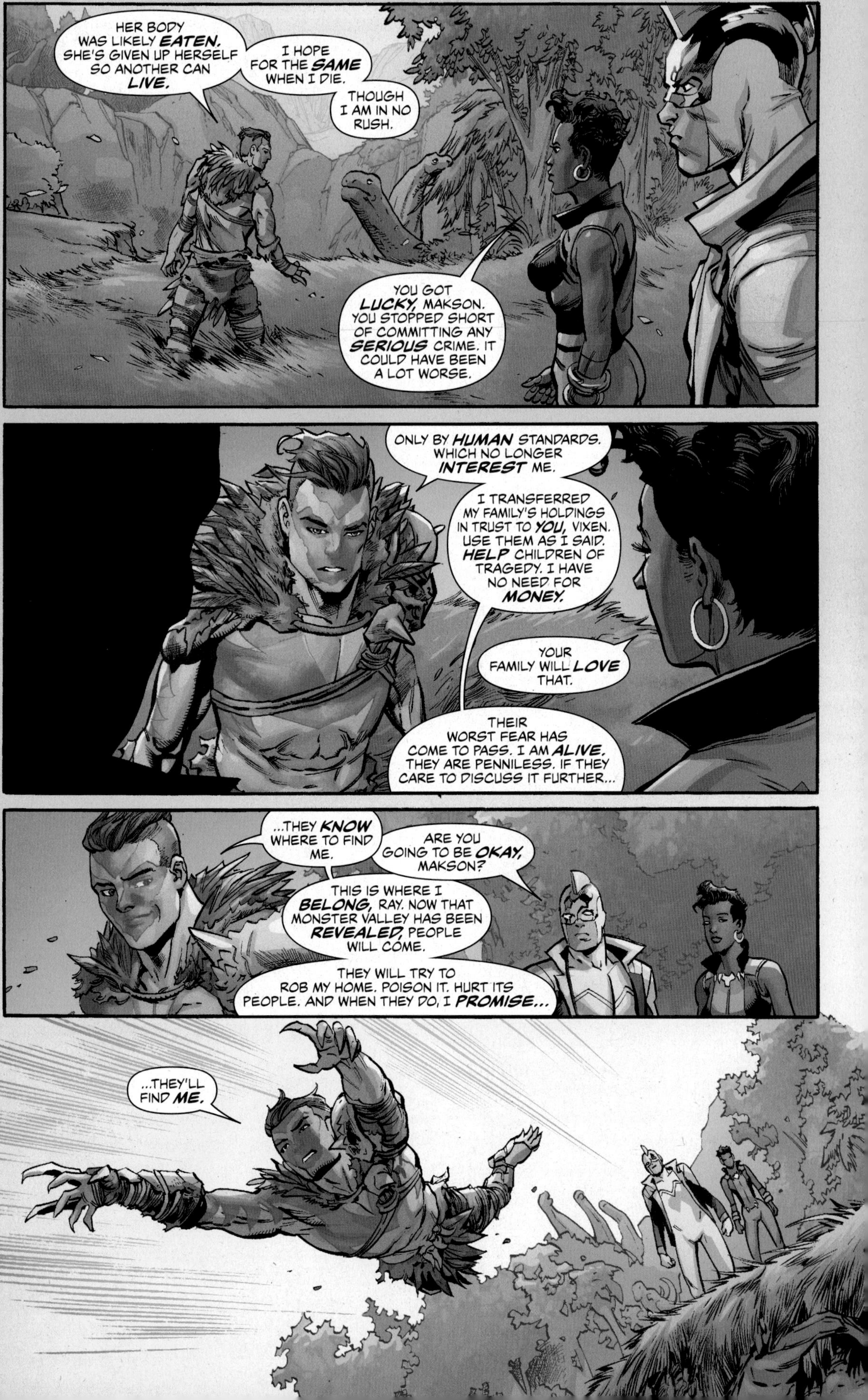

HER BODY WAS LIKELY EATEN. SHE'S GIVEN UP HERSELF SO ANOTHER CAN LIVE.
I HOPE FOR THE SAME WHEN I DIE.
THOUGH I AM IN NO RUSH.
YOU GOT LUCKY, MAKSON. YOU STOPPED SHORT OF COMMITTING ANY SERIOUS CRIME. IT COULD HAVE BEEN A LOT WORSE.
ONLY BY HUMAN STANDARDS. WHICH NO LONGER INTEREST ME.
I TRANSFERRED MY FAMILY'S HOLDINGS IN TRUST TO YOU, VIXEN. USE THEM AS I SAID. HELP CHILDREN OF TRAGEDY. I HAVE NO NEED FOR MONEY.
YOUR FAMILY WILL LOVE THAT.
THEIR WORST FEAR HAS COME TO PASS. I AM ALIVE. THEY ARE PENNILESS. IF THEY CARE TO DISCUSS IT FURTHER...
...THEY KNOW WHERE TO FIND ME.
ARE YOU GOING TO BE OKAY, MAKSON?
THIS IS WHERE I BELONG, RAY. NOW THAT MONSTER VALLEY HAS BEEN REVEALED, PEOPLE WILL COME.
THEY WILL TRY TO ROB MY HOME. POISON IT. HURT ITS PEOPLE. AND WHEN THEY DO, I PROMISE...
...THEY'LL FIND ME.

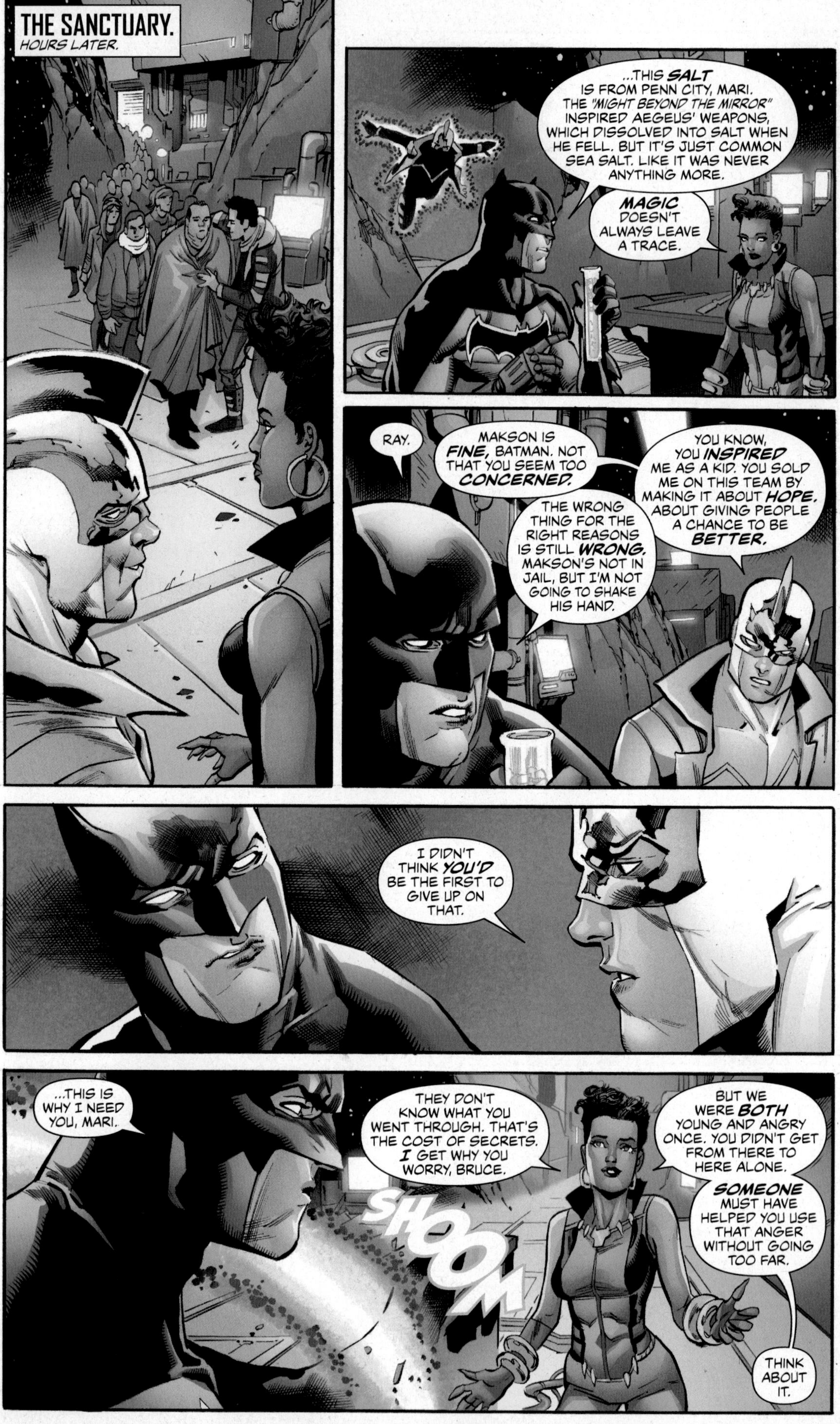
THE SANCTUARY.
HOURS LATER.
...THIS SALT IS FROM PENN CITY, MARI. THE "MIGHT BEYOND THE MIRROR" INSPIRED AEGEUS' WEAPONS, WHICH DISSOLVED INTO SALT WHEN HE FELL. BUT IT'S JUST COMMON SEA SALT. LIKE IT WAS NEVER ANYTHING MORE.
MAGIC DOESN'T ALWAYS LEAVE A TRACE.
RAY.
MAKSON IS FINE, BATMAN. NOT THAT YOU SEEM TOO CONCERNED.
THE WRONG THING FOR THE RIGHT REASONS IS STILL WRONG. MAKSON'S NOT IN JAIL, BUT I'M NOT GOING TO SHAKE HIS HAND.
YOU KNOW, YOU INSPIRED ME AS A KID. YOU SOLD ME ON THIS TEAM BY MAKING IT ABOUT HOPE. ABOUT GIVING PEOPLE A CHANCE TO BE BETTER.
I DIDN'T THINK YOU'D BE THE FIRST TO GIVE UP ON THAT.
...THIS IS WHY I NEED YOU, MARI.
THEY DON'T KNOW WHAT YOU WENT THROUGH. THAT'S THE COST OF SECRETS. I GET WHY YOU WORRY, BRUCE.
BUT WE WERE BOTH YOUNG AND ANGRY ONCE. YOU DIDN'T GET FROM THERE TO HERE ALONE.
SOMEONE MUST HAVE HELPED YOU USE THAT ANGER WITHOUT GOING TOO FAR.
SHOOOM
THINK ABOUT IT.

SO I AIN'T SLEPT IN TWO WEEKS, BUT THE *CATHEXIS*, THEY GOT A DIFFERENT TYPE A' TIME THAN US. THAT'S WHEN THEY TELL ME WE AIN'T EVEN DONE WITH *FOREPLAY*, AN' I--

I DON'T NEED TO HEAR *MORE*, LOBO.

FINE, BUT DON'T SAY THE MAIN MAN DIDN'T TRY TA TEACH YA 'BOUT *STAMINA*, KID. WHAT'S ON YER MIND?

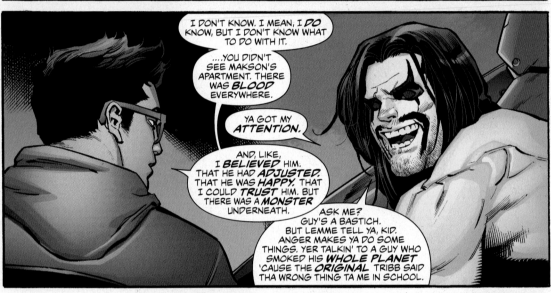

I DON'T KNOW. I MEAN, I *DO* KNOW, BUT I DON'T KNOW WHAT TO DO WITH IT.

....YOU DIDN'T SEE MAKSON'S APARTMENT. THERE WAS *BLOOD* EVERYWHERE.

YA GOT MY *ATTENTION*.

AND, LIKE, I *BELIEVED* HIM. THAT HE HAD *ADJUSTED*. THAT HE WAS *HAPPY*. THAT I COULD *TRUST* HIM. BUT THERE WAS A *MONSTER* UNDERNEATH.

ASK ME? GUY'S A BASTICH. BUT LEMME TELL YA, KID. ANGER MAKES YA DO SOME THINGS. YER TALKIN' TO A GUY WHO SMOKED HIS *WHOLE PLANET* 'CAUSE THE *ORIGINAL* TRIBB SAID THA WRONG THING TA ME IN SCHOOL.

AN' YA *AIN'T* AN IDIOT. YA *KNOW* WHAT I'M TALKIN' ABOUT. FACT IS, YER NOT *AFRAID* A' MONSTERS.

FROM WHAT I CAN SEE, YER MOVIN' IN ON THE *COLDEST* WE GOT. AN' IT AIN'T *FEAR* DRIVIN' YA.

I DON'T KNOW WHAT YOU'RE TALKING ABOUT, LOBO. AND IF I *DID* I WOULDN'T WANT YOUR ADVICE.

SURE, KID. WHAT'S THE *MAIN MAN* KNOW? DUMBER THAN A ZWENIAN FERTILITY RITUAL, RIGHT? BUT YA KNOW WHAT?

HE AIN'T *NEVER* BEEN AFRAID TA MAKE HIS FRAGGIN' INTENTIONS KNOWN.

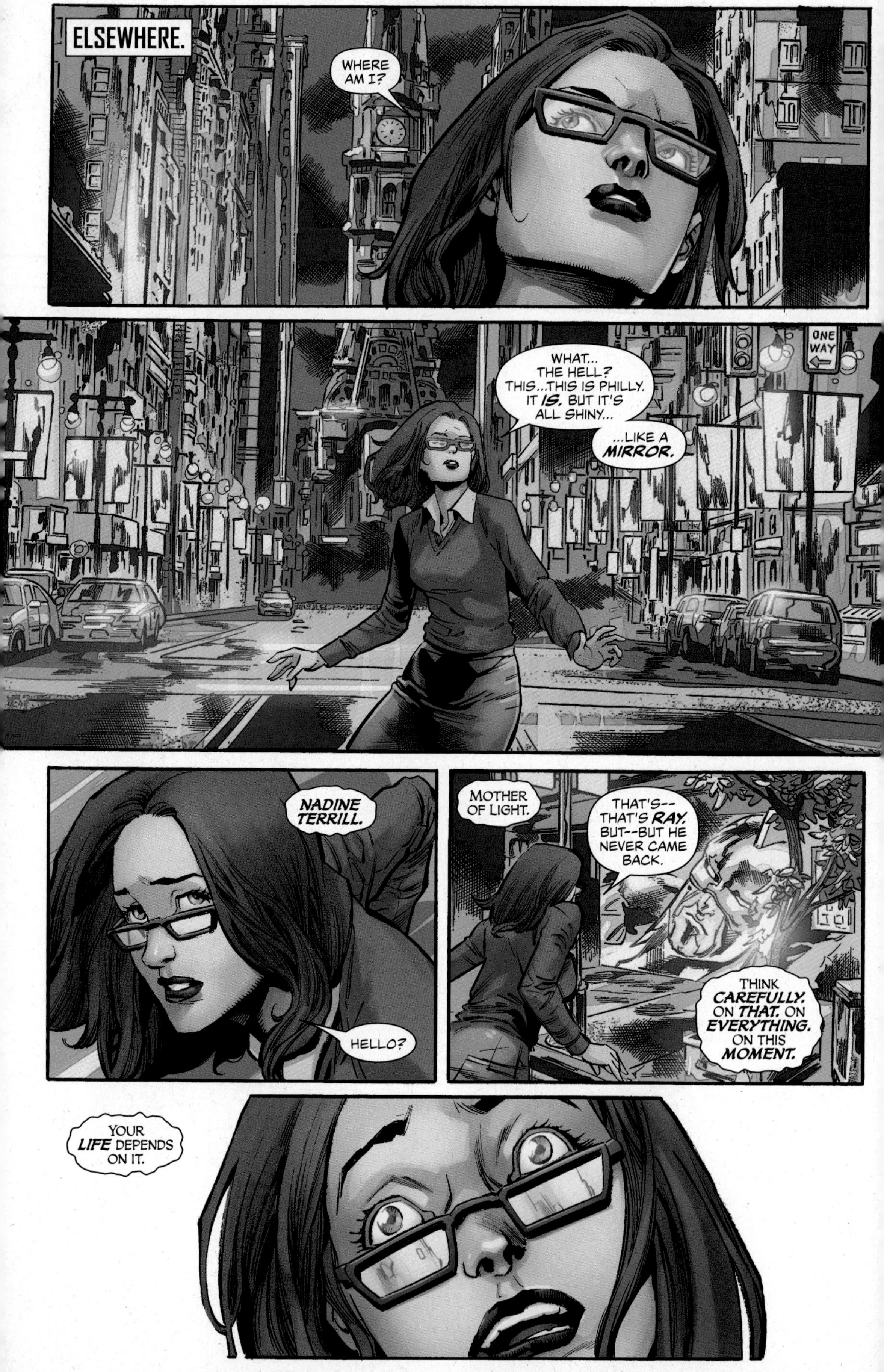
ELSEWHERE.
WHERE AM I?
WHAT... THE HELL? THIS...THIS IS PHILLY. IT IS. BUT IT'S ALL SHINY...
...LIKE A MIRROR.
NADINE TERRILL.
HELLO?
MOTHER OF LIGHT.
THAT'S-- THAT'S RAY. BUT--BUT HE NEVER CAME BACK.
THINK CAREFULLY. ON THAT. ON EVERYTHING. ON THIS MOMENT.
YOUR LIFE DEPENDS ON IT.

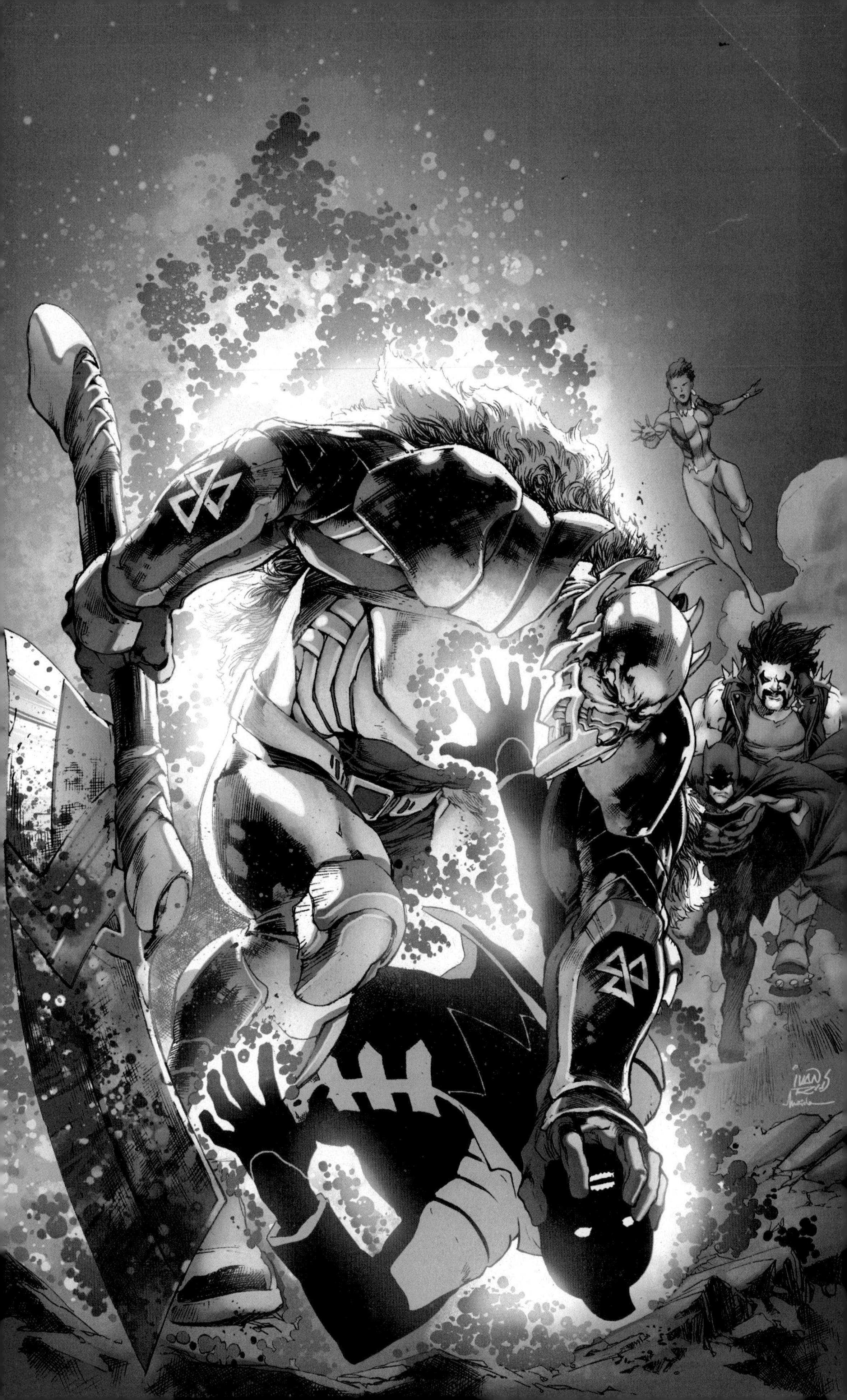

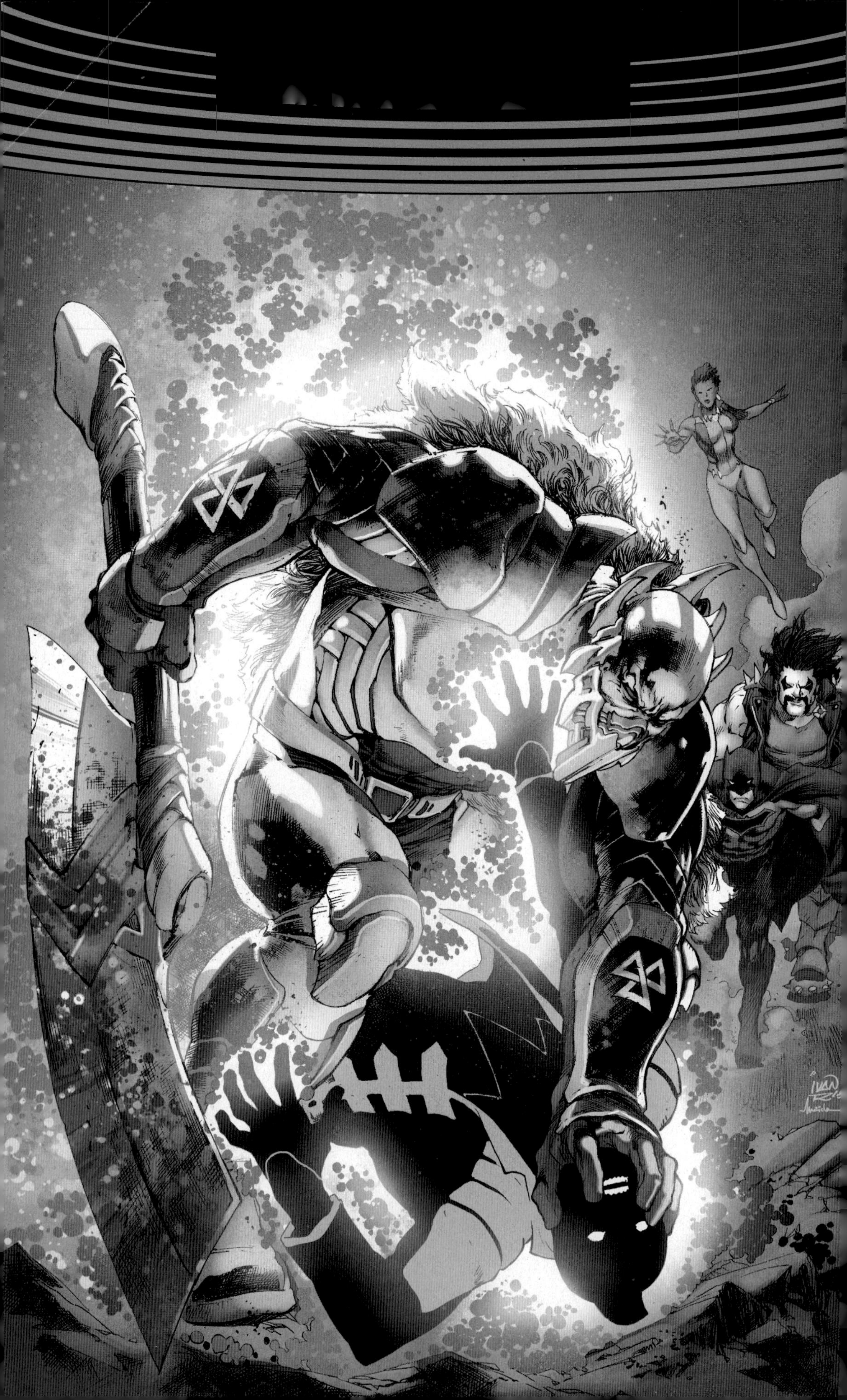

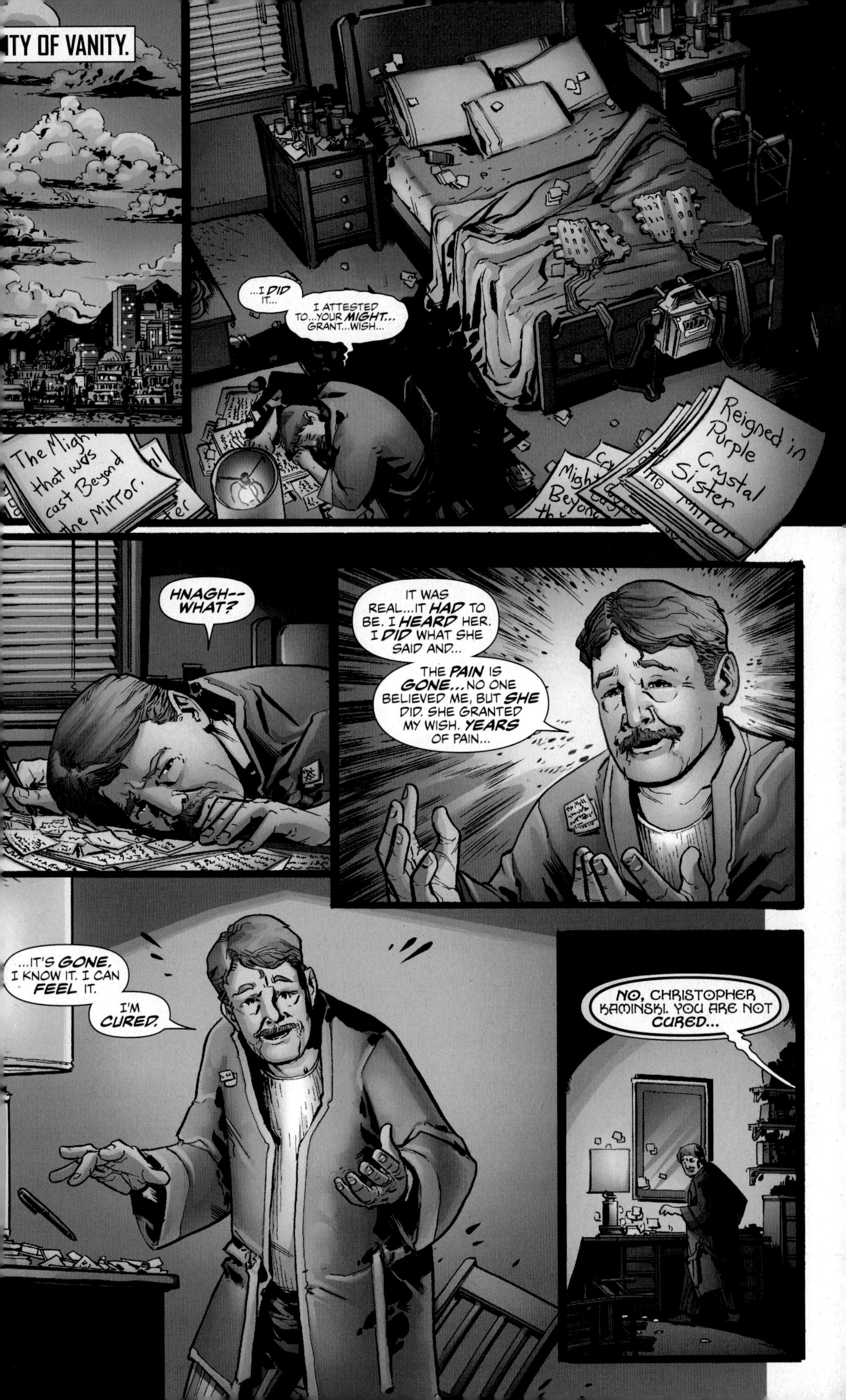

ITY OF VANITY.
...I DID IT...
I ATTESTED TO...YOUR MIGHT... GRANT...WISH...
that was cast Beyond the Mirror.
Reigned in Purple Crystal Sister
HNAGH-- WHAT?
IT WAS REAL...IT HAD TO BE. I HEARD HER. I DID WHAT SHE SAID AND...
THE PAIN IS GONE...NO ONE BELIEVED ME, BUT SHE DID. SHE GRANTED MY WISH. YEARS OF PAIN...
...IT'S GONE. I KNOW IT. I CAN FEEL IT.
I'M CURED.
NO, CHRISTOPHER KAMINSKI. YOU ARE NOT CURED...

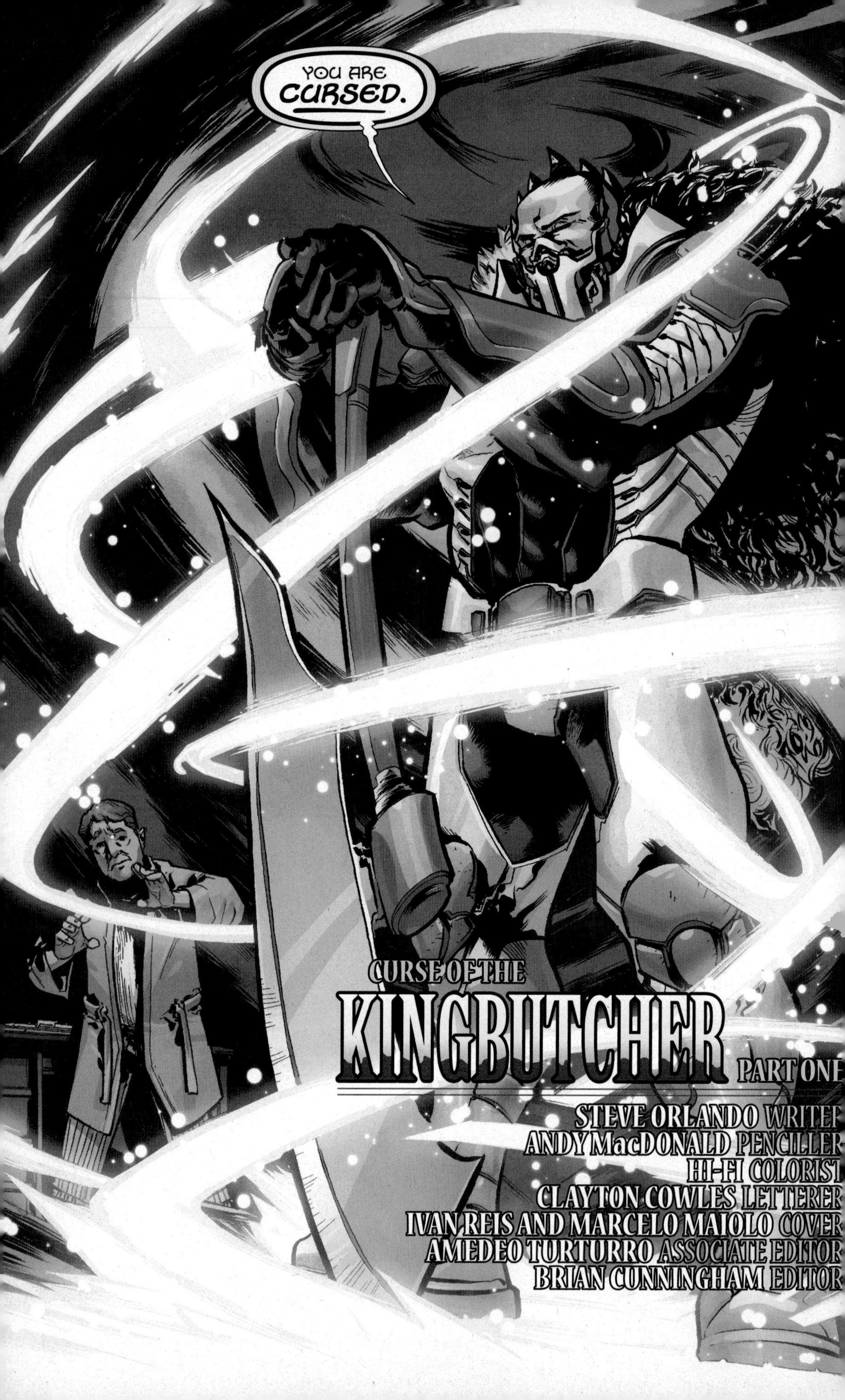
YOU ARE CURSED.
CURSE OF THE
KINGBUTCHER
PART ONE
STEVE ORLANDO WRITER
ANDY MacDONALD PENCILLER
HI-FI COLORIST
CLAYTON COWLES LETTERER
IVAN REIS AND MARCELO MAIOLO COVER
AMEDEO TURTURRO ASSOCIATE EDITOR
BRIAN CUNNINGHAM EDITOR

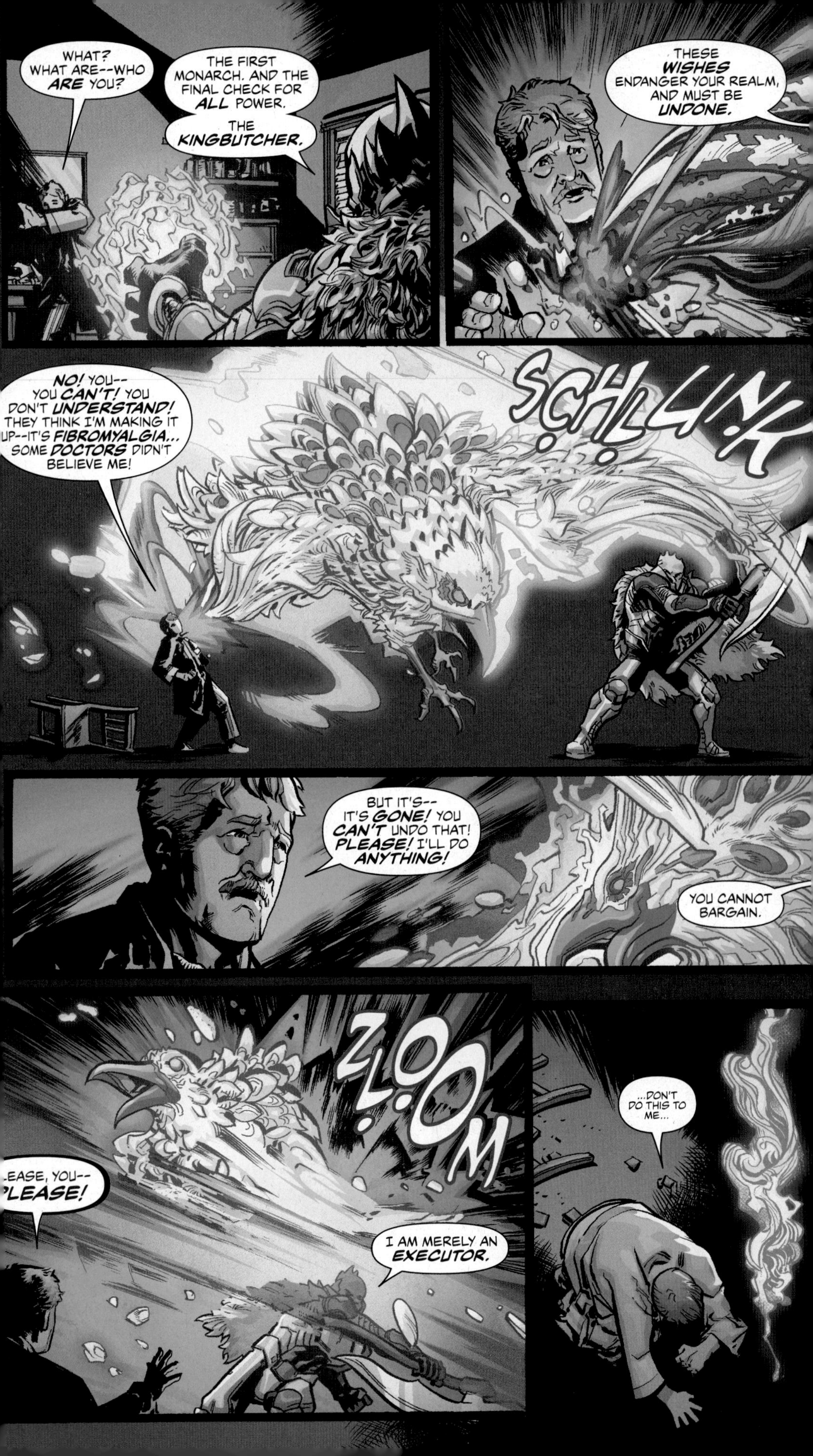
WHAT? WHAT ARE--WHO ARE YOU?
THE FIRST MONARCH. AND THE FINAL CHECK FOR ALL POWER.
THE KINGBUTCHER.
THESE WISHES ENDANGER YOUR REALM, AND MUST BE UNDONE.
NO! YOU-- YOU CAN'T! YOU DON'T UNDERSTAND! THEY THINK I'M MAKING IT UP--IT'S FIBROMYALGIA... SOME DOCTORS DIDN'T BELIEVE ME!
SCHLUNK
BUT IT'S-- IT'S GONE! YOU CAN'T UNDO THAT! PLEASE! I'LL DO ANYTHING!
YOU CANNOT BARGAIN.
ZOOM
LEASE, YOU-- PLEASE!
I AM MERELY AN EXECUTOR.
...DON'T DO THIS TO ME...

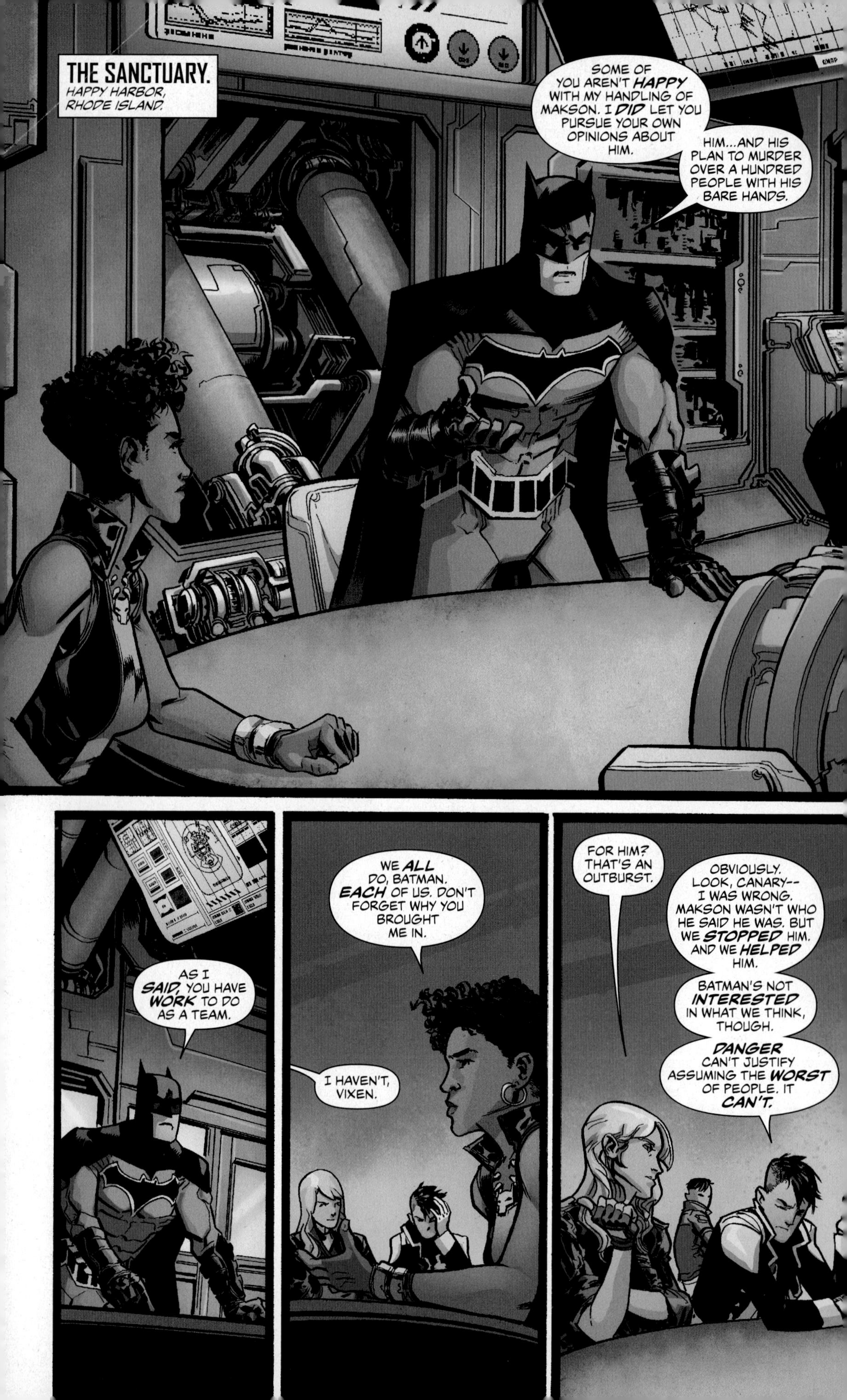
THE SANCTUARY.
HAPPY HARBOR, RHODE ISLAND.
SOME OF YOU AREN'T HAPPY WITH MY HANDLING OF MAKSON. I DID LET YOU PURSUE YOUR OWN OPINIONS ABOUT HIM.
HIM...AND HIS PLAN TO MURDER OVER A HUNDRED PEOPLE WITH HIS BARE HANDS.
AS I SAID, YOU HAVE WORK TO DO AS A TEAM.
WE ALL DO, BATMAN. EACH OF US. DON'T FORGET WHY YOU BROUGHT ME IN.
I HAVEN'T, VIXEN.
FOR HIM? THAT'S AN OUTBURST.
OBVIOUSLY. LOOK, CANARY-- I WAS WRONG. MAKSON WASN'T WHO HE SAID HE WAS. BUT WE STOPPED HIM. AND WE HELPED HIM.
BATMAN'S NOT INTERESTED IN WHAT WE THINK, THOUGH.
DANGER CAN'T JUSTIFY ASSUMING THE WORST OF PEOPLE. IT CAN'T.

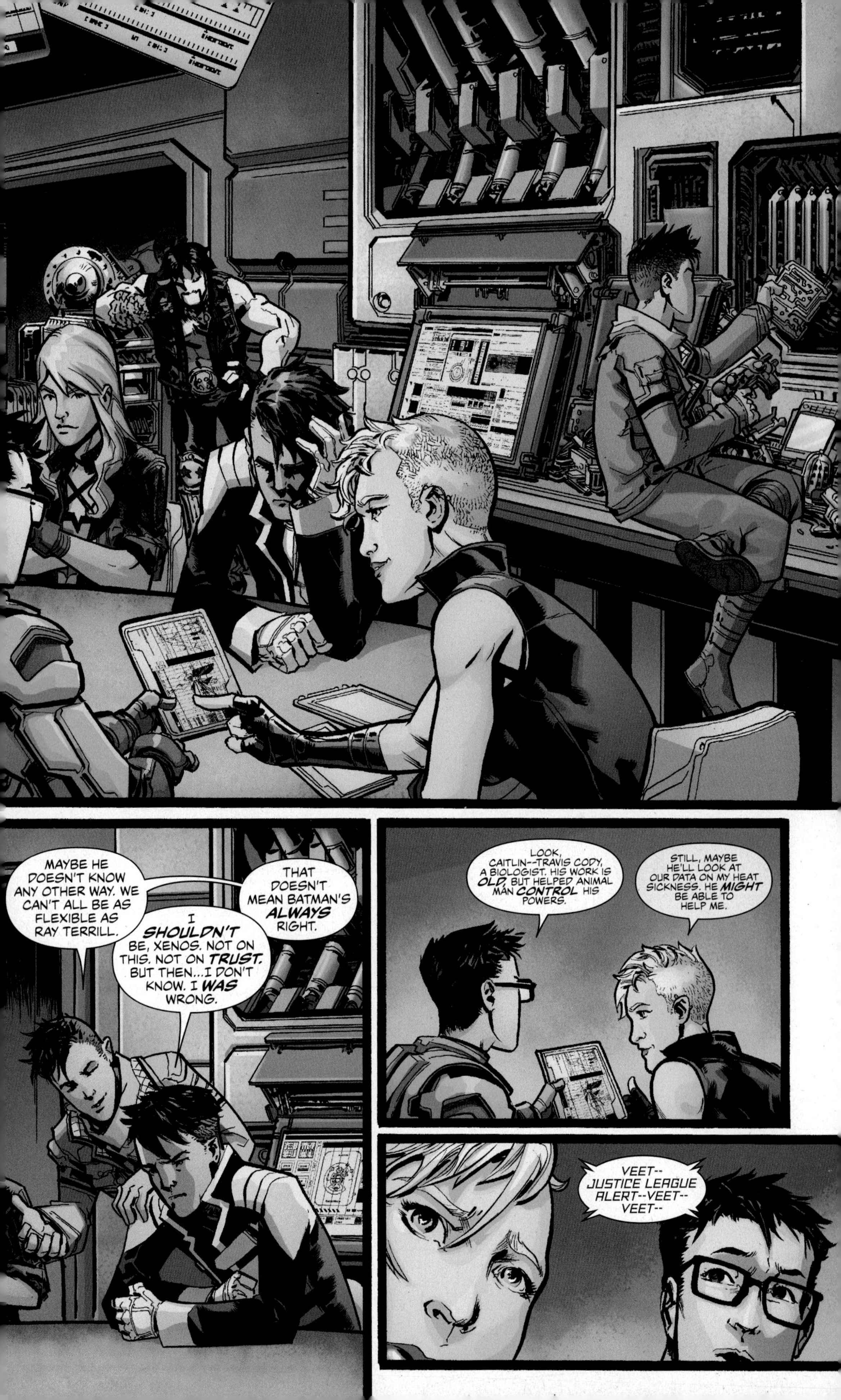
MAYBE HE DOESN'T KNOW ANY OTHER WAY. WE CAN'T ALL BE AS FLEXIBLE AS RAY TERRILL.
THAT DOESN'T MEAN BATMAN'S ALWAYS RIGHT.
I SHOULDN'T BE, XENOS. NOT ON THIS. NOT ON TRUST. BUT THEN...I DON'T KNOW. I WAS WRONG.
LOOK, CAITLIN--TRAVIS CODY, A BIOLOGIST. HIS WORK IS OLD, BUT HELPED ANIMAL MAN CONTROL HIS POWERS.
STILL, MAYBE HE'LL LOOK AT OUR DATA ON MY HEAT SICKNESS. HE MIGHT BE ABLE TO HELP ME.
VEET-- JUSTICE LEAGUE ALERT--VEET-- VEET--

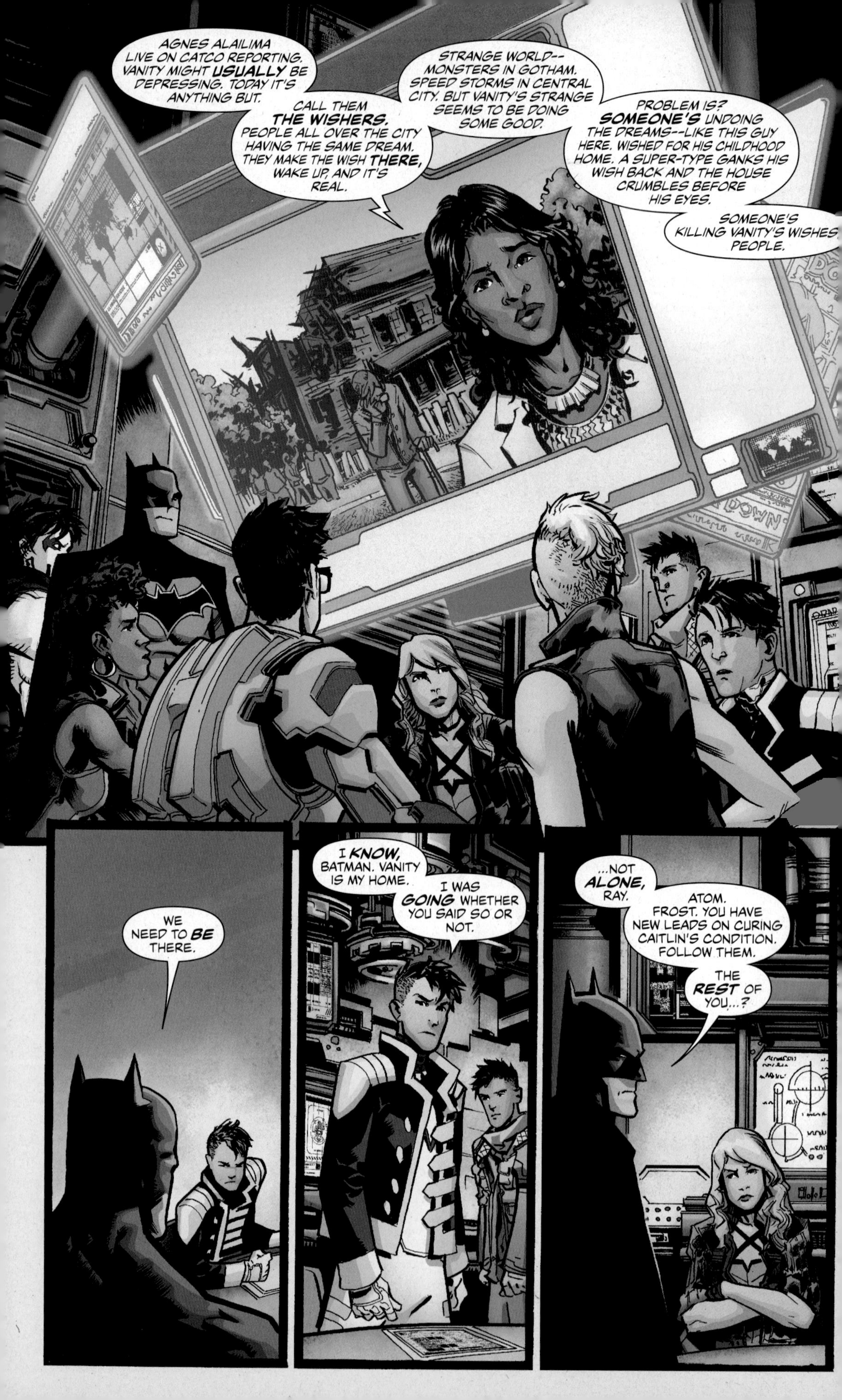
AGNES ALAILIMA LIVE ON CATCO REPORTING. VANITY MIGHT **USUALLY** BE DEPRESSING. TODAY IT'S ANYTHING BUT.
CALL THEM **THE WISHERS.** PEOPLE ALL OVER THE CITY HAVING THE SAME DREAM. THEY MAKE THE WISH **THERE,** WAKE UP, AND IT'S REAL.
STRANGE WORLD--MONSTERS IN GOTHAM. SPEED STORMS IN CENTRAL CITY. BUT VANITY'S STRANGE SEEMS TO BE DOING SOME GOOD.
PROBLEM IS? **SOMEONE'S** UNDOING THE DREAMS--LIKE THIS GUY HERE. WISHED FOR HIS CHILDHOOD HOME. A SUPER-TYPE GANKS HIS WISH BACK AND THE HOUSE CRUMBLES BEFORE HIS EYES.
SOMEONE'S KILLING VANITY'S WISHES PEOPLE.
WE NEED TO **BE** THERE.
I **KNOW,** BATMAN. VANITY IS MY HOME.
I WAS **GOING** WHETHER YOU SAID SO OR NOT.
...NOT **ALONE,** RAY.
ATOM. FROST. YOU HAVE NEW LEADS ON CURING CAITLIN'S CONDITION. FOLLOW THEM.
THE **REST** OF YOU...?

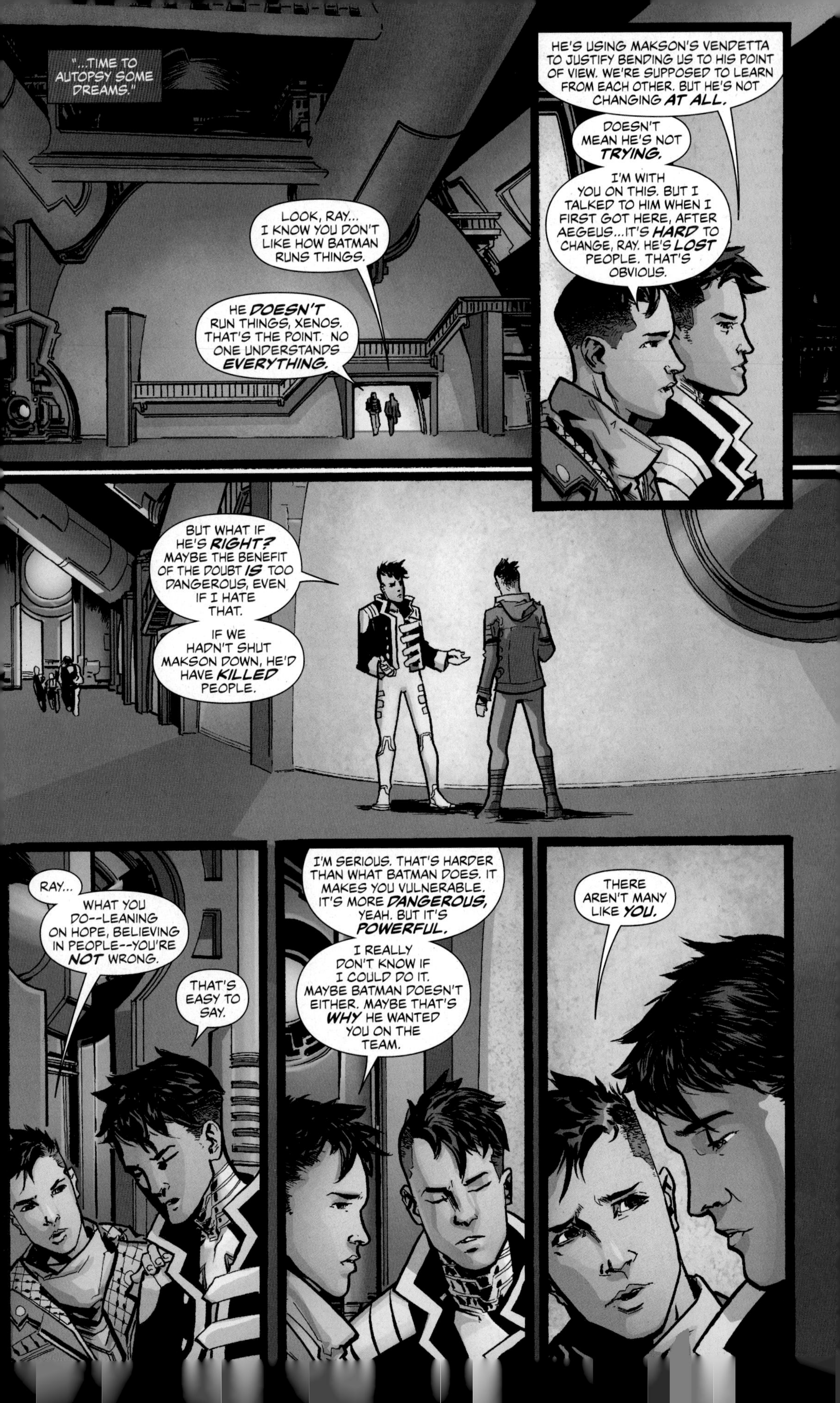
"...TIME TO AUTOPSY SOME DREAMS."
LOOK, RAY... I KNOW YOU DON'T LIKE HOW BATMAN RUNS THINGS.
HE DOESN'T RUN THINGS, XENOS. THAT'S THE POINT. NO ONE UNDERSTANDS EVERYTHING.
HE'S USING MAKSON'S VENDETTA TO JUSTIFY BENDING US TO HIS POINT OF VIEW. WE'RE SUPPOSED TO LEARN FROM EACH OTHER. BUT HE'S NOT CHANGING AT ALL.
DOESN'T MEAN HE'S NOT TRYING.
I'M WITH YOU ON THIS. BUT I TALKED TO HIM WHEN I FIRST GOT HERE, AFTER AEGEUS...IT'S HARD TO CHANGE, RAY. HE'S LOST PEOPLE. THAT'S OBVIOUS.
BUT WHAT IF HE'S RIGHT? MAYBE THE BENEFIT OF THE DOUBT IS TOO DANGEROUS, EVEN IF I HATE THAT.
IF WE HADN'T SHUT MAKSON DOWN, HE'D HAVE KILLED PEOPLE.
RAY...
WHAT YOU DO--LEANING ON HOPE, BELIEVING IN PEOPLE--YOU'RE NOT WRONG.
THAT'S EASY TO SAY.
I'M SERIOUS. THAT'S HARDER THAN WHAT BATMAN DOES. IT MAKES YOU VULNERABLE. IT'S MORE DANGEROUS, YEAH. BUT IT'S POWERFUL.
I REALLY DON'T KNOW IF I COULD DO IT. MAYBE BATMAN DOESN'T EITHER. MAYBE THAT'S WHY HE WANTED YOU ON THE TEAM.
THERE AREN'T MANY LIKE YOU.

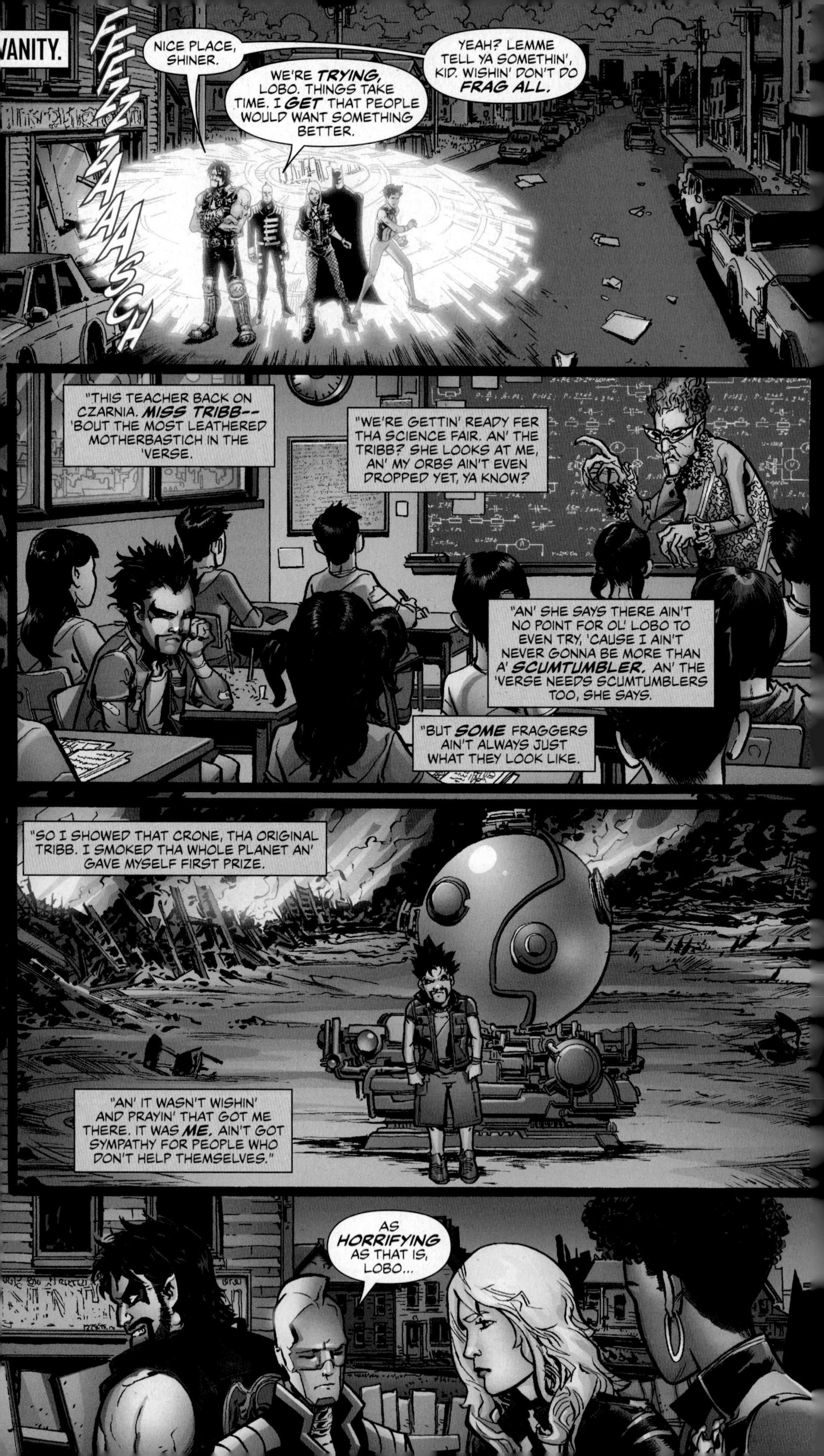

VANITY.
FFEZZZAAAASCH
NICE PLACE, SHINER.
WE'RE TRYING, LOBO. THINGS TAKE TIME. I GET THAT PEOPLE WOULD WANT SOMETHING BETTER.
YEAH? LEMME TELL YA SOMETHIN', KID. WISHIN' DON'T DO FRAG ALL.
"THIS TEACHER BACK ON CZARNIA. MISS TRIBB-- 'BOUT THE MOST LEATHERED MOTHERBASTICH IN THE 'VERSE.
"WE'RE GETTIN' READY FER THA SCIENCE FAIR. AN' THE TRIBB? SHE LOOKS AT ME, AN' MY ORBS AIN'T EVEN DROPPED YET, YA KNOW?
"AN' SHE SAYS THERE AIN'T NO POINT FOR OL' LOBO TO EVEN TRY, 'CAUSE I AIN'T NEVER GONNA BE MORE THAN A' SCUMTUMBLER. AN' THE 'VERSE NEEDS SCUMTUMBLERS TOO, SHE SAYS.
"BUT SOME FRAGGERS AIN'T ALWAYS JUST WHAT THEY LOOK LIKE.
"SO I SHOWED THAT CRONE, THA ORIGINAL TRIBB. I SMOKED THA WHOLE PLANET AN' GAVE MYSELF FIRST PRIZE.
"AN' IT WASN'T WISHIN' AND PRAYIN' THAT GOT ME THERE. IT WAS ME. AIN'T GOT SYMPATHY FOR PEOPLE WHO DON'T HELP THEMSELVES."
AS HORRIFYING AS THAT IS, LOBO...

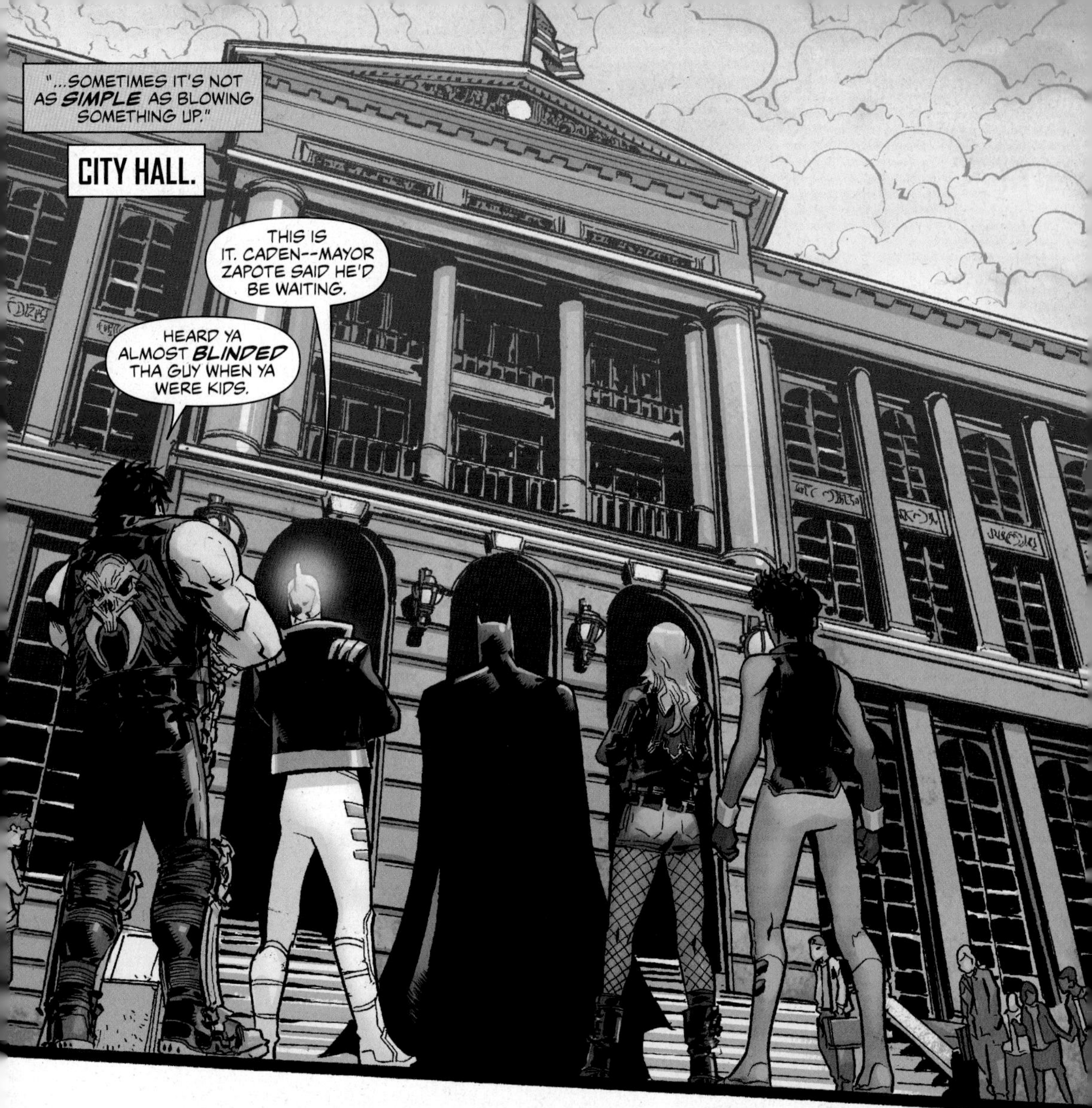
"...SOMETIMES IT'S NOT AS SIMPLE AS BLOWING SOMETHING UP."
CITY HALL.
THIS IS IT. CADEN--MAYOR ZAPOTE SAID HE'D BE WAITING.
HEARD YA ALMOST BLINDED THA GUY WHEN YA WERE KIDS.

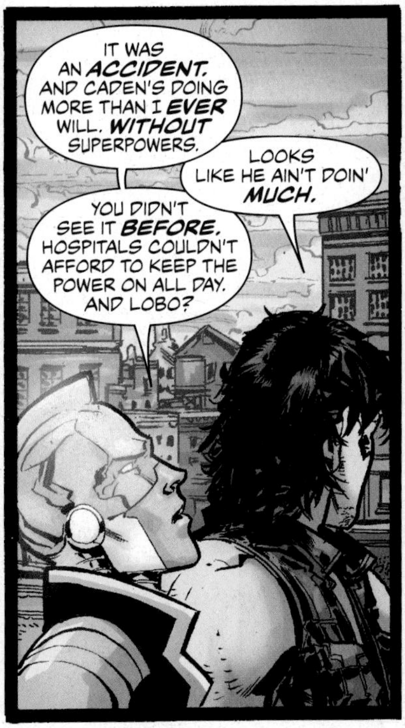
IT WAS AN ACCIDENT. AND CADEN'S DOING MORE THAN I EVER WILL. WITHOUT SUPERPOWERS.
LOOKS LIKE HE AIN'T DOIN' MUCH.
YOU DIDN'T SEE IT BEFORE. HOSPITALS COULDN'T AFFORD TO KEEP THE POWER ON ALL DAY. AND LOBO?

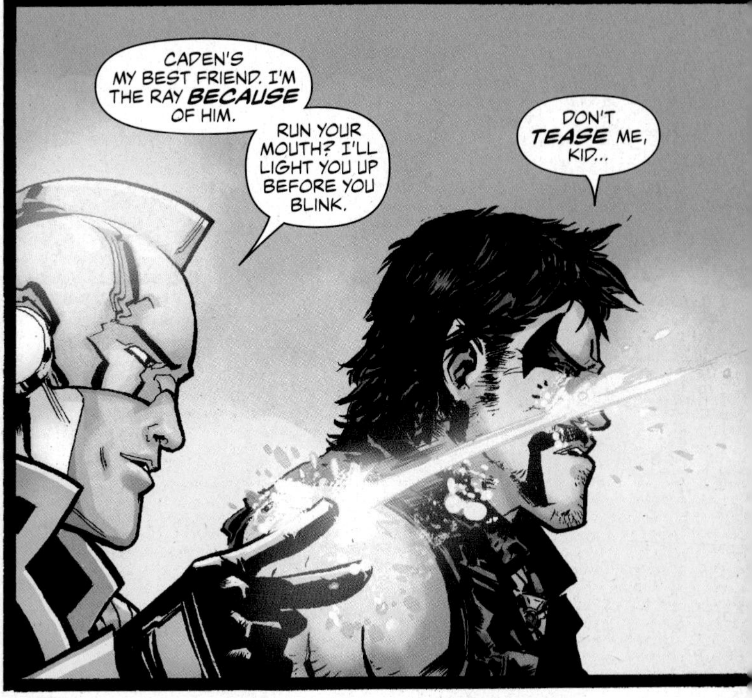
CADEN'S MY BEST FRIEND. I'M THE RAY BECAUSE OF HIM.
RUN YOUR MOUTH? I'LL LIGHT YOU UP BEFORE YOU BLINK.
DON'T TEASE ME, KID...

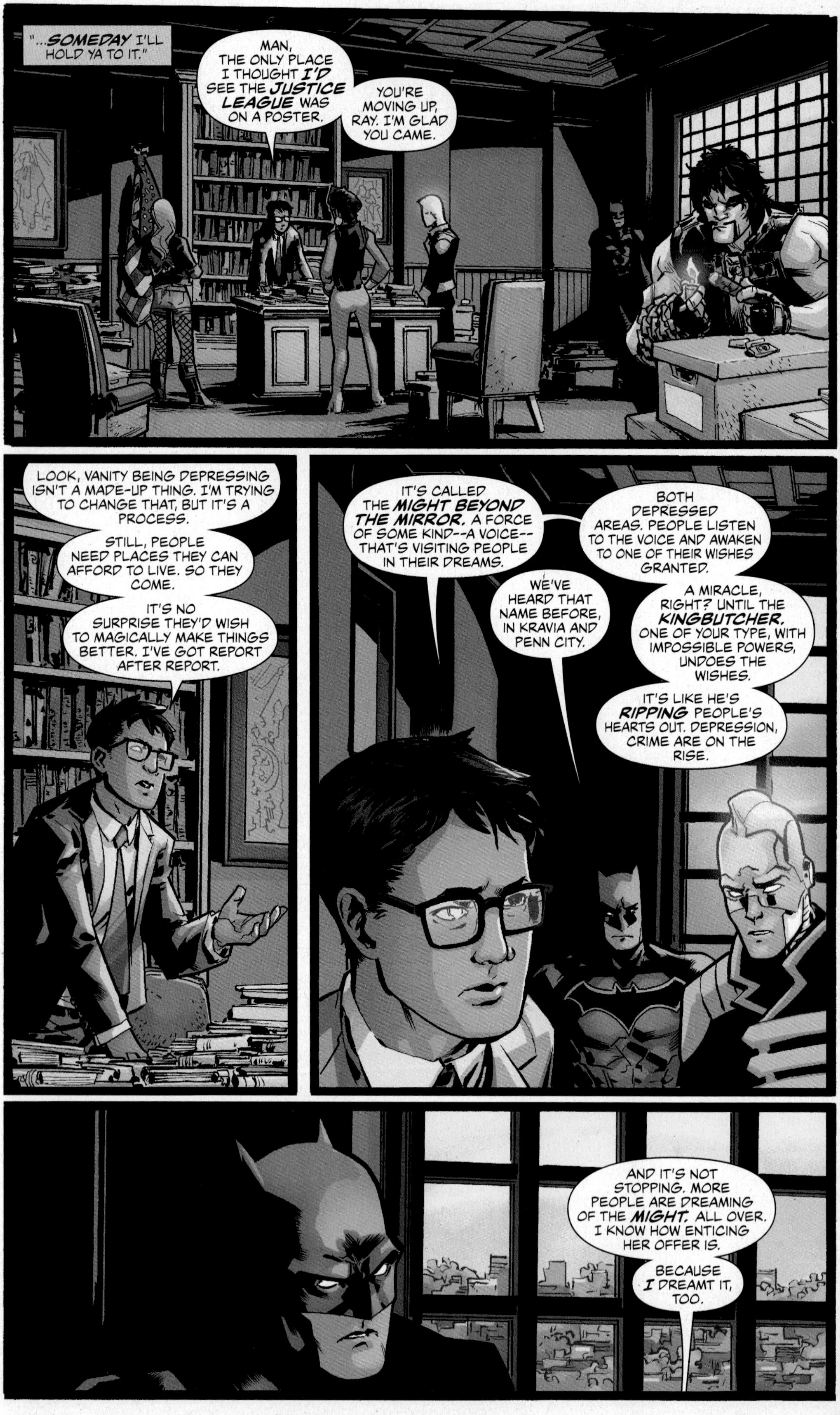
"...SOMEDAY I'LL HOLD YA TO IT."
MAN, THE ONLY PLACE I THOUGHT I'D SEE THE JUSTICE LEAGUE WAS ON A POSTER.
YOU'RE MOVING UP, RAY. I'M GLAD YOU CAME.
LOOK, VANITY BEING DEPRESSING ISN'T A MADE-UP THING. I'M TRYING TO CHANGE THAT, BUT IT'S A PROCESS.
STILL, PEOPLE NEED PLACES THEY CAN AFFORD TO LIVE. SO THEY COME.
IT'S NO SURPRISE THEY'D WISH TO MAGICALLY MAKE THINGS BETTER. I'VE GOT REPORT AFTER REPORT.
IT'S CALLED THE MIGHT BEYOND THE MIRROR. A FORCE OF SOME KIND--A VOICE--THAT'S VISITING PEOPLE IN THEIR DREAMS.
BOTH DEPRESSED AREAS. PEOPLE LISTEN TO THE VOICE AND AWAKEN TO ONE OF THEIR WISHES GRANTED.
WE'VE HEARD THAT NAME BEFORE, IN KRAVIA AND PENN CITY.
A MIRACLE, RIGHT? UNTIL THE KINGBUTCHER. ONE OF YOUR TYPE, WITH IMPOSSIBLE POWERS, UNDOES THE WISHES.
IT'S LIKE HE'S RIPPING PEOPLE'S HEARTS OUT. DEPRESSION, CRIME ARE ON THE RISE.
AND IT'S NOT STOPPING. MORE PEOPLE ARE DREAMING OF THE MIGHT. ALL OVER. I KNOW HOW ENTICING HER OFFER IS.
BECAUSE I DREAMT IT, TOO.

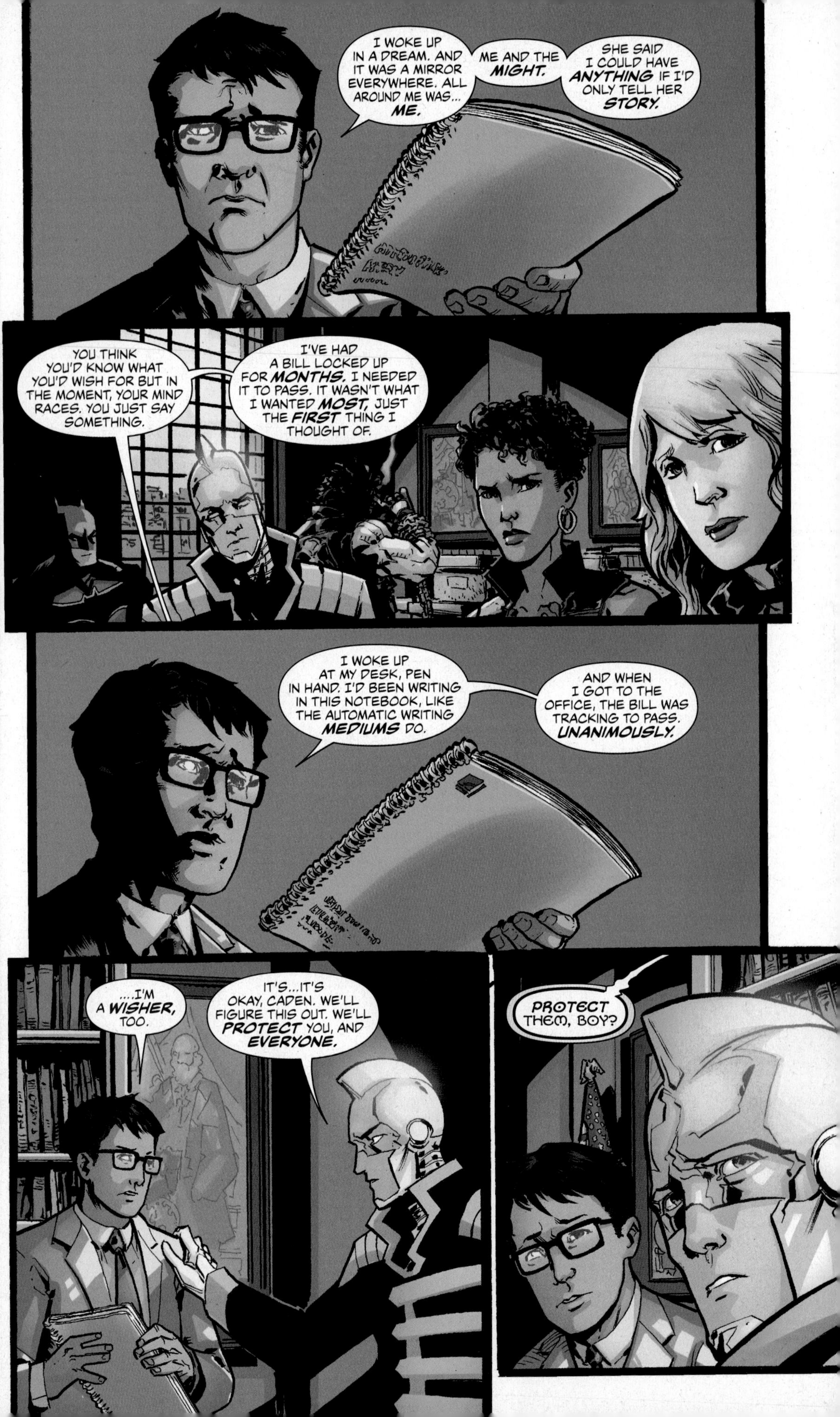

I WOKE UP IN A DREAM. AND IT WAS A MIRROR EVERYWHERE. ALL AROUND ME WAS... ME.
ME AND THE MIGHT.
SHE SAID I COULD HAVE ANYTHING IF I'D ONLY TELL HER STORY.
YOU THINK YOU'D KNOW WHAT YOU'D WISH FOR BUT IN THE MOMENT, YOUR MIND RACES. YOU JUST SAY SOMETHING.
I'VE HAD A BILL LOCKED UP FOR MONTHS. I NEEDED IT TO PASS. IT WASN'T WHAT I WANTED MOST, JUST THE FIRST THING I THOUGHT OF.
I WOKE UP AT MY DESK, PEN IN HAND. I'D BEEN WRITING IN THIS NOTEBOOK, LIKE THE AUTOMATIC WRITING MEDIUMS DO.
AND WHEN I GOT TO THE OFFICE, THE BILL WAS TRACKING TO PASS. UNANIMOUSLY.
....I'M A WISHER, TOO.
IT'S...IT'S OKAY, CADEN. WE'LL FIGURE THIS OUT. WE'LL PROTECT YOU, AND EVERYONE.
PROTECT THEM, BOY?

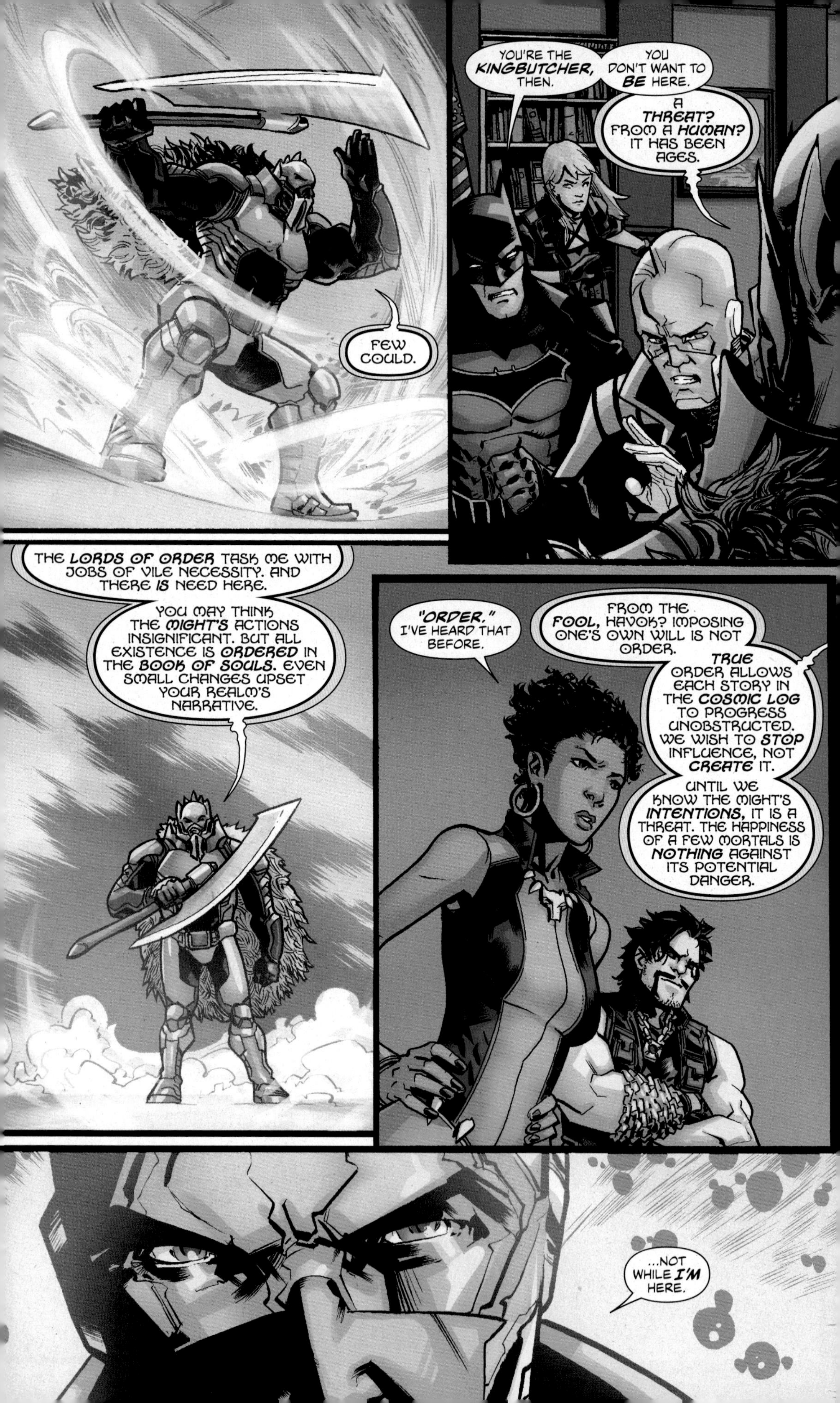
FEW COULD.
YOU'RE THE KINGBUTCHER, THEN.
YOU DON'T WANT TO BE HERE.
A THREAT? FROM A HUMAN? IT HAS BEEN AGES.
THE LORDS OF ORDER TASK ME WITH JOBS OF VILE NECESSITY. AND THERE IS NEED HERE.
YOU MAY THINK THE MIGHT'S ACTIONS INSIGNIFICANT. BUT ALL EXISTENCE IS ORDERED IN THE BOOK OF SOULS. EVEN SMALL CHANGES UPSET YOUR REALM'S NARRATIVE.
"ORDER." I'VE HEARD THAT BEFORE.
FROM THE FOOL, HAVOK? IMPOSING ONE'S OWN WILL IS NOT ORDER.
TRUE ORDER ALLOWS EACH STORY IN THE COSMIC LOG TO PROGRESS UNOBSTRUCTED. WE WISH TO STOP INFLUENCE, NOT CREATE IT.
UNTIL WE KNOW THE MIGHT'S INTENTIONS, IT IS A THREAT. THE HAPPINESS OF A FEW MORTALS IS NOTHING AGAINST ITS POTENTIAL DANGER.
...NOT WHILE I'M HERE.

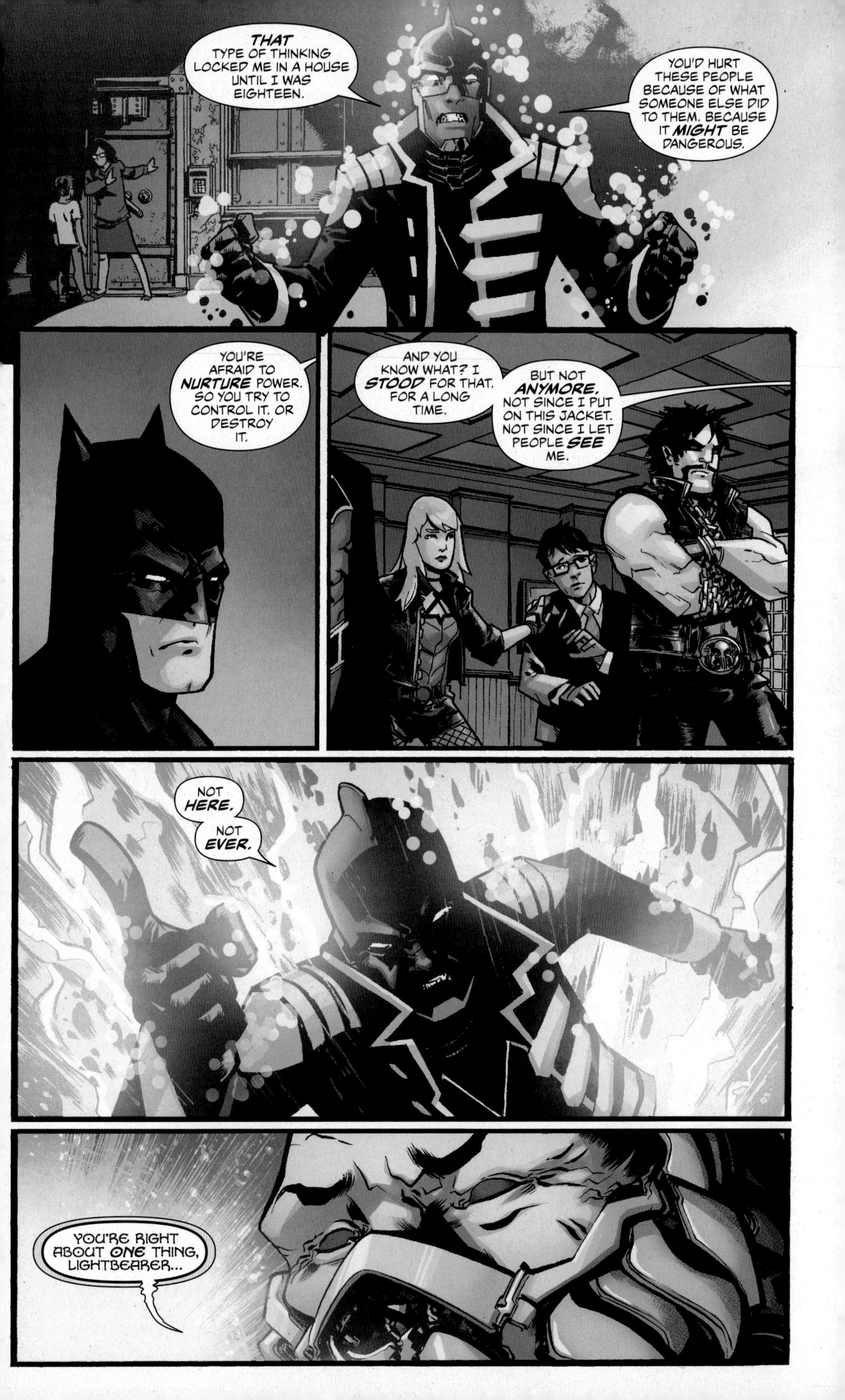

THAT TYPE OF THINKING LOCKED ME IN A HOUSE UNTIL I WAS EIGHTEEN.
YOU'D HURT THESE PEOPLE BECAUSE OF WHAT SOMEONE ELSE DID TO THEM. BECAUSE IT MIGHT BE DANGEROUS.
YOU'RE AFRAID TO NURTURE POWER. SO YOU TRY TO CONTROL IT. OR DESTROY IT.
AND YOU KNOW WHAT? I STOOD FOR THAT. FOR A LONG TIME.
BUT NOT ANYMORE. NOT SINCE I PUT ON THIS JACKET. NOT SINCE I LET PEOPLE SEE ME.
NOT HERE.
NOT EVER.
YOU'RE RIGHT ABOUT ONE THING, LIGHTBEARER...

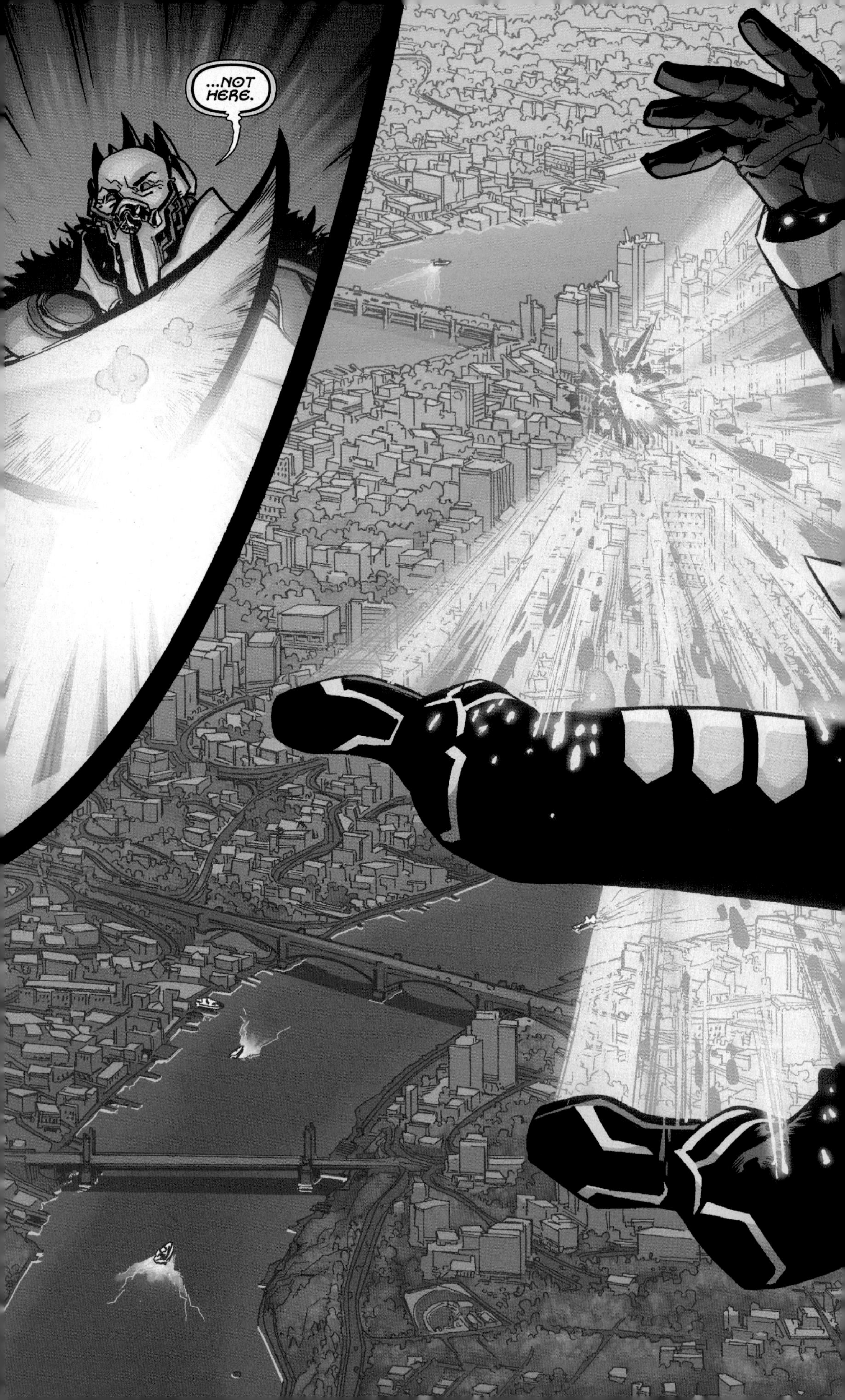
...NOT HERE.

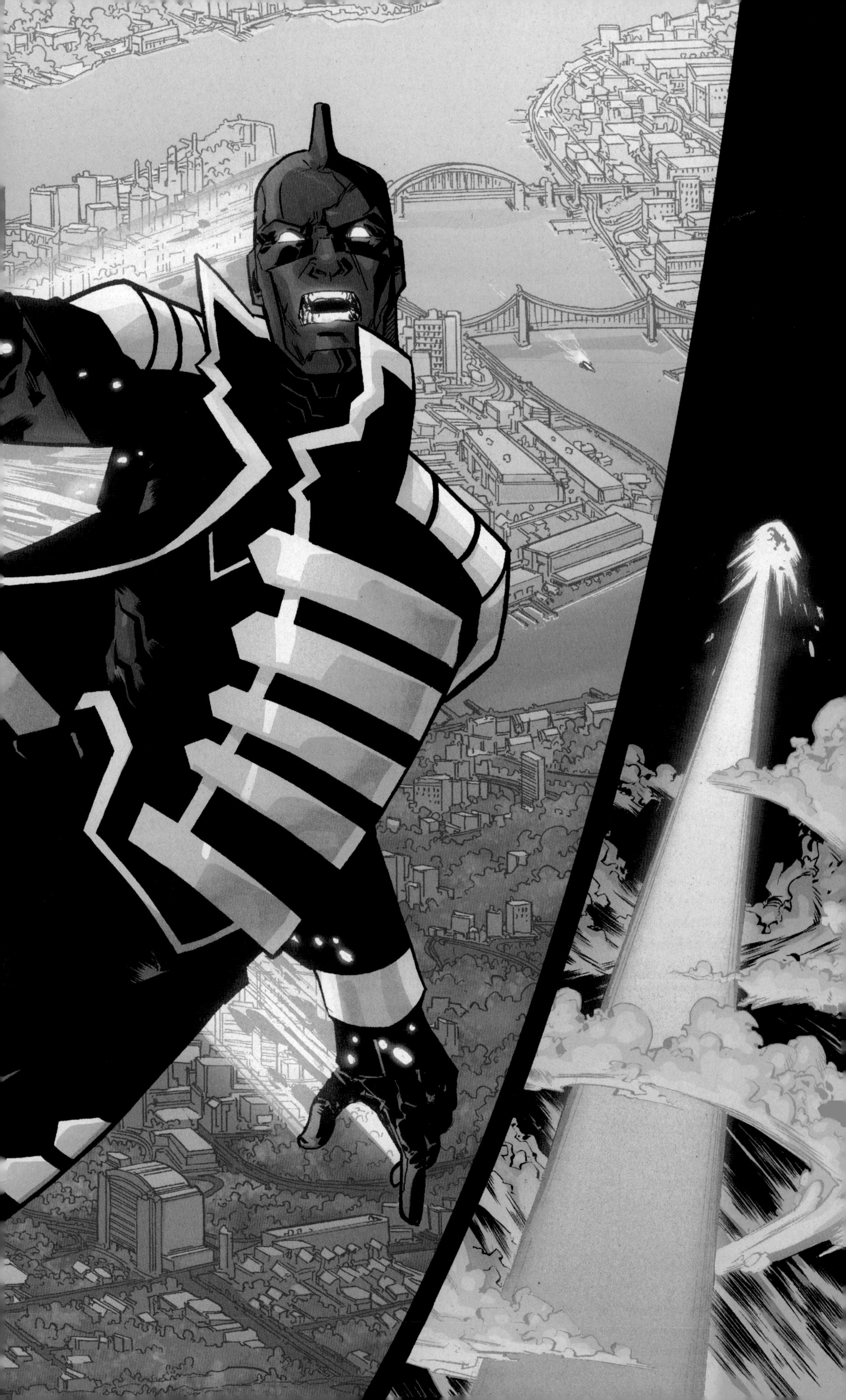

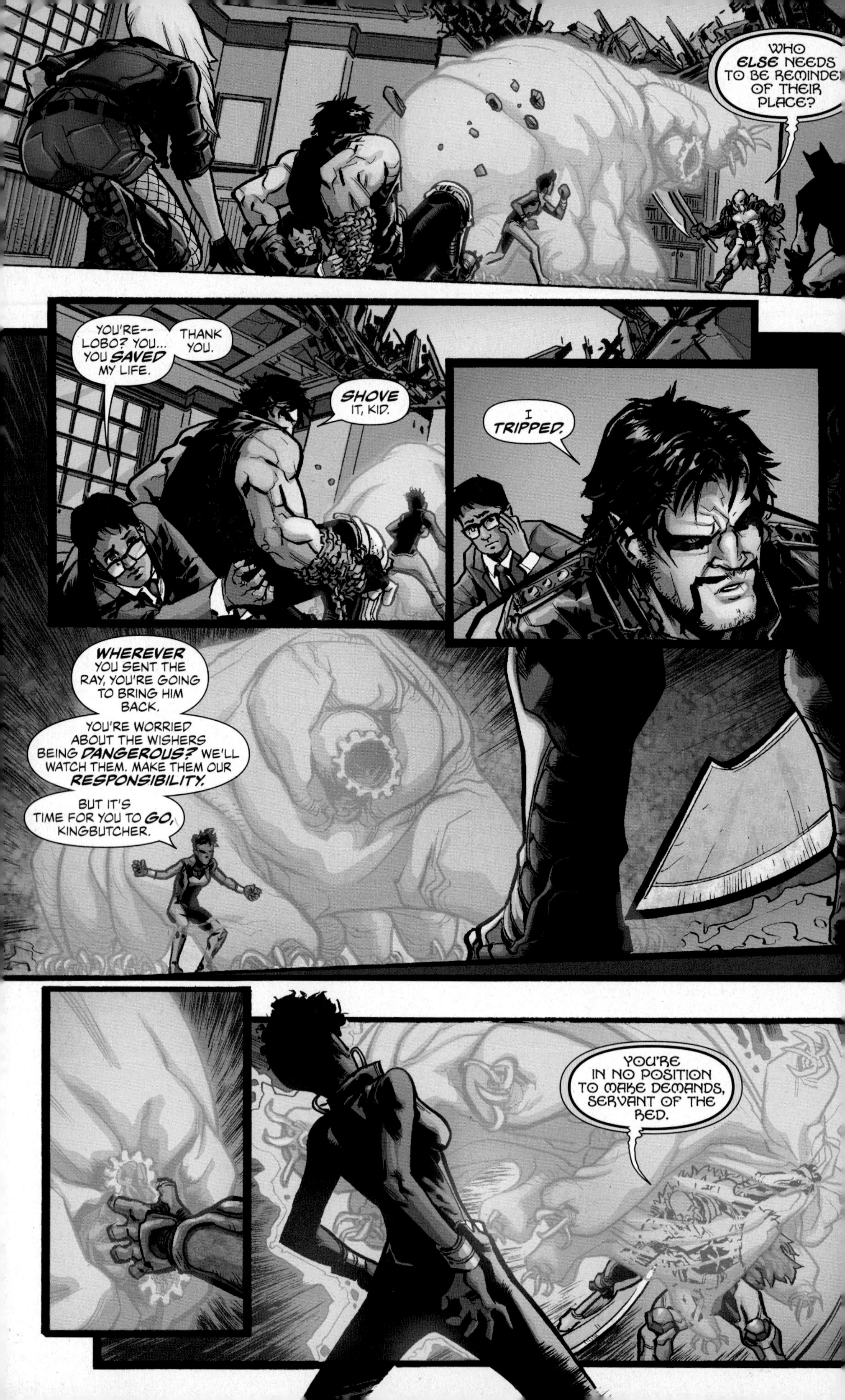
WHO ELSE NEEDS TO BE REMINDED OF THEIR PLACE?
YOU'RE-- LOBO? YOU... YOU SAVED MY LIFE.
THANK YOU.
SHOVE IT, KID.
I TRIPPED.
WHEREVER YOU SENT THE RAY, YOU'RE GOING TO BRING HIM BACK.
YOU'RE WORRIED ABOUT THE WISHERS BEING DANGEROUS? WE'LL WATCH THEM. MAKE THEM OUR RESPONSIBILITY.
BUT IT'S TIME FOR YOU TO GO, KINGBUTCHER.
YOU'RE IN NO POSITION TO MAKE DEMANDS, SERVANT OF THE RED.

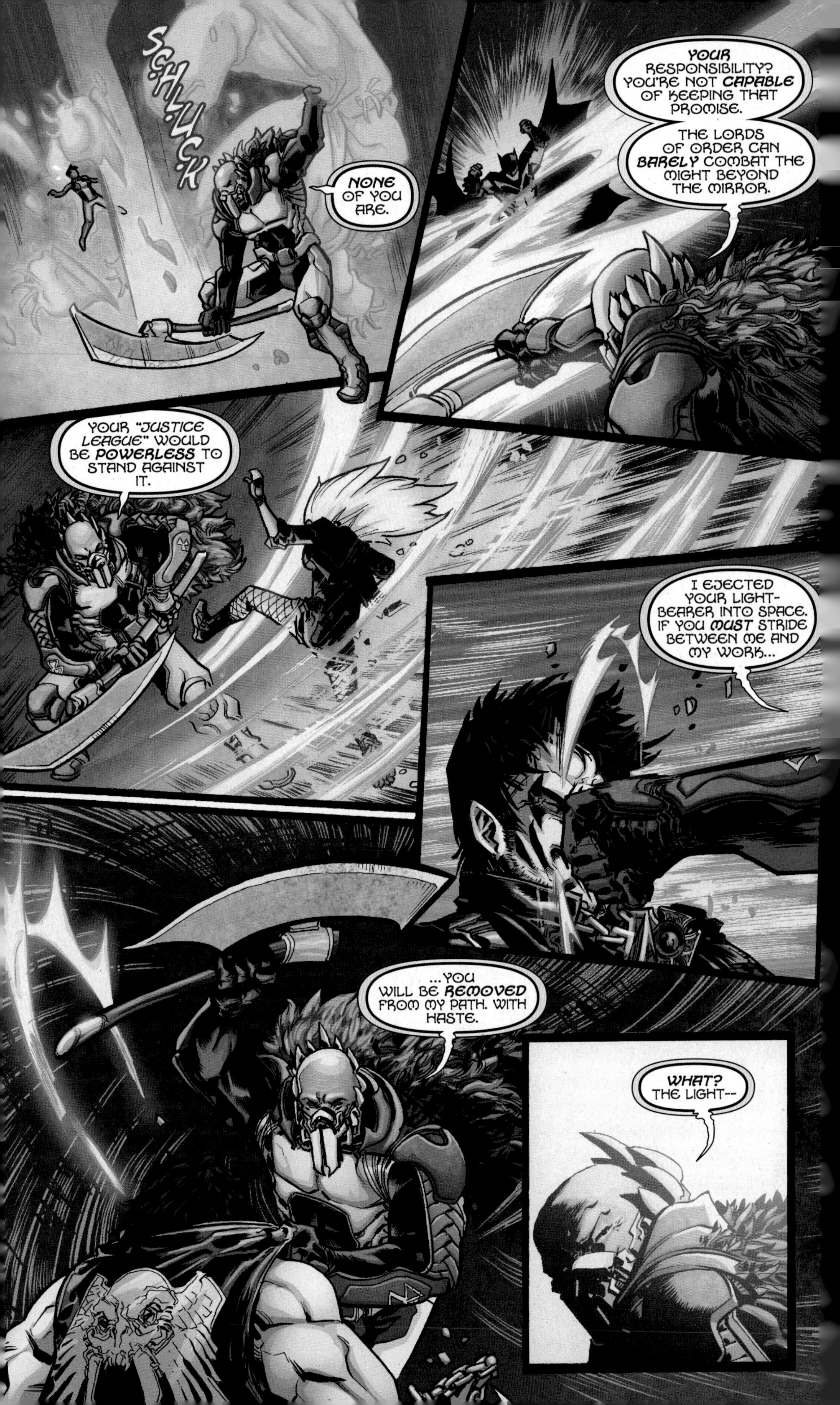
SCHLUCK
NONE OF YOU ARE.
YOUR RESPONSIBILITY? YOU'RE NOT CAPABLE OF KEEPING THAT PROMISE.
THE LORDS OF ORDER CAN BARELY COMBAT THE MIGHT BEYOND THE MIRROR.
YOUR "JUSTICE LEAGUE" WOULD BE POWERLESS TO STAND AGAINST IT.
I EJECTED YOUR LIGHT-BEARER INTO SPACE. IF YOU MUST STRIDE BETWEEN ME AND MY WORK...
...YOU WILL BE REMOVED FROM MY PATH. WITH HASTE.
WHAT? THE LIGHT--

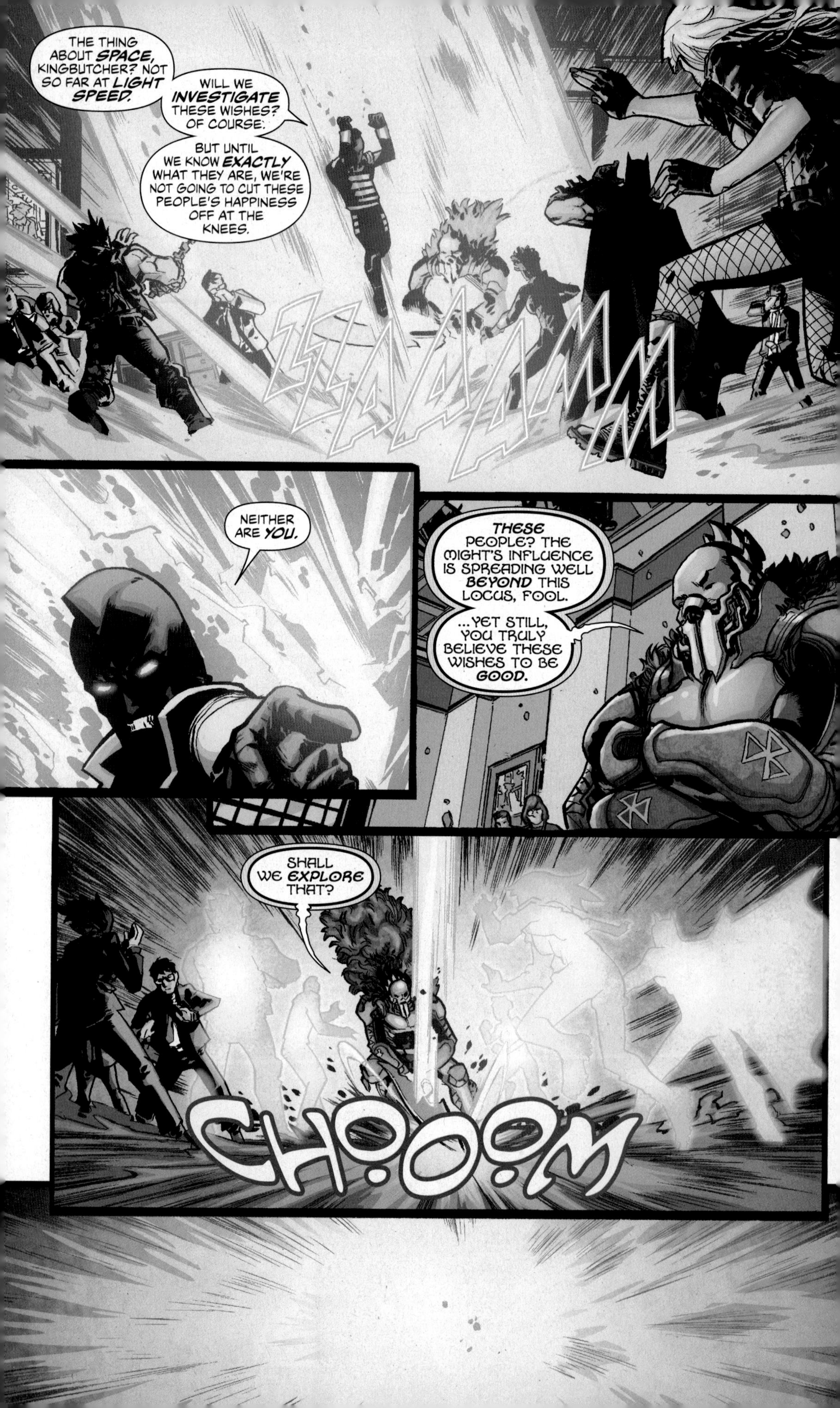
THE THING ABOUT SPACE, KINGBUTCHER? NOT SO FAR AT LIGHT SPEED.
WILL WE INVESTIGATE THESE WISHES? OF COURSE.
BUT UNTIL WE KNOW EXACTLY WHAT THEY ARE, WE'RE NOT GOING TO CUT THESE PEOPLE'S HAPPINESS OFF AT THE KNEES.
ZZZAAAMMM
NEITHER ARE YOU.
THESE PEOPLE? THE MIGHT'S INFLUENCE IS SPREADING WELL BEYOND THIS LOCUS, FOOL.
...YET STILL, YOU TRULY BELIEVE THESE WISHES TO BE GOOD.
SHALL WE EXPLORE THAT?
CHOOOM

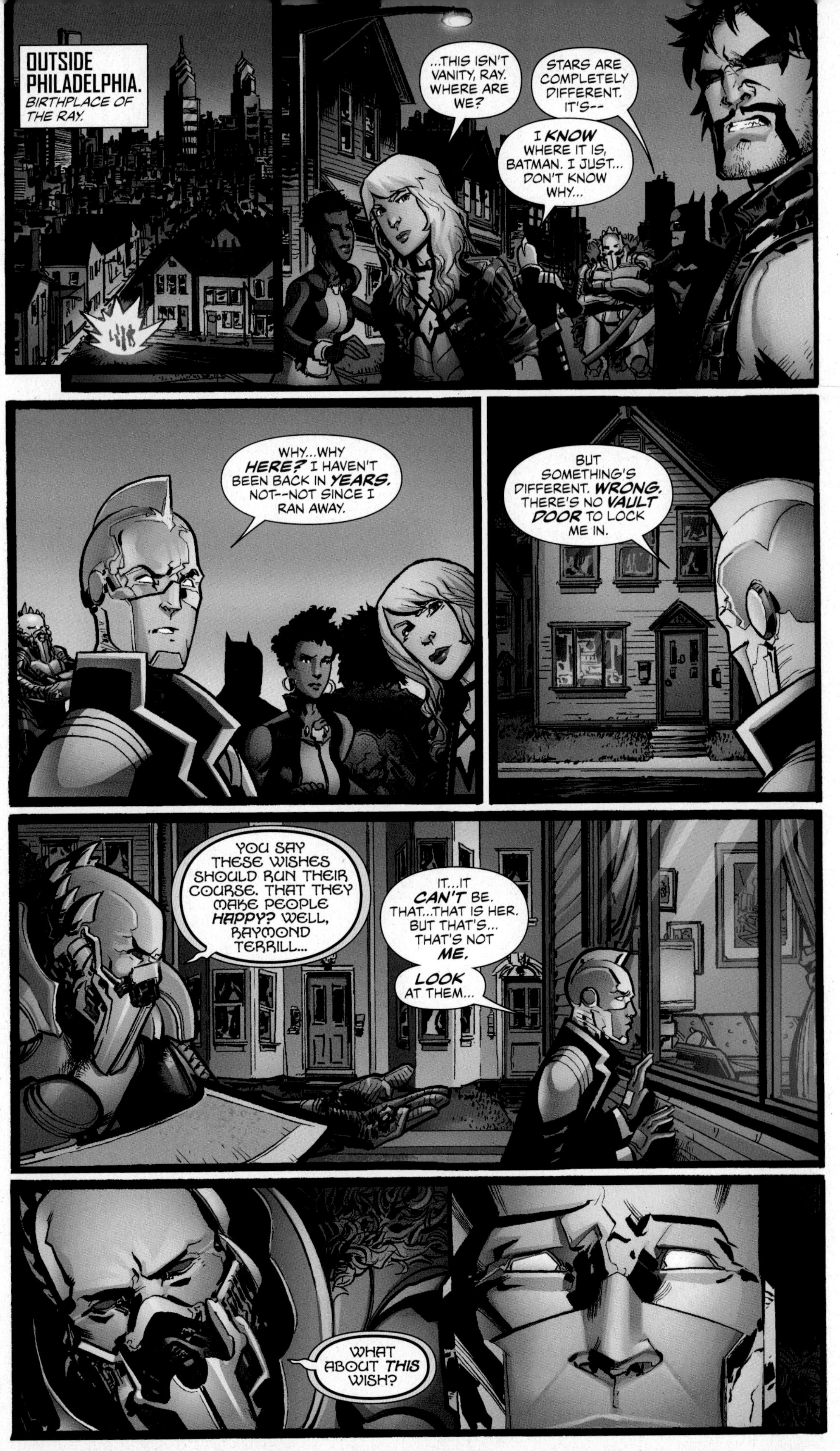
OUTSIDE PHILADELPHIA.
BIRTHPLACE OF THE RAY.
...THIS ISN'T VANITY, RAY. WHERE ARE WE?
STARS ARE COMPLETELY DIFFERENT. IT'S--
I KNOW WHERE IT IS, BATMAN. I JUST... DON'T KNOW WHY...
WHY...WHY HERE? I HAVEN'T BEEN BACK IN YEARS. NOT--NOT SINCE I RAN AWAY.
BUT SOMETHING'S DIFFERENT. WRONG. THERE'S NO VAULT DOOR TO LOCK ME IN.
YOU SAY THESE WISHES SHOULD RUN THEIR COURSE. THAT THEY MAKE PEOPLE HAPPY? WELL, RAYMOND TERRILL...
IT...IT CAN'T BE. THAT...THAT IS HER. BUT THAT'S... THAT'S NOT ME.
LOOK AT THEM...
WHAT ABOUT THIS WISH?

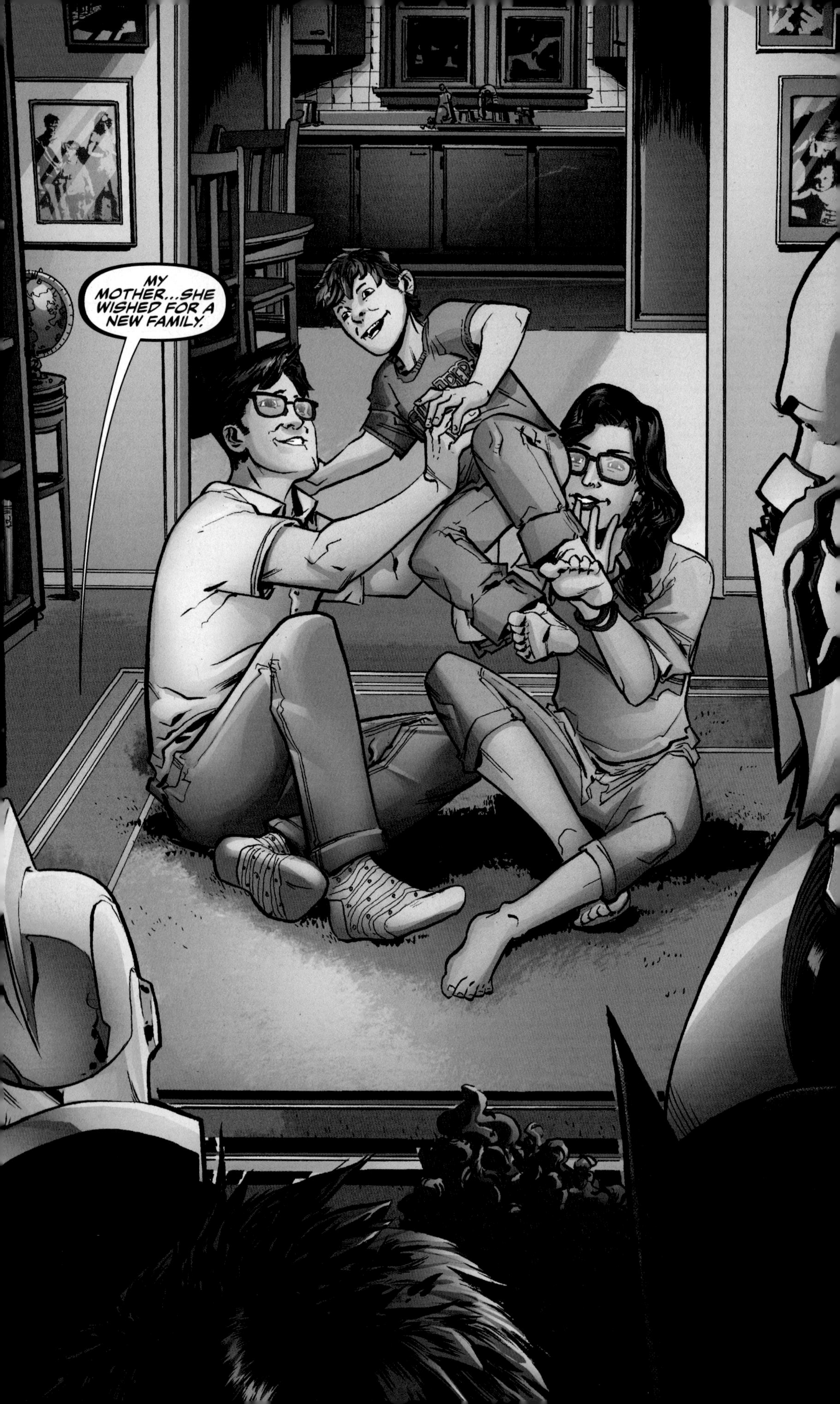
MY MOTHER...SHE WISHED FOR A NEW FAMILY.

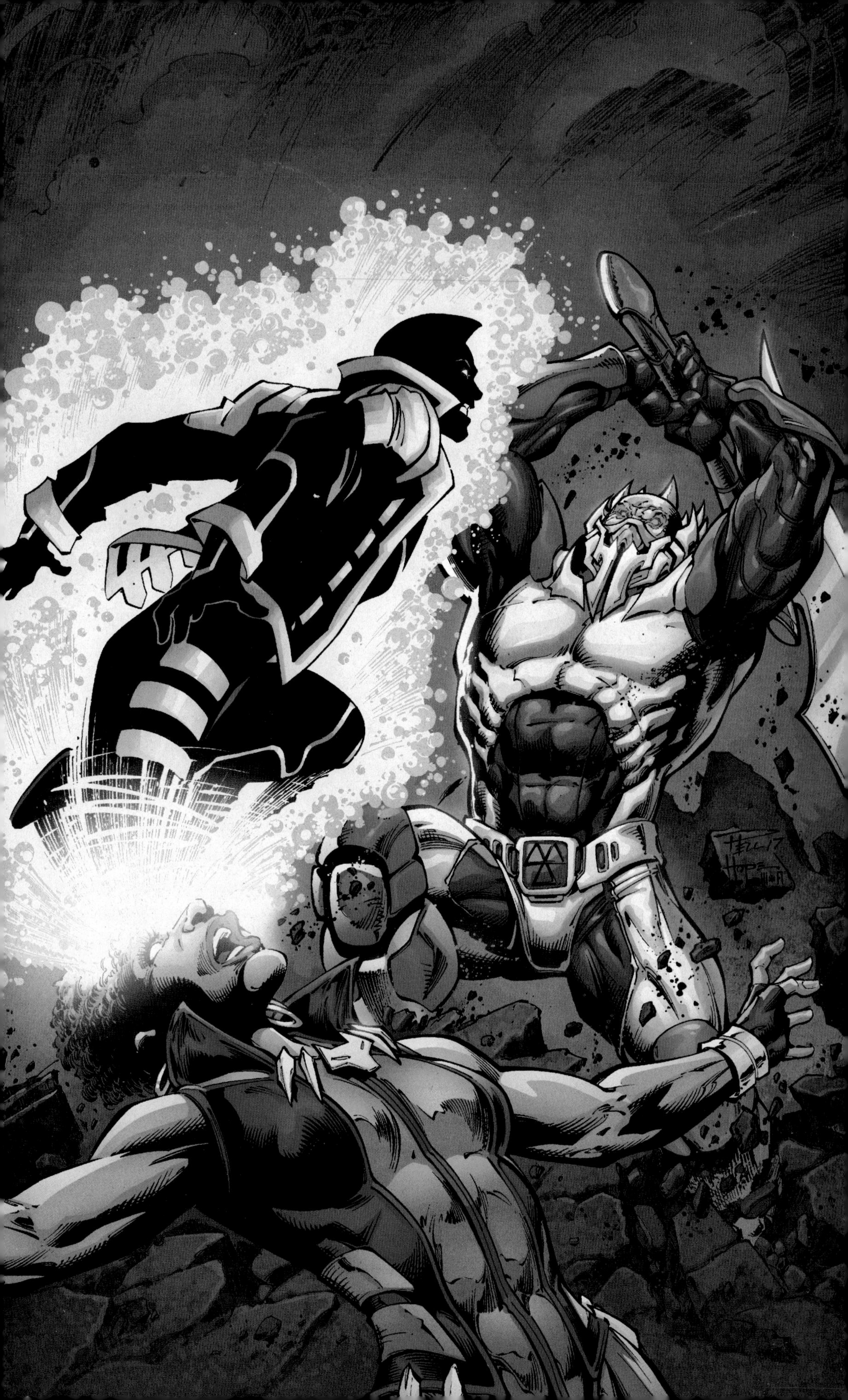

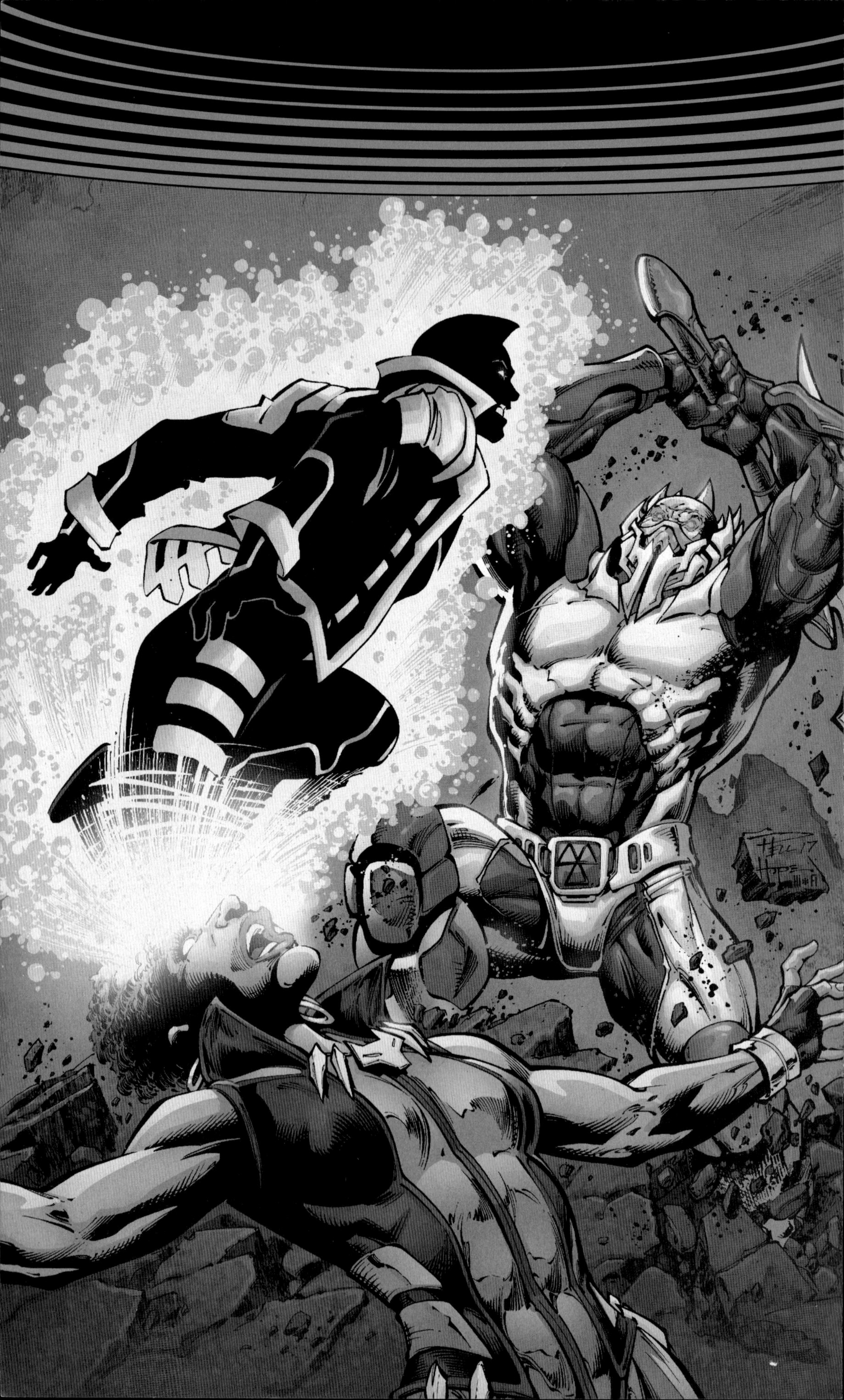

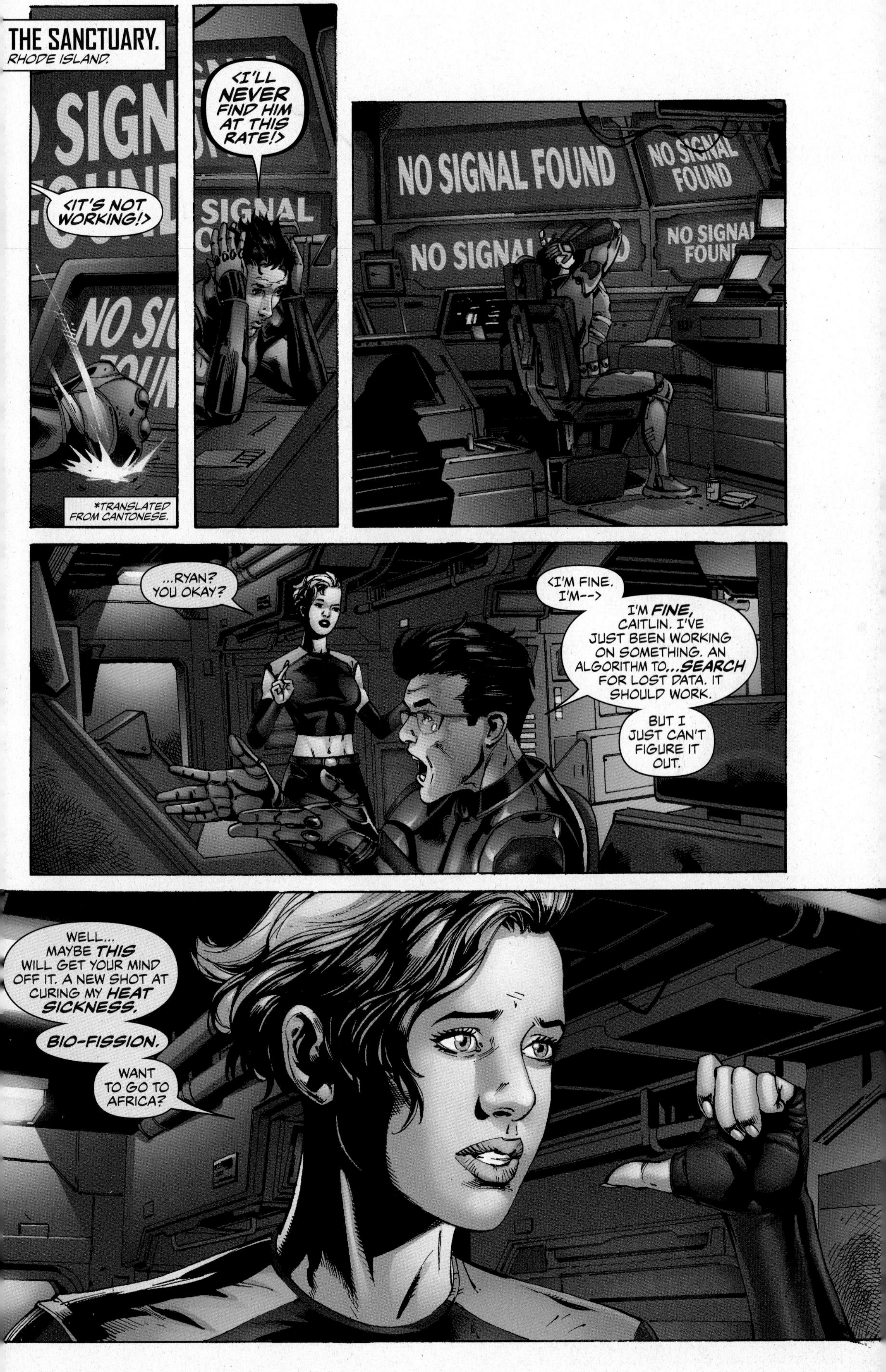
THE SANCTUARY.
RHODE ISLAND.
NO SIGN FOUND
<IT'S NOT WORKING!>
NO SIG FOUN
*TRANSLATED FROM CANTONESE.
SIGNAL
<I'LL NEVER FIND HIM AT THIS RATE!>
NO SIGNAL FOUND
NO SIGNAL FOUND
NO SIGNAL
NO SIGNAL FOUND
...RYAN? YOU OKAY?
<I'M FINE. I'M-->
I'M FINE, CAITLIN. I'VE JUST BEEN WORKING ON SOMETHING. AN ALGORITHM TO...SEARCH FOR LOST DATA. IT SHOULD WORK.
BUT I JUST CAN'T FIGURE IT OUT.
WELL... MAYBE THIS WILL GET YOUR MIND OFF IT. A NEW SHOT AT CURING MY HEAT SICKNESS.
BIO-FISSION.
WANT TO GO TO AFRICA?

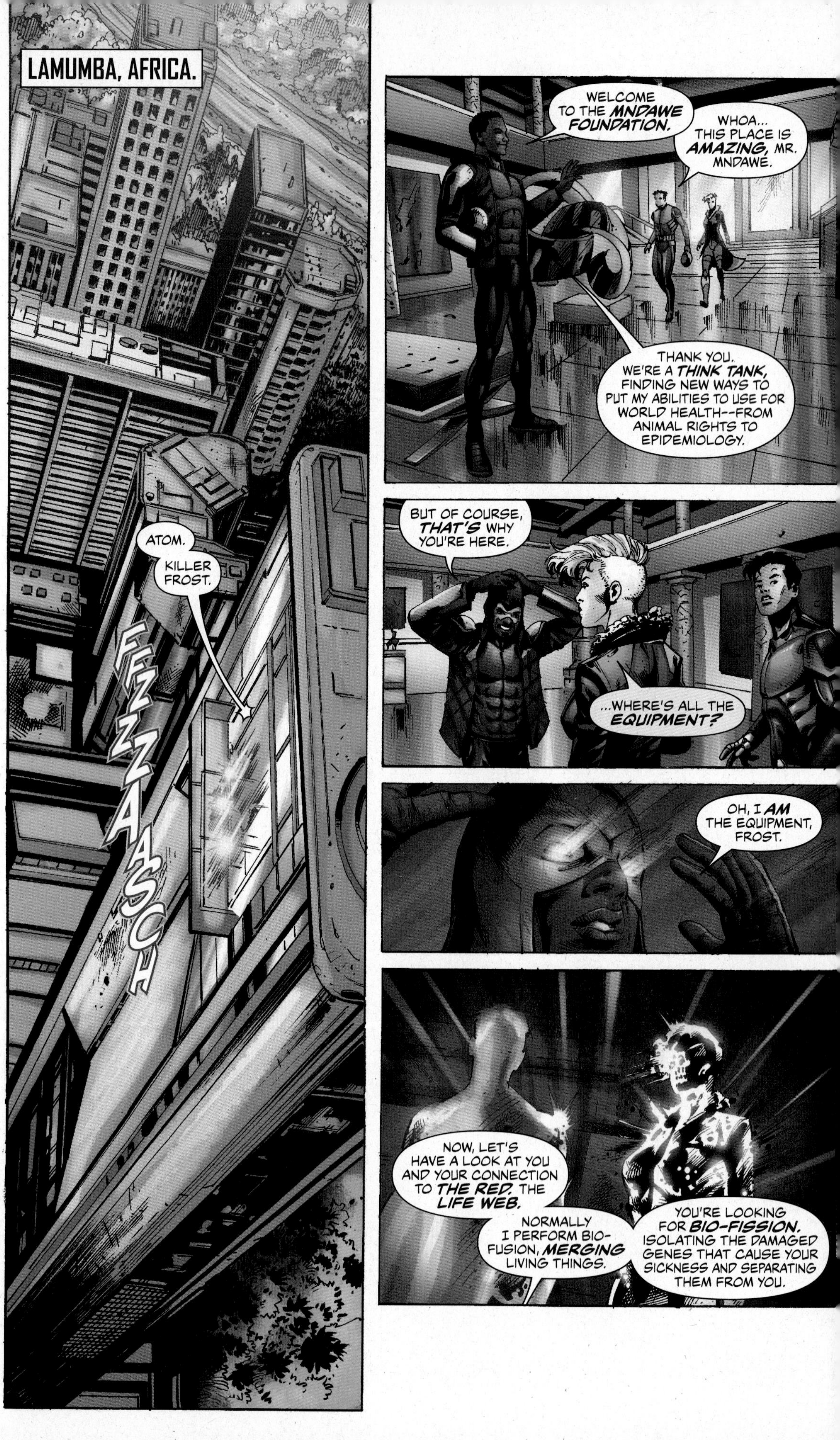
LAMUMBA, AFRICA.
ATOM.
KILLER FROST.
FFZZZAASCH
WELCOME TO THE MNDAWE FOUNDATION.
WHOA... THIS PLACE IS AMAZING, MR. MNDAWE.
THANK YOU. WE'RE A THINK TANK, FINDING NEW WAYS TO PUT MY ABILITIES TO USE FOR WORLD HEALTH--FROM ANIMAL RIGHTS TO EPIDEMIOLOGY.
BUT OF COURSE, THAT'S WHY YOU'RE HERE.
...WHERE'S ALL THE EQUIPMENT?
OH, I AM THE EQUIPMENT, FROST.
NOW, LET'S HAVE A LOOK AT YOU AND YOUR CONNECTION TO THE RED. THE LIFE WEB.
NORMALLY I PERFORM BIO-FUSION, MERGING LIVING THINGS.
YOU'RE LOOKING FOR BIO-FISSION. ISOLATING THE DAMAGED GENES THAT CAUSE YOUR SICKNESS AND SEPARATING THEM FROM YOU.

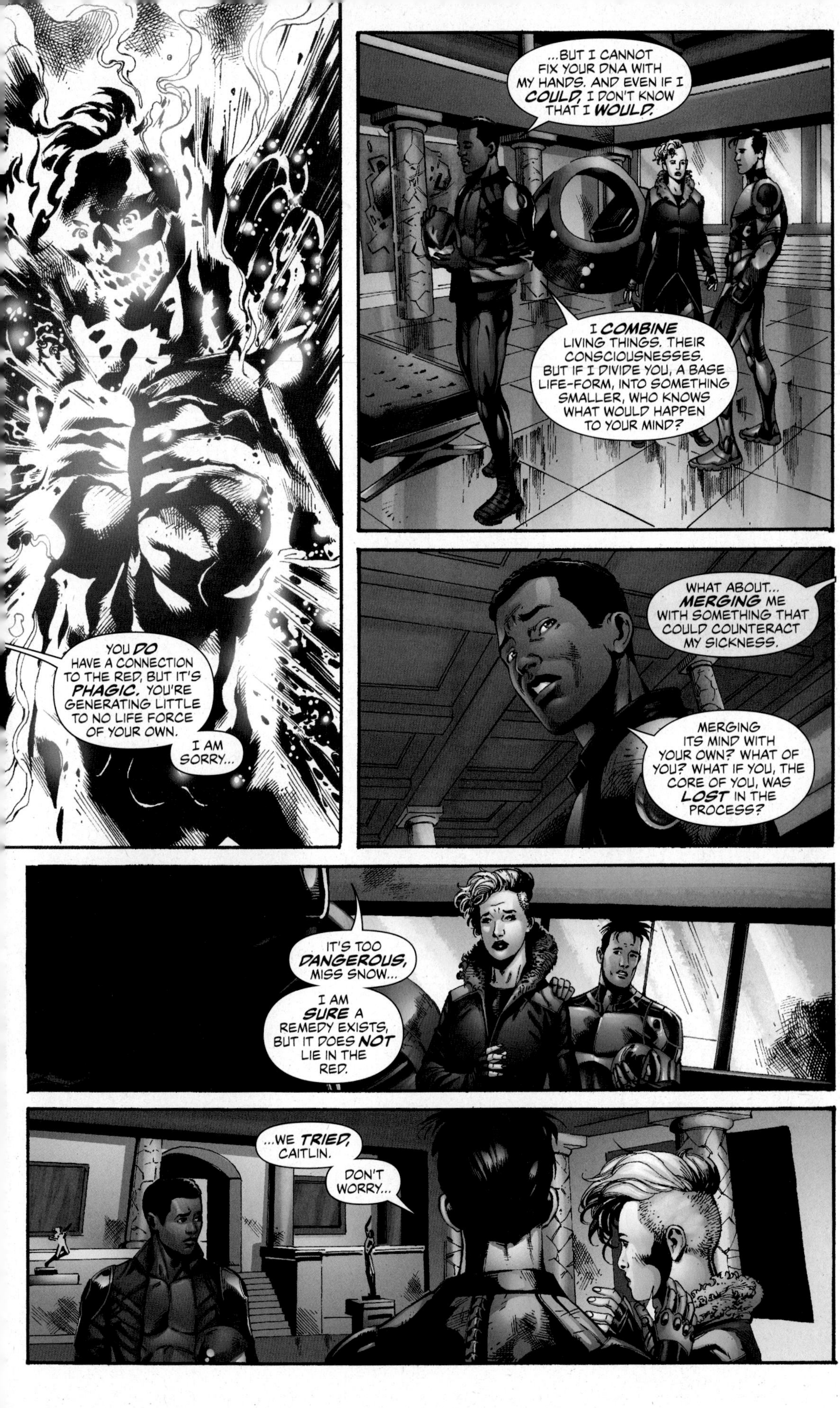
YOU DO HAVE A CONNECTION TO THE RED, BUT IT'S PHAGIC. YOU'RE GENERATING LITTLE TO NO LIFE FORCE OF YOUR OWN.
I AM SORRY...
...BUT I CANNOT FIX YOUR DNA WITH MY HANDS. AND EVEN IF I COULD, I DON'T KNOW THAT I WOULD.
I COMBINE LIVING THINGS. THEIR CONSCIOUSNESSES. BUT IF I DIVIDE YOU, A BASE LIFE-FORM, INTO SOMETHING SMALLER, WHO KNOWS WHAT WOULD HAPPEN TO YOUR MIND?
WHAT ABOUT... MERGING ME WITH SOMETHING THAT COULD COUNTERACT MY SICKNESS.
MERGING ITS MIND WITH YOUR OWN? WHAT OF YOU? WHAT IF YOU, THE CORE OF YOU, WAS LOST IN THE PROCESS?
IT'S TOO DANGEROUS, MISS SNOW...
I AM SURE A REMEDY EXISTS, BUT IT DOES NOT LIE IN THE RED.
...WE TRIED, CAITLIN.
DON'T WORRY...

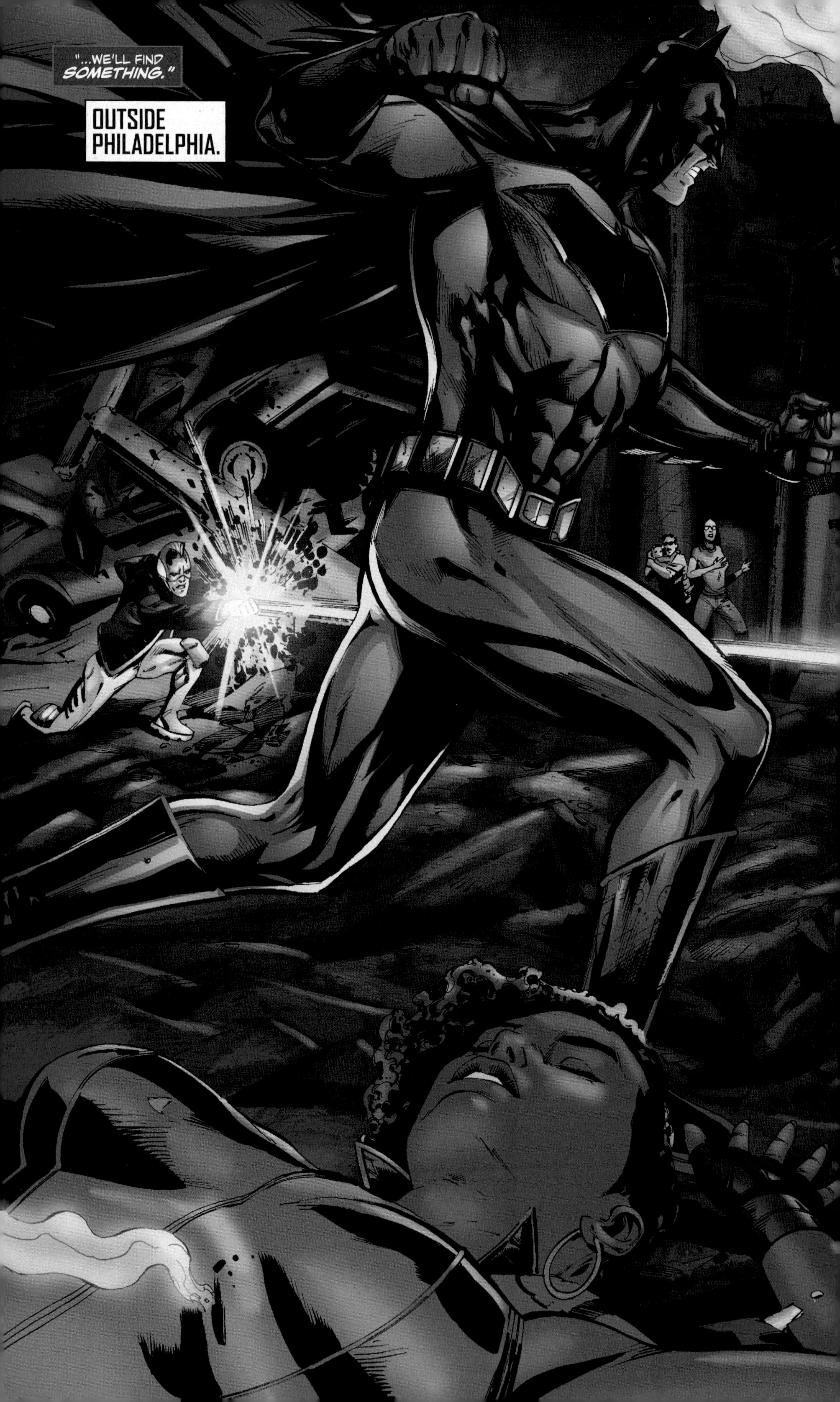
"...WE'LL FIND SOMETHING."
OUTSIDE PHILADELPHIA.

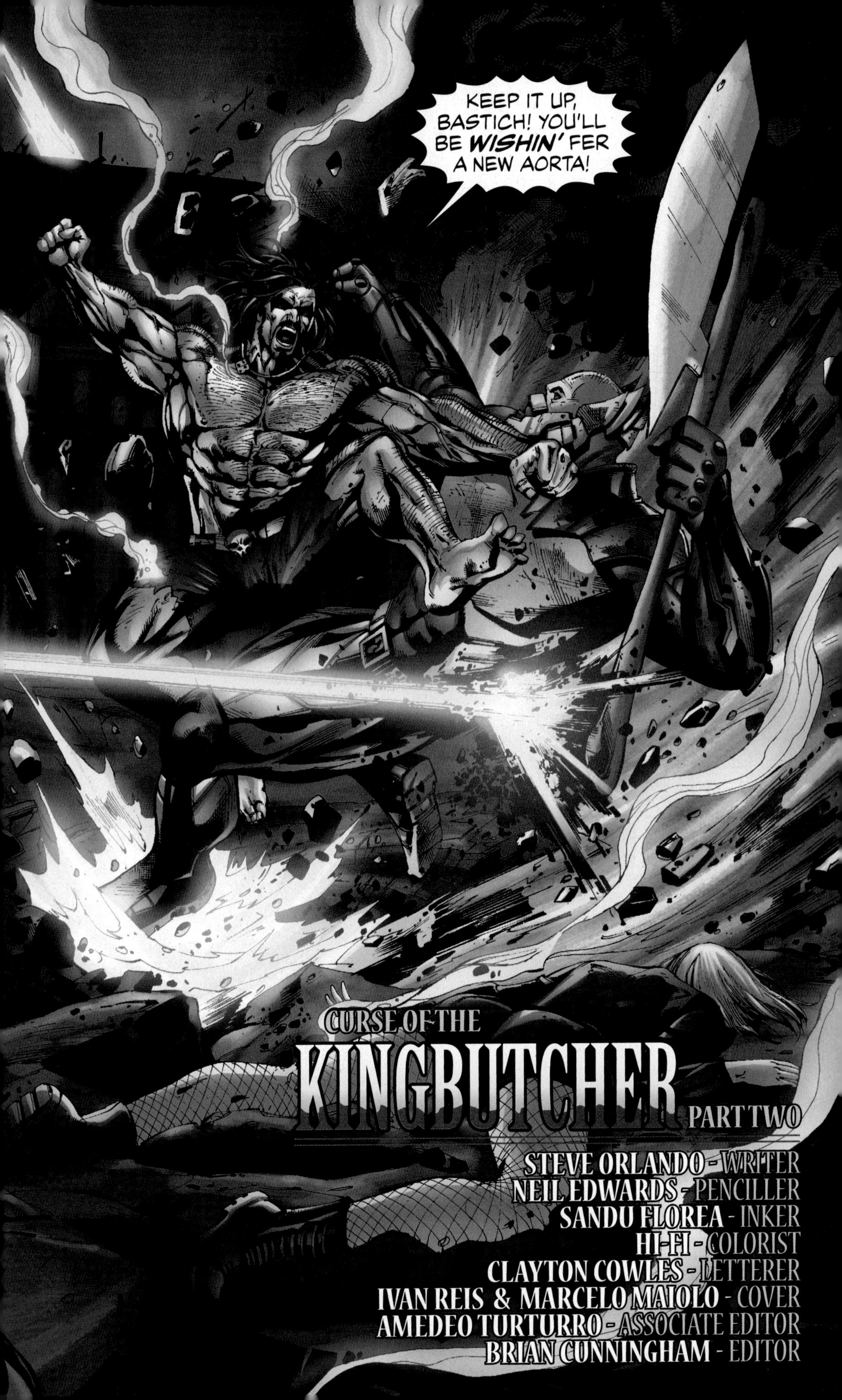

KEEP IT UP, BASTICH! YOU'LL BE WISHIN' FER A NEW AORTA!
CURSE OF THE
KINGBUTCHER
PART TWO
STEVE ORLANDO - WRITER
NEIL EDWARDS - PENCILLER
SANDU FLOREA - INKER
HI-FI - COLORIST
CLAYTON COWLES - LETTERER
IVAN REIS & MARCELO MAIOLO - COVER
AMEDEO TURTURRO - ASSOCIATE EDITOR
BRIAN CUNNINGHAM - EDITOR

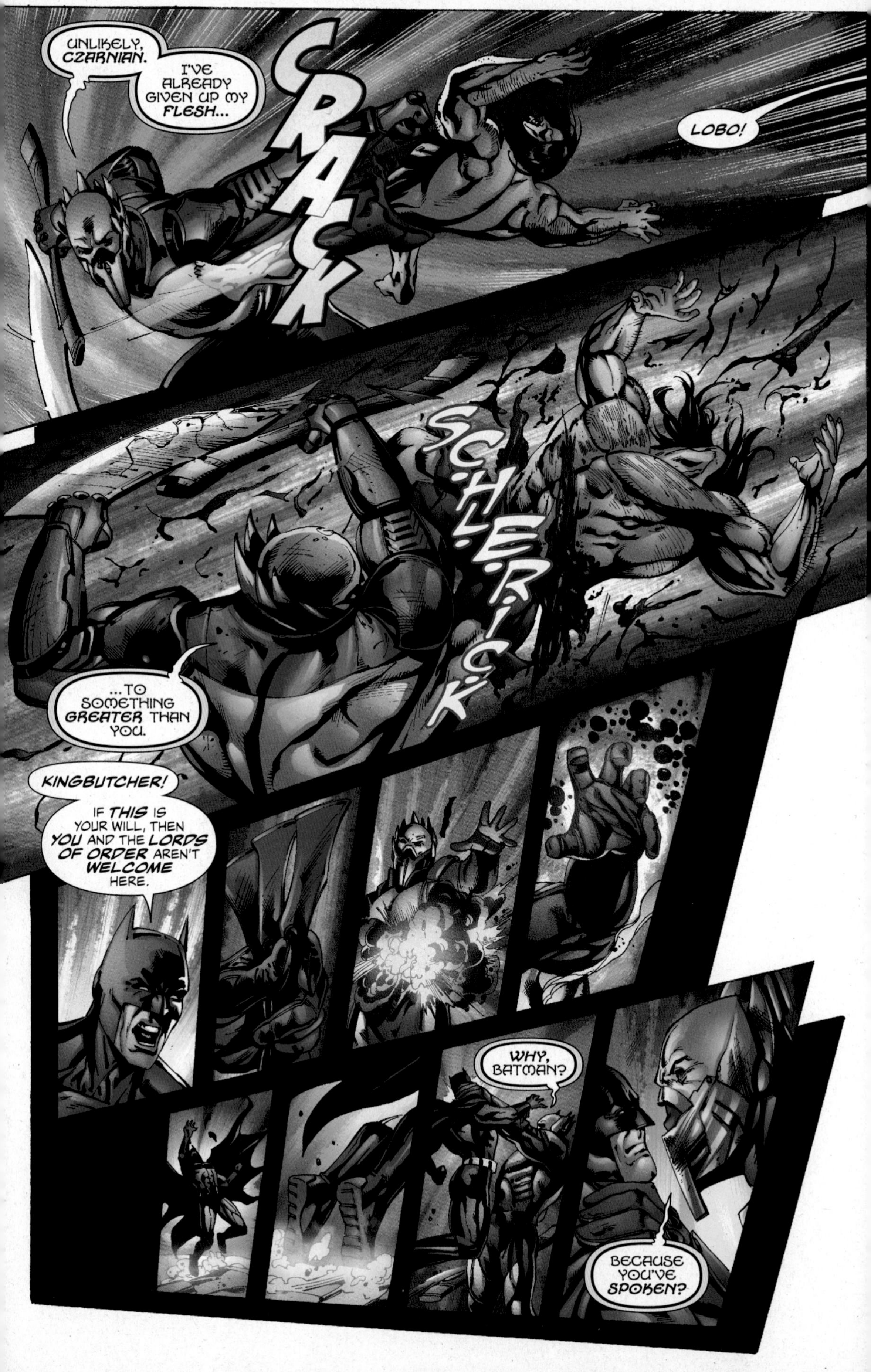

UNLIKELY, CZARNIAN.
I'VE ALREADY GIVEN UP MY FLESH...
CRACK
LOBO!
SCHLERICK
...TO SOMETHING GREATER THAN YOU.
KINGBUTCHER!
IF THIS IS YOUR WILL, THEN YOU AND THE LORDS OF ORDER AREN'T WELCOME HERE.
WHY, BATMAN?
BECAUSE YOU'VE SPOKEN?

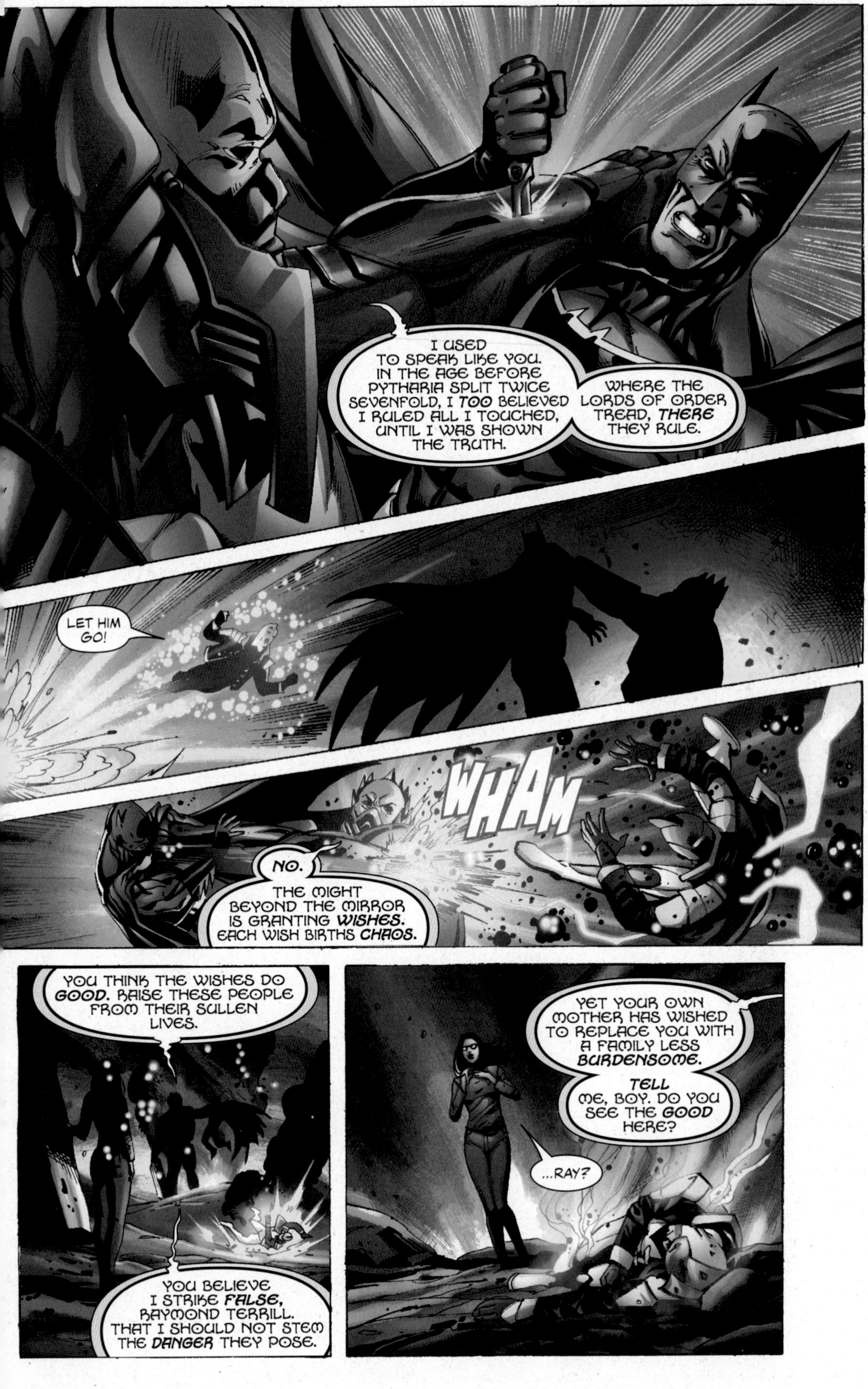
I USED TO SPEAK LIKE YOU. IN THE AGE BEFORE PYTHARIA SPLIT TWICE SEVENFOLD, I TOO BELIEVED I RULED ALL I TOUCHED, UNTIL I WAS SHOWN THE TRUTH.
WHERE THE LORDS OF ORDER TREAD, THERE THEY RULE.
LET HIM GO!
WHAM
NO.
THE MIGHT BEYOND THE MIRROR IS GRANTING WISHES. EACH WISH BIRTHS CHAOS.
YOU THINK THE WISHES DO GOOD. RAISE THESE PEOPLE FROM THEIR SULLEN LIVES.
YOU BELIEVE I STRIKE FALSE, RAYMOND TERRILL. THAT I SHOULD NOT STEM THE DANGER THEY POSE.
YET YOUR OWN MOTHER HAS WISHED TO REPLACE YOU WITH A FAMILY LESS BURDENSOME.
TELL ME, BOY. DO YOU SEE THE GOOD HERE?
...RAY?

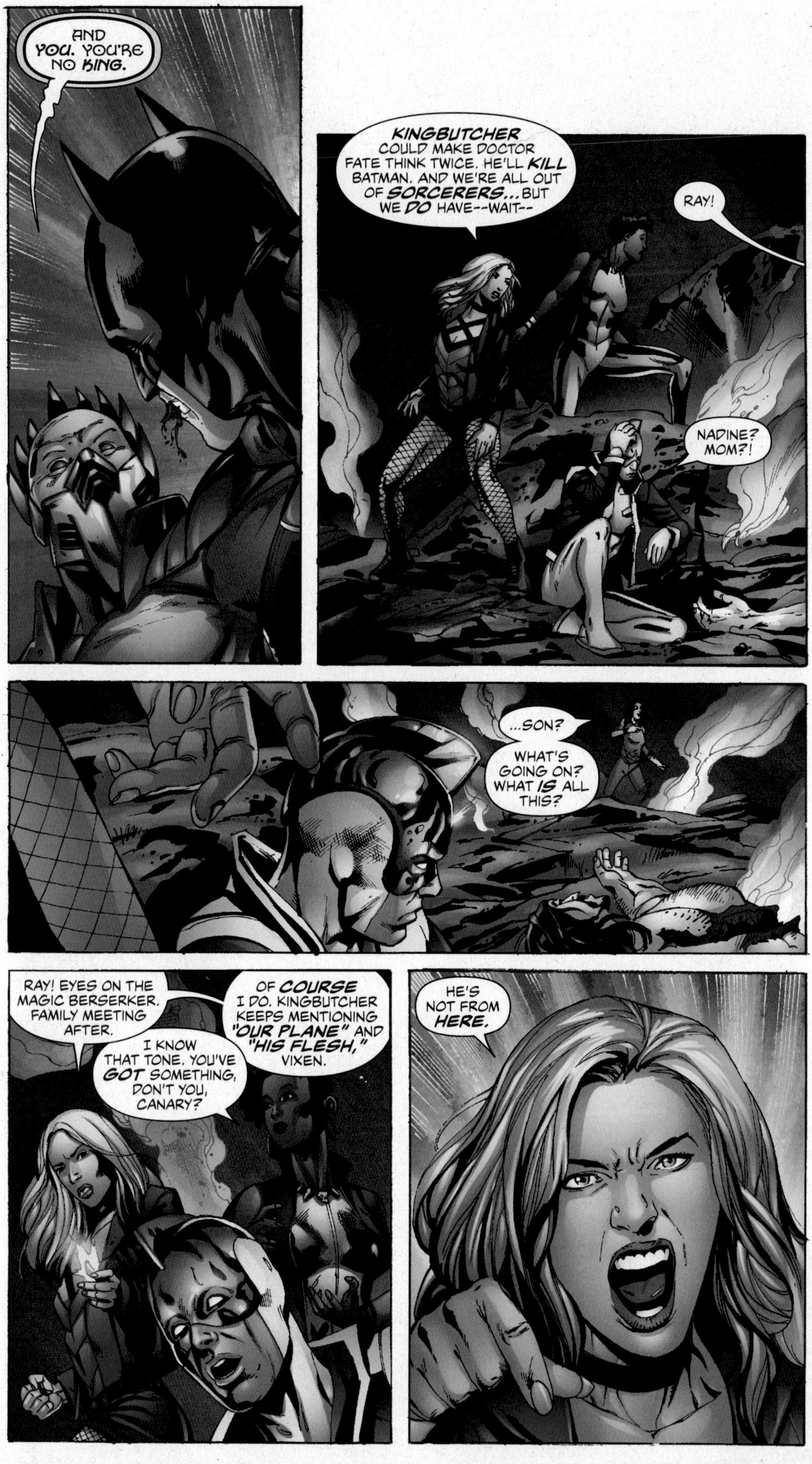
AND YOU. YOU'RE NO KING.
KINGBUTCHER COULD MAKE DOCTOR FATE THINK TWICE. HE'LL KILL BATMAN. AND WE'RE ALL OUT OF SORCERERS... BUT WE DO HAVE--WAIT--
RAY!
NADINE? MOM?!
...SON?
WHAT'S GOING ON? WHAT IS ALL THIS?
RAY! EYES ON THE MAGIC BERSERKER. FAMILY MEETING AFTER.
I KNOW THAT TONE. YOU'VE GOT SOMETHING, DON'T YOU, CANARY?
OF COURSE I DO. KINGBUTCHER KEEPS MENTIONING "OUR PLANE" AND "HIS FLESH," VIXEN.
HE'S NOT FROM HERE.

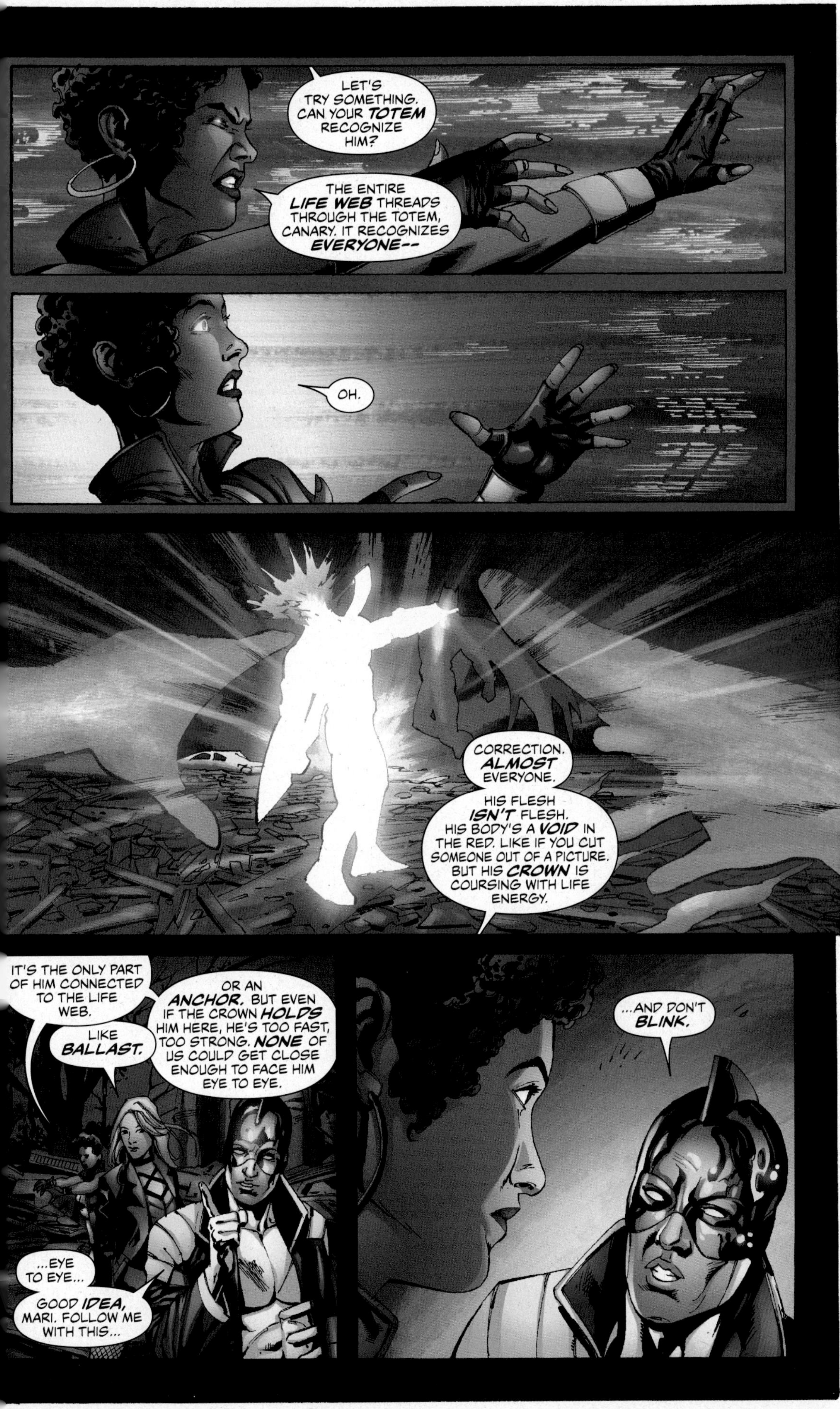
LET'S TRY SOMETHING. CAN YOUR TOTEM RECOGNIZE HIM?
THE ENTIRE LIFE WEB THREADS THROUGH THE TOTEM, CANARY. IT RECOGNIZES EVERYONE--
OH.
CORRECTION. ALMOST EVERYONE.
HIS FLESH ISN'T FLESH. HIS BODY'S A VOID IN THE RED. LIKE IF YOU CUT SOMEONE OUT OF A PICTURE. BUT HIS CROWN IS COURSING WITH LIFE ENERGY.
IT'S THE ONLY PART OF HIM CONNECTED TO THE LIFE WEB.
LIKE BALLAST.
OR AN ANCHOR. BUT EVEN IF THE CROWN HOLDS HIM HERE, HE'S TOO FAST, TOO STRONG. NONE OF US COULD GET CLOSE ENOUGH TO FACE HIM EYE TO EYE.
...EYE TO EYE...
GOOD IDEA, MARI. FOLLOW ME WITH THIS...
...AND DON'T BLINK.

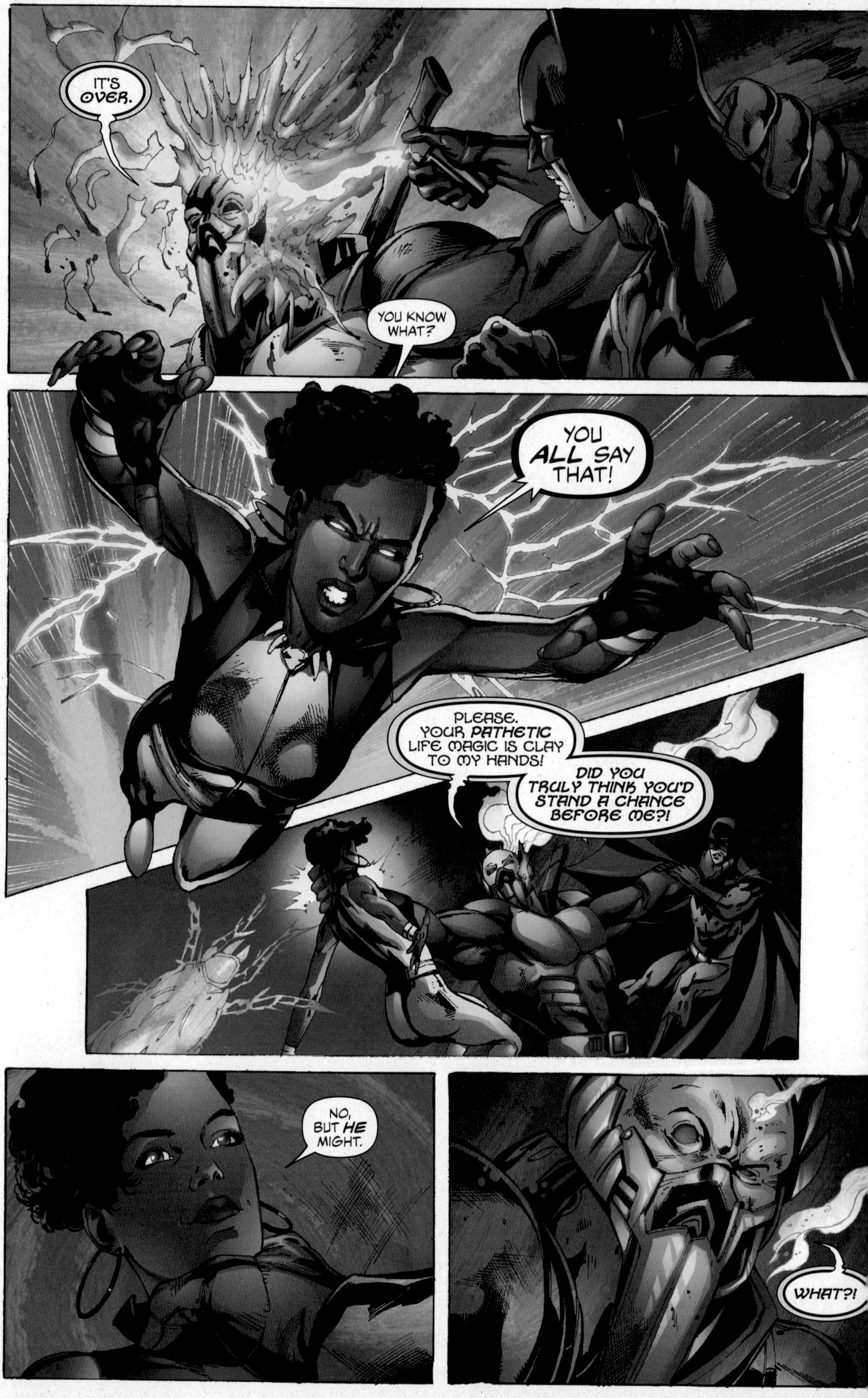
IT'S OVER.
YOU KNOW WHAT?
YOU ALL SAY THAT!
PLEASE. YOUR PATHETIC LIFE MAGIC IS CLAY TO MY HANDS!
DID YOU TRULY THINK YOU'D STAND A CHANCE BEFORE ME?!
NO, BUT HE MIGHT.
WHAT?!

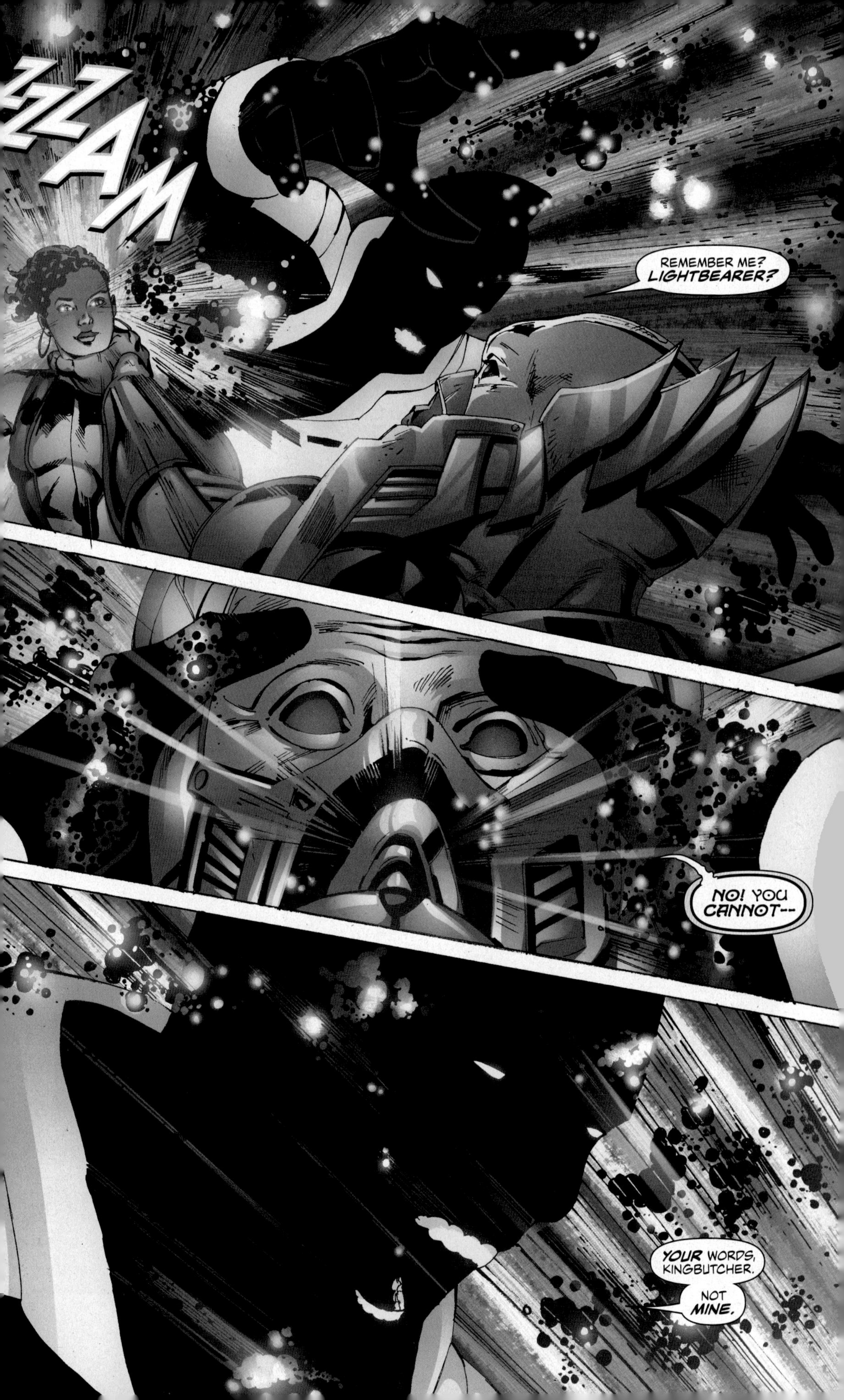
ZZZAM
REMEMBER ME? LIGHTBEARER?
NO! YOU CANNOT--
YOUR WORDS, KINGBUTCHER.
NOT MINE.

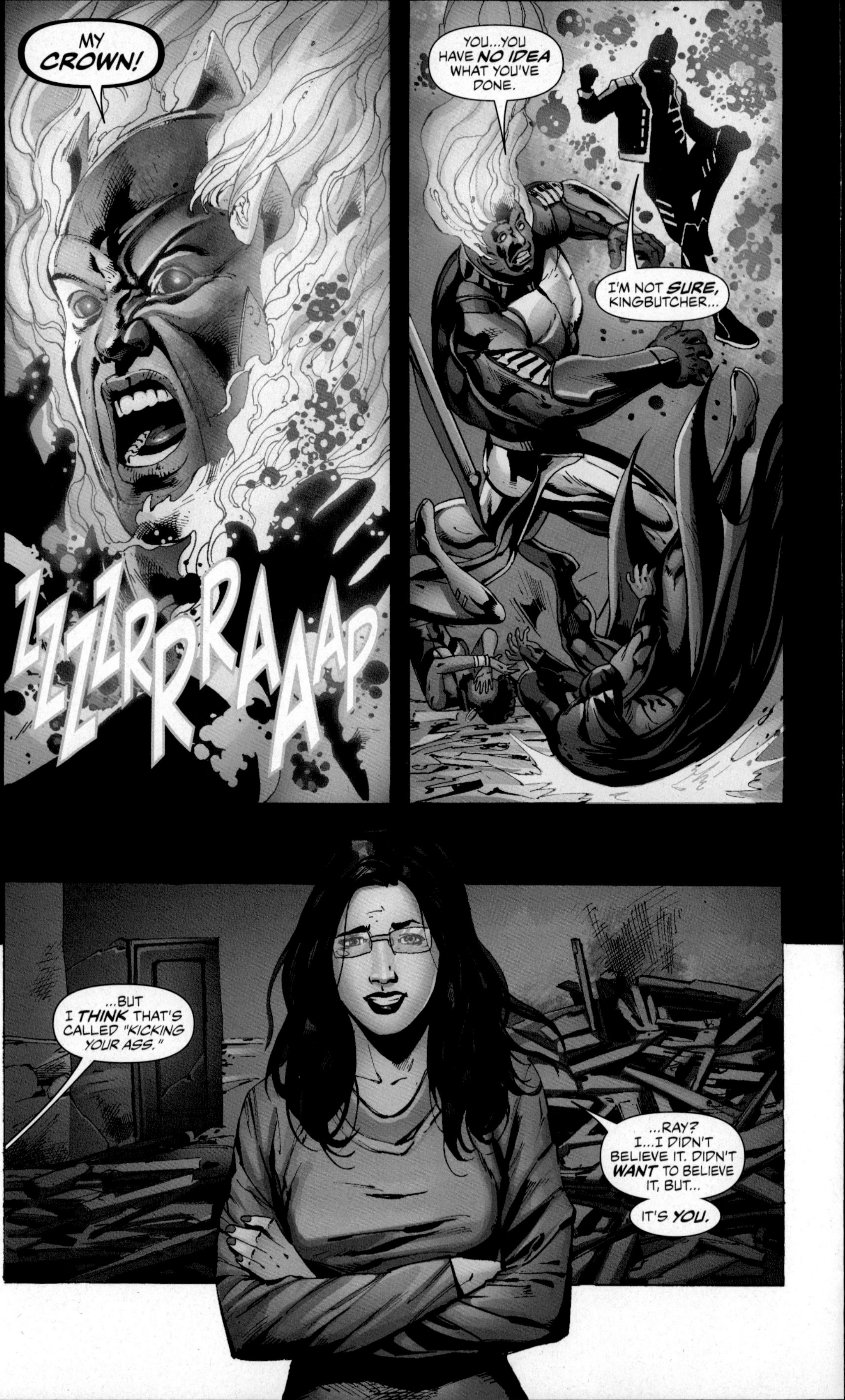
MY CROWN!
ZZZZRRRRAAAAP
YOU...YOU HAVE NO IDEA WHAT YOU'VE DONE.
I'M NOT SURE, KINGBUTCHER...
...BUT I THINK THAT'S CALLED "KICKING YOUR ASS."
...RAY? I...I DIDN'T BELIEVE IT. DIDN'T WANT TO BELIEVE IT, BUT...
IT'S YOU.

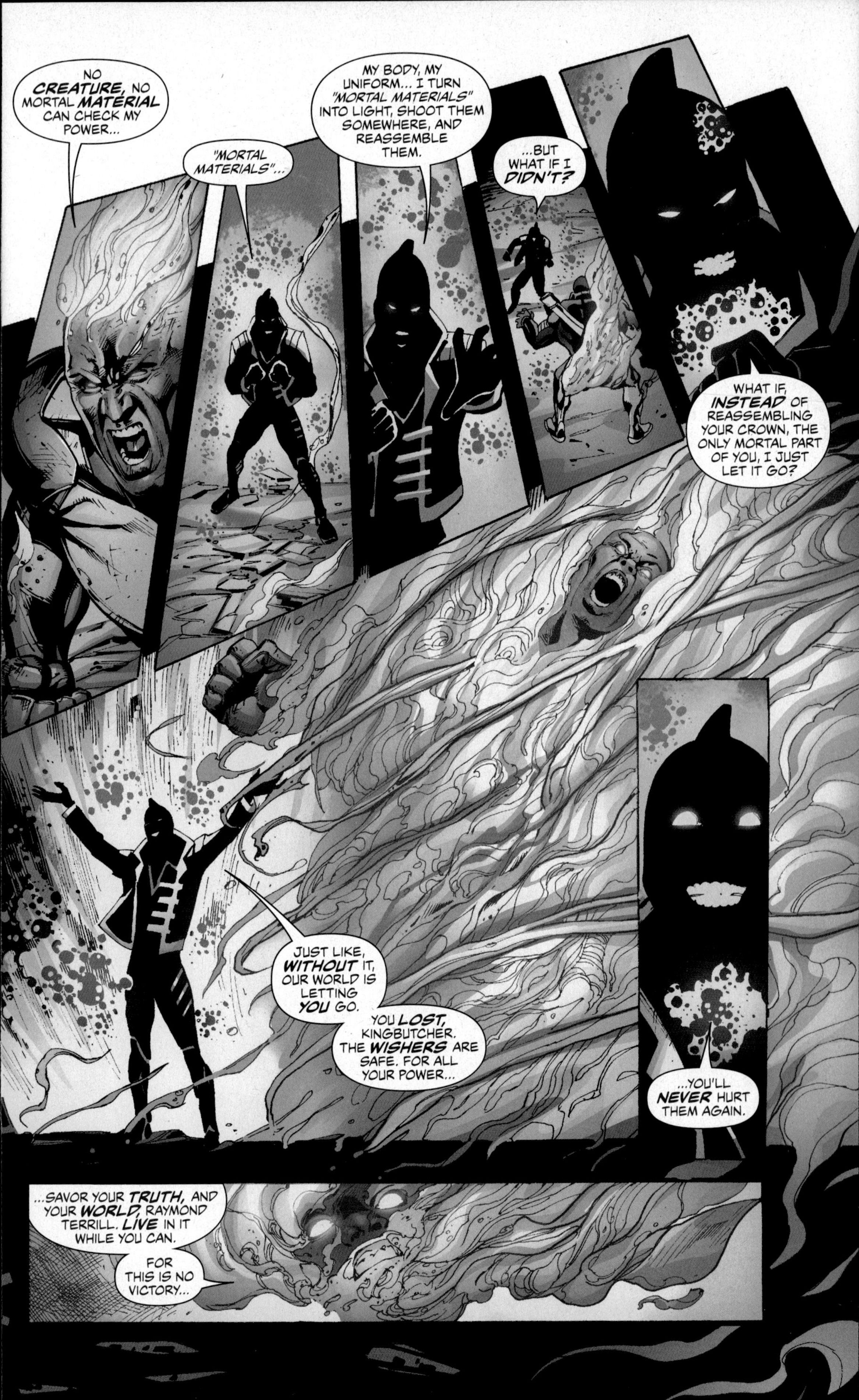
NO CREATURE, NO MORTAL MATERIAL CAN CHECK MY POWER...
"MORTAL MATERIALS"...
MY BODY, MY UNIFORM... I TURN "MORTAL MATERIALS" INTO LIGHT, SHOOT THEM SOMEWHERE, AND REASSEMBLE THEM.
...BUT WHAT IF I DIDN'T?
WHAT IF, INSTEAD OF REASSEMBLING YOUR CROWN, THE ONLY MORTAL PART OF YOU, I JUST LET IT GO?
JUST LIKE, WITHOUT IT, OUR WORLD IS LETTING YOU GO.
YOU LOST, KINGBUTCHER. THE WISHERS ARE SAFE. FOR ALL YOUR POWER...
...YOU'LL NEVER HURT THEM AGAIN.
...SAVOR YOUR TRUTH, AND YOUR WORLD, RAYMOND TERRILL. LIVE IN IT WHILE YOU CAN.
FOR THIS IS NO VICTORY...

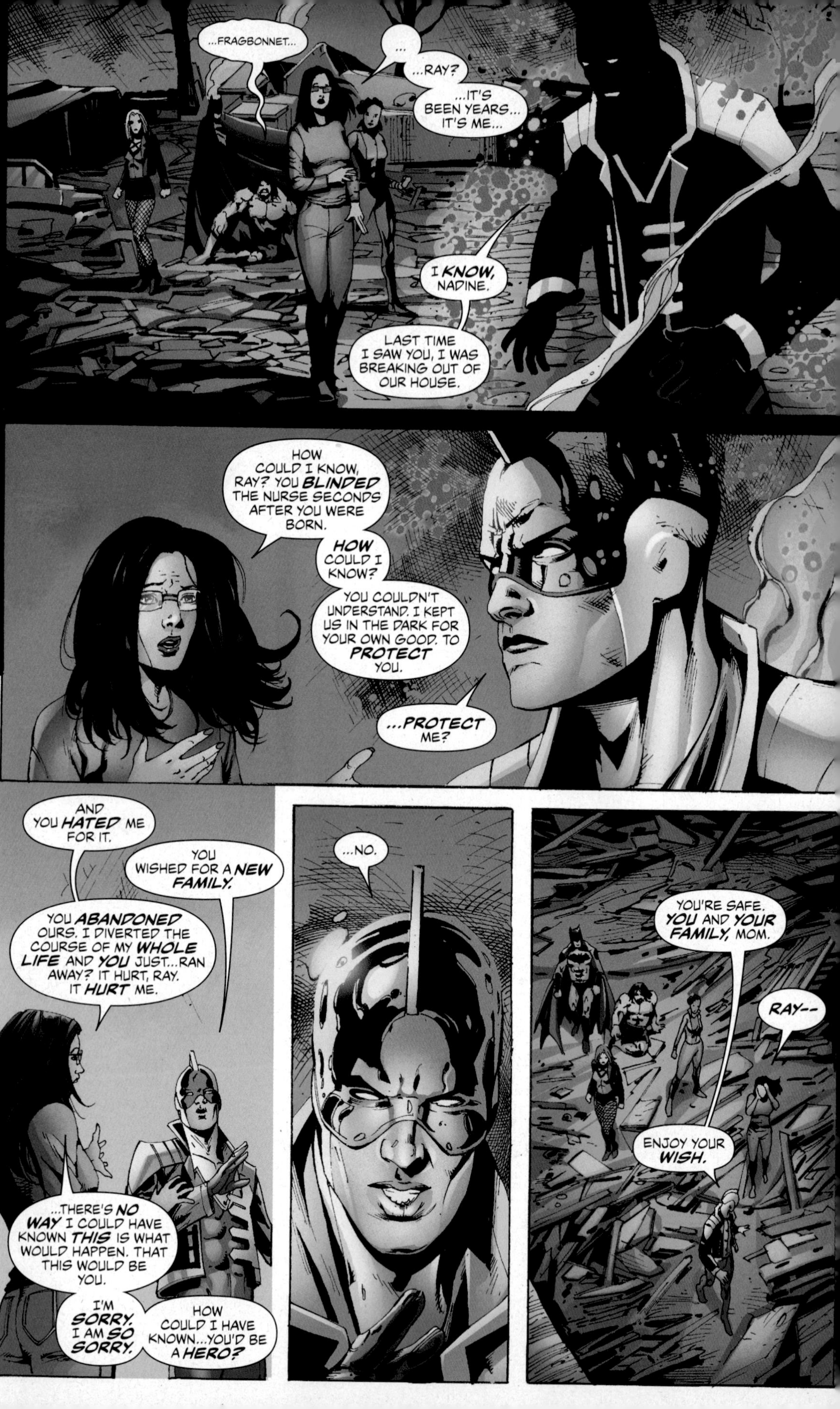
...FRAGBONNET...
...
...RAY?
...IT'S BEEN YEARS... IT'S ME...
I KNOW, NADINE.
LAST TIME I SAW YOU, I WAS BREAKING OUT OF OUR HOUSE.
HOW COULD I KNOW, RAY? YOU BLINDED THE NURSE SECONDS AFTER YOU WERE BORN.
HOW COULD I KNOW?
YOU COULDN'T UNDERSTAND. I KEPT US IN THE DARK FOR YOUR OWN GOOD. TO PROTECT YOU.
...PROTECT ME?
AND YOU HATED ME FOR IT.
YOU WISHED FOR A NEW FAMILY.
YOU ABANDONED OURS. I DIVERTED THE COURSE OF MY WHOLE LIFE AND YOU JUST...RAN AWAY? IT HURT, RAY. IT HURT ME.
...THERE'S NO WAY I COULD HAVE KNOWN THIS IS WHAT WOULD HAPPEN. THAT THIS WOULD BE YOU.
I'M SORRY. I AM SO SORRY.
HOW COULD I HAVE KNOWN...YOU'D BE A HERO?
...NO.
YOU'RE SAFE. YOU AND YOUR FAMILY, MOM.
RAY--
ENJOY YOUR WISH.

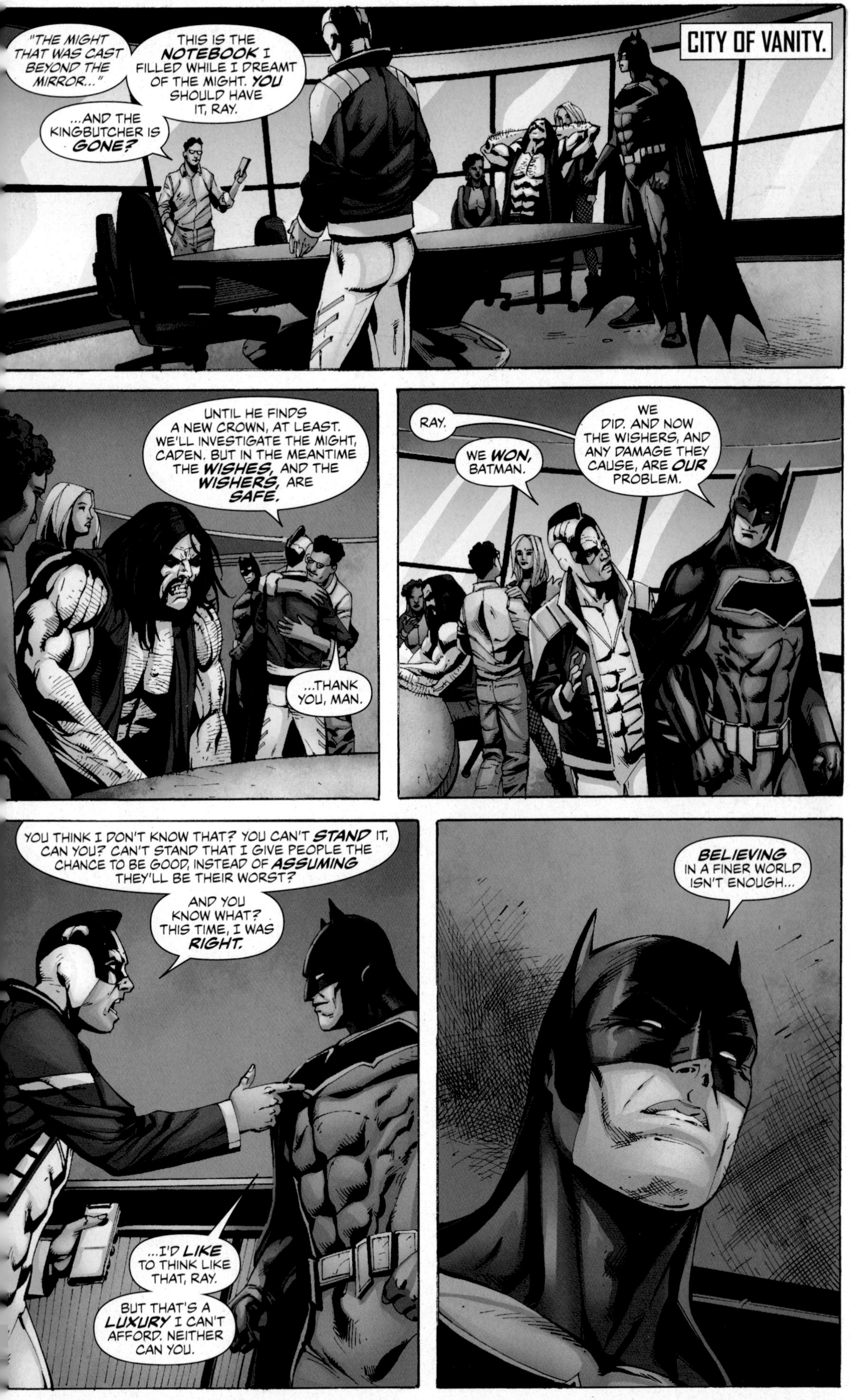
CITY OF VANITY.
"THE MIGHT THAT WAS CAST BEYOND THE MIRROR..."
THIS IS THE NOTEBOOK I FILLED WHILE I DREAMT OF THE MIGHT. YOU SHOULD HAVE IT, RAY.
...AND THE KINGBUTCHER IS GONE?
UNTIL HE FINDS A NEW CROWN, AT LEAST. WE'LL INVESTIGATE THE MIGHT, CADEN. BUT IN THE MEANTIME THE WISHES, AND THE WISHERS, ARE SAFE.
...THANK YOU, MAN.
RAY.
WE WON, BATMAN.
WE DID. AND NOW THE WISHERS, AND ANY DAMAGE THEY CAUSE, ARE OUR PROBLEM.
YOU THINK I DON'T KNOW THAT? YOU CAN'T STAND IT, CAN YOU? CAN'T STAND THAT I GIVE PEOPLE THE CHANCE TO BE GOOD, INSTEAD OF ASSUMING THEY'LL BE THEIR WORST?
AND YOU KNOW WHAT? THIS TIME, I WAS RIGHT.
...I'D LIKE TO THINK LIKE THAT, RAY.
BUT THAT'S A LUXURY I CAN'T AFFORD. NEITHER CAN YOU.
BELIEVING IN A FINER WORLD ISN'T ENOUGH...

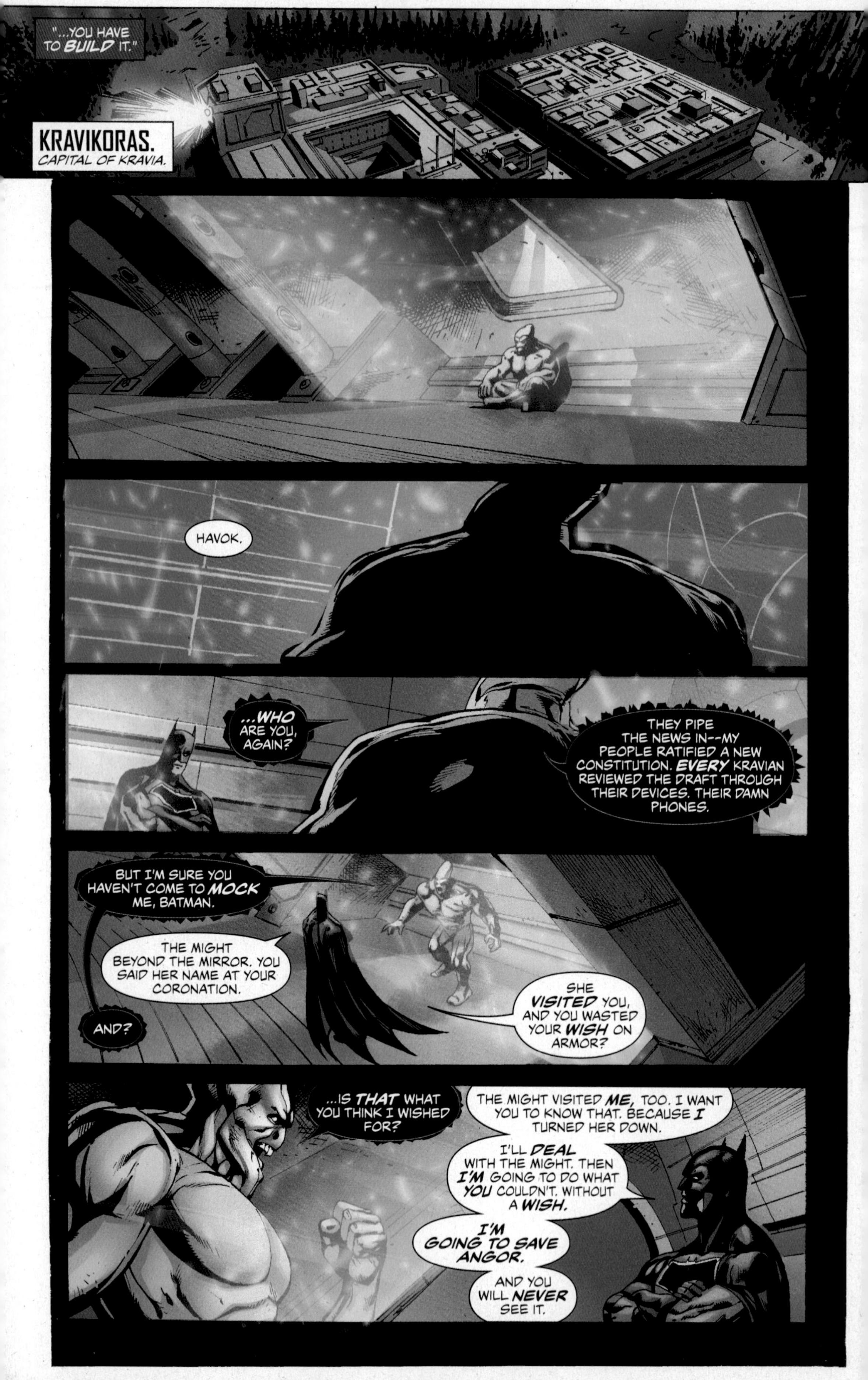
"...YOU HAVE TO BUILD IT."
KRAVIKORAS. CAPITAL OF KRAVIA.
HAVOK.
...WHO ARE YOU, AGAIN?
THEY PIPE THE NEWS IN--MY PEOPLE RATIFIED A NEW CONSTITUTION. EVERY KRAVIAN REVIEWED THE DRAFT THROUGH THEIR DEVICES. THEIR DAMN PHONES.
BUT I'M SURE YOU HAVEN'T COME TO MOCK ME, BATMAN.
THE MIGHT BEYOND THE MIRROR. YOU SAID HER NAME AT YOUR CORONATION.
AND?
SHE VISITED YOU, AND YOU WASTED YOUR WISH ON ARMOR?
...IS THAT WHAT YOU THINK I WISHED FOR?
THE MIGHT VISITED ME, TOO. I WANT YOU TO KNOW THAT. BECAUSE I TURNED HER DOWN.
I'LL DEAL WITH THE MIGHT. THEN I'M GOING TO DO WHAT YOU COULDN'T. WITHOUT A WISH.
I'M GOING TO SAVE ANGOR.
AND YOU WILL NEVER SEE IT.

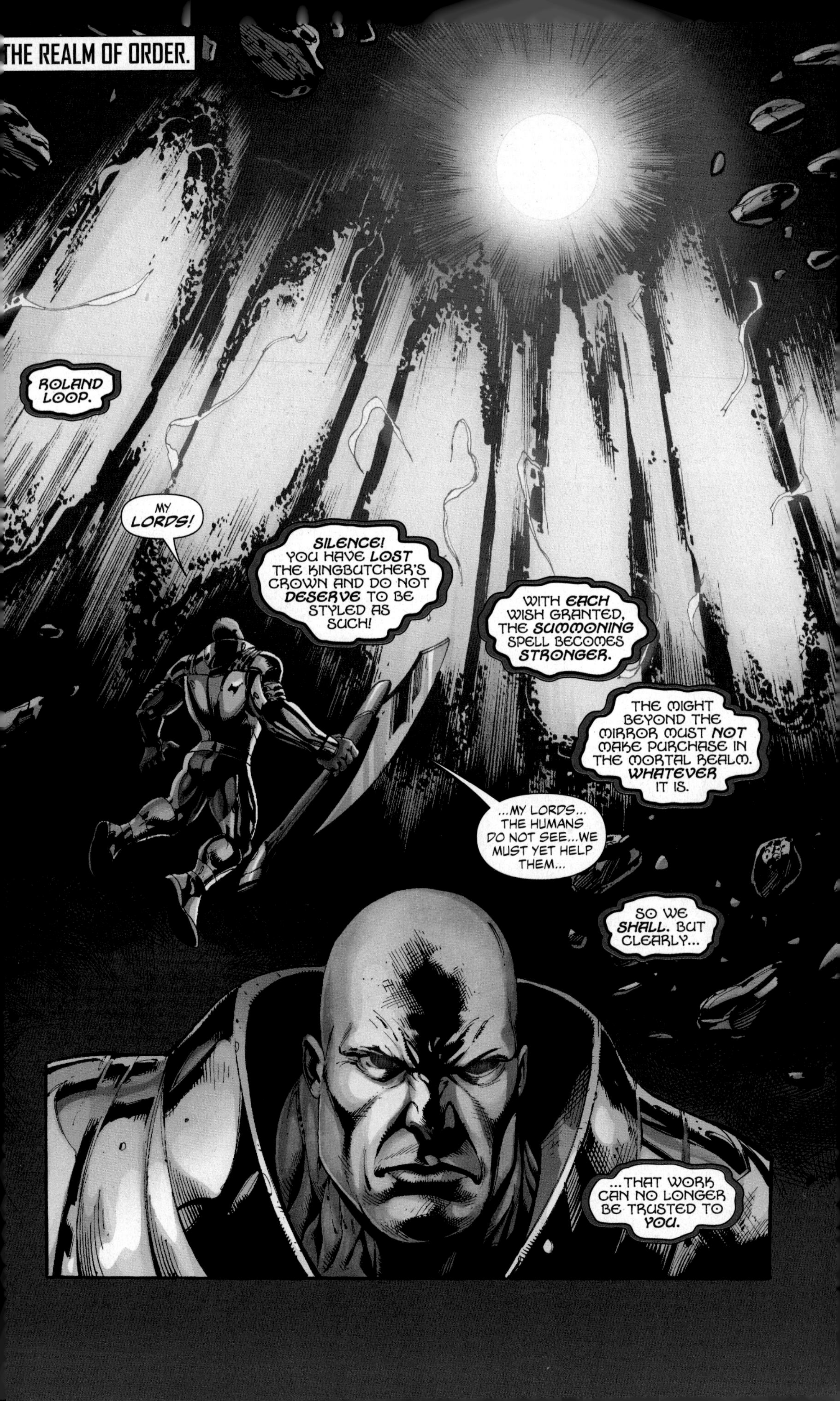
THE REALM OF ORDER.
ROLAND LOOP.
MY LORDS!
SILENCE! YOU HAVE LOST THE KINGBUTCHER'S CROWN AND DO NOT DESERVE TO BE STYLED AS SUCH!
WITH EACH WISH GRANTED, THE SUMMONING SPELL BECOMES STRONGER.
THE MIGHT BEYOND THE MIRROR MUST NOT MAKE PURCHASE IN THE MORTAL REALM. WHATEVER IT IS.
...MY LORDS... THE HUMANS DO NOT SEE...WE MUST YET HELP THEM...
SO WE SHALL. BUT CLEARLY...
...THAT WORK CAN NO LONGER BE TRUSTED TO YOU.

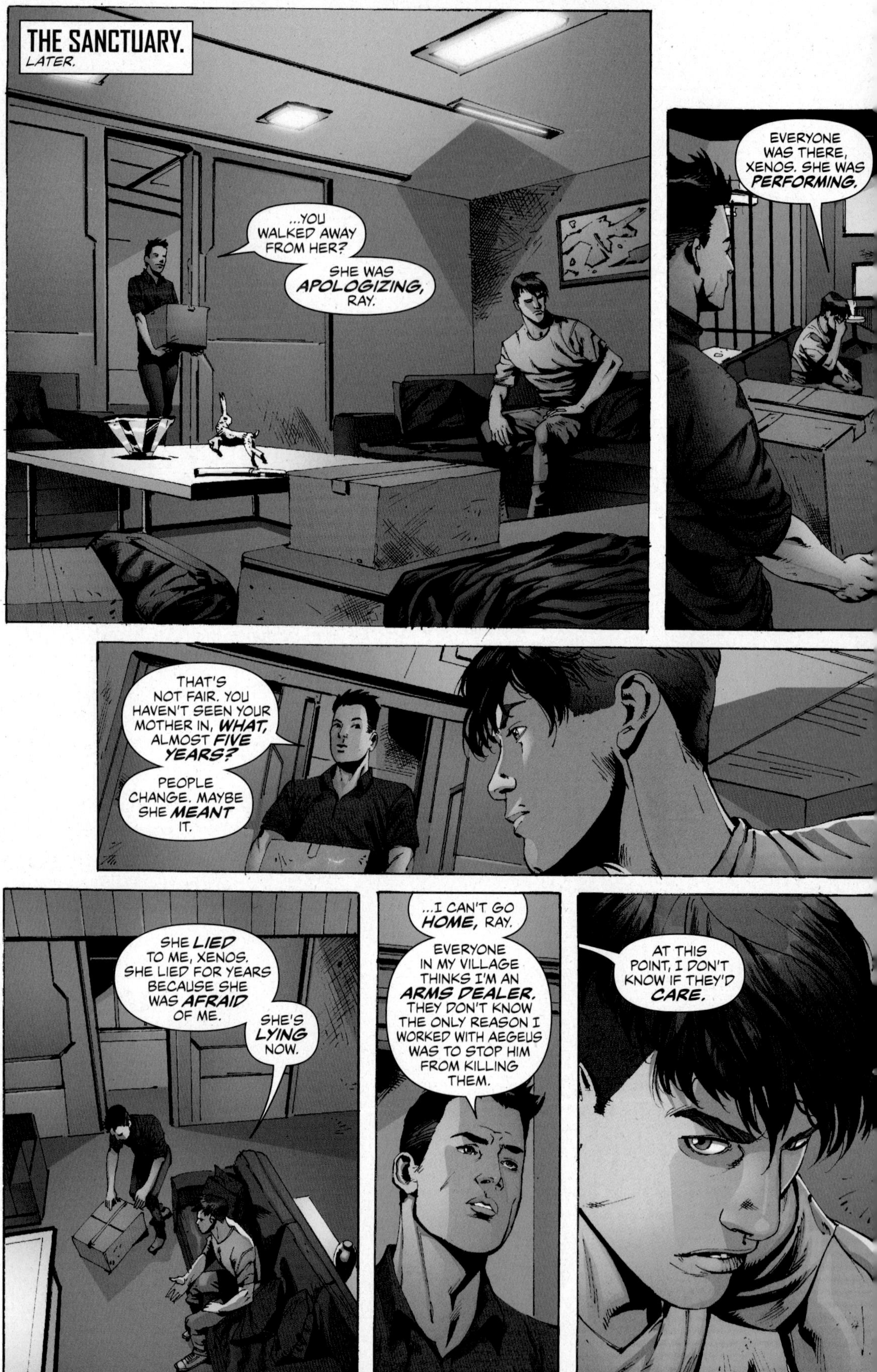
THE SANCTUARY.
LATER.
...YOU WALKED AWAY FROM HER?
SHE WAS APOLOGIZING, RAY.
EVERYONE WAS THERE, XENOS. SHE WAS PERFORMING.
THAT'S NOT FAIR. YOU HAVEN'T SEEN YOUR MOTHER IN, WHAT, ALMOST FIVE YEARS?
PEOPLE CHANGE. MAYBE SHE MEANT IT.
SHE LIED TO ME, XENOS. SHE LIED FOR YEARS BECAUSE SHE WAS AFRAID OF ME.
SHE'S LYING NOW.
...I CAN'T GO HOME, RAY.
EVERYONE IN MY VILLAGE THINKS I'M AN ARMS DEALER. THEY DON'T KNOW THE ONLY REASON I WORKED WITH AEGEUS WAS TO STOP HIM FROM KILLING THEM.
AT THIS POINT, I DON'T KNOW IF THEY'D CARE.

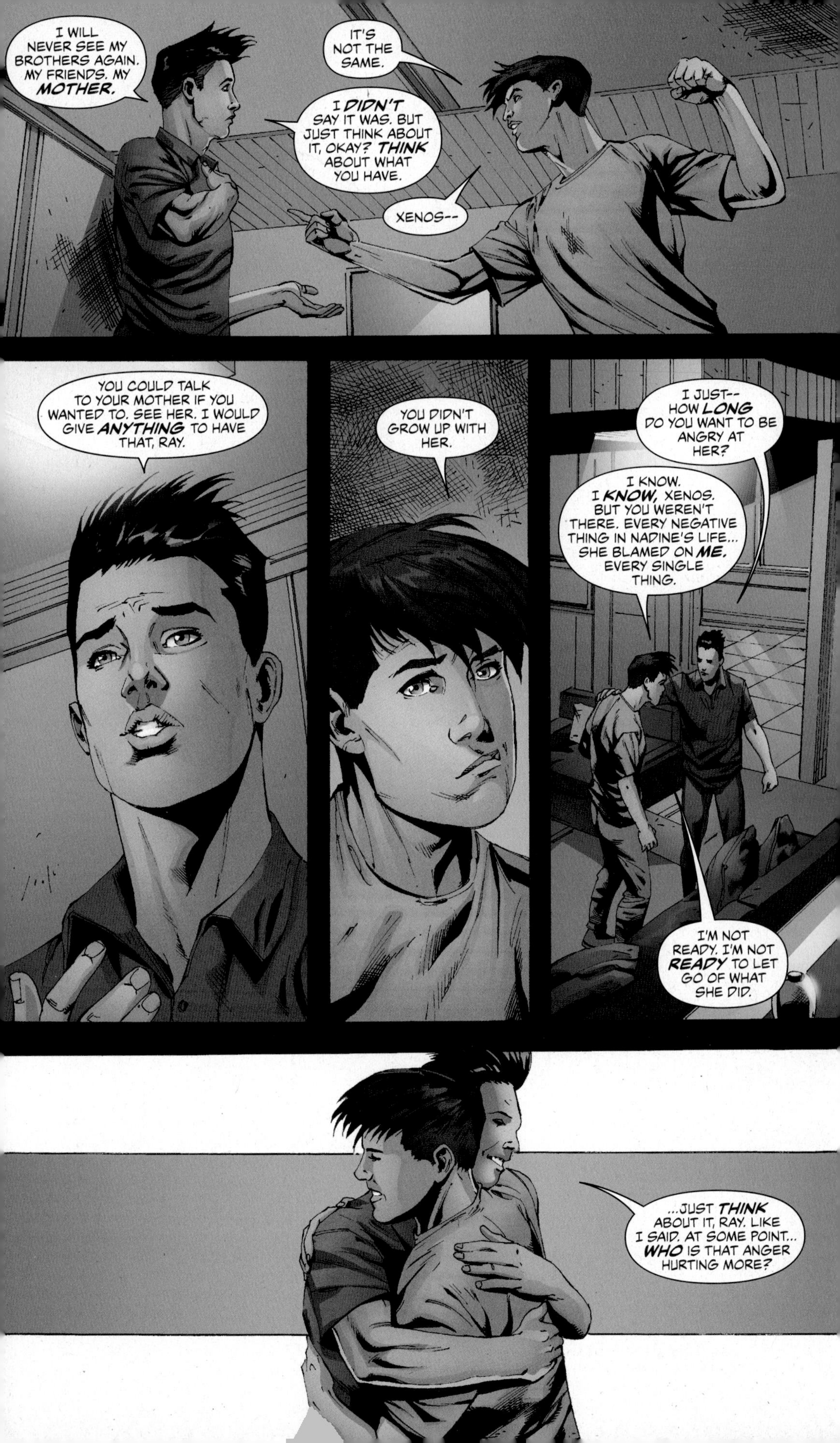
I WILL NEVER SEE MY BROTHERS AGAIN. MY FRIENDS. MY MOTHER.
IT'S NOT THE SAME.
I DIDN'T SAY IT WAS. BUT JUST THINK ABOUT IT, OKAY? THINK ABOUT WHAT YOU HAVE.
XENOS--
YOU COULD TALK TO YOUR MOTHER IF YOU WANTED TO. SEE HER. I WOULD GIVE ANYTHING TO HAVE THAT, RAY.
YOU DIDN'T GROW UP WITH HER.
I JUST-- HOW LONG DO YOU WANT TO BE ANGRY AT HER?
I KNOW. I KNOW, XENOS. BUT YOU WEREN'T THERE. EVERY NEGATIVE THING IN NADINE'S LIFE... SHE BLAMED ON ME. EVERY SINGLE THING.
I'M NOT READY. I'M NOT READY TO LET GO OF WHAT SHE DID.
...JUST THINK ABOUT IT, RAY. LIKE I SAID. AT SOME POINT... WHO IS THAT ANGER HURTING MORE?

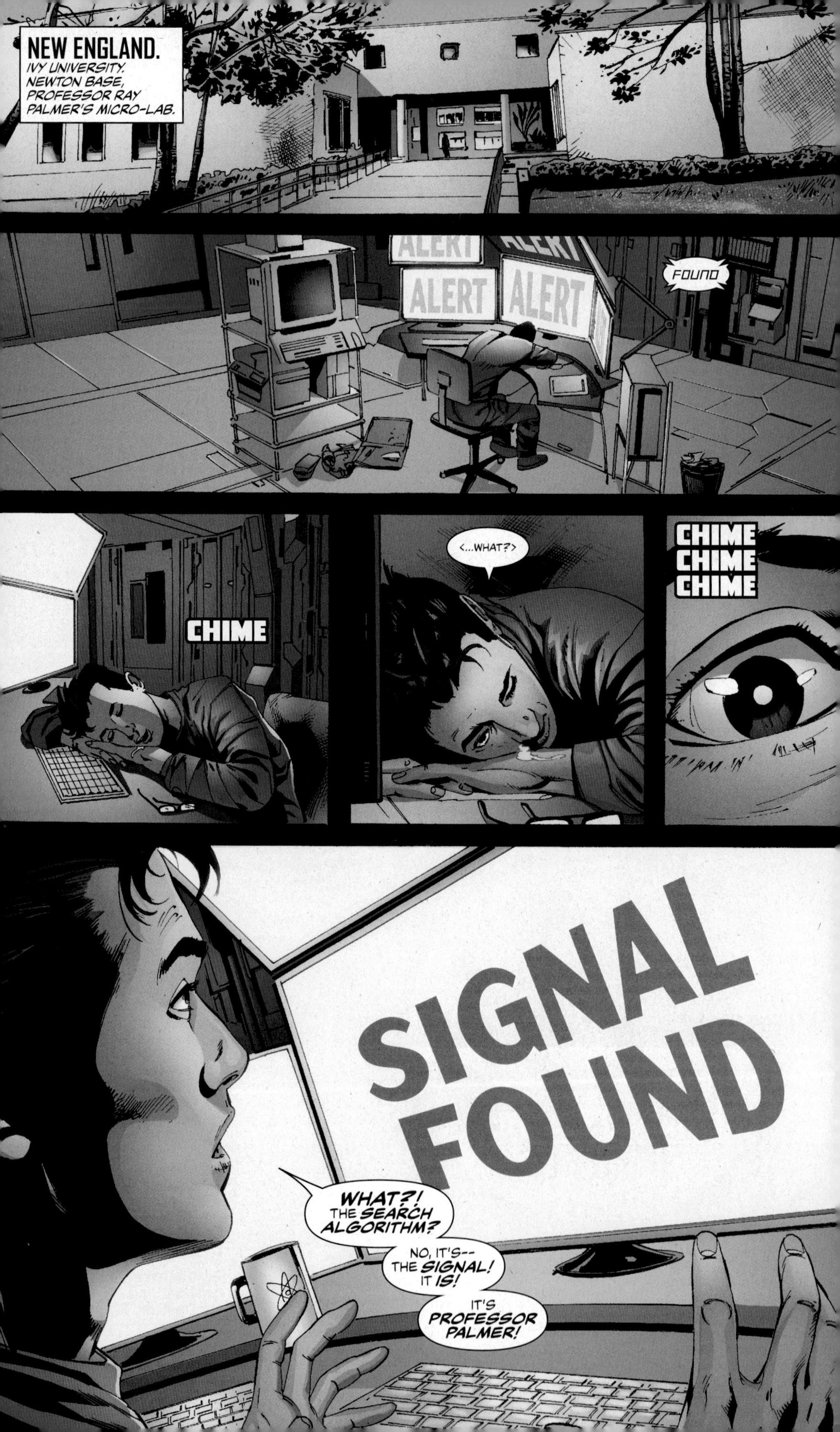
NEW ENGLAND.
IVY UNIVERSITY.
NEWTON BASE,
PROFESSOR RAY
PALMER'S MICRO-LAB.
ALERT
ALERT
ALERT
ALERT
FOUND
CHIME
<...WHAT?>
CHIME
CHIME
CHIME
SIGNAL
FOUND
WHAT?! THE SEARCH ALGORITHM?
NO, IT'S-- THE SIGNAL! IT IS!
IT'S PROFESSOR PALMER!

VARIANT COVER GALLERY

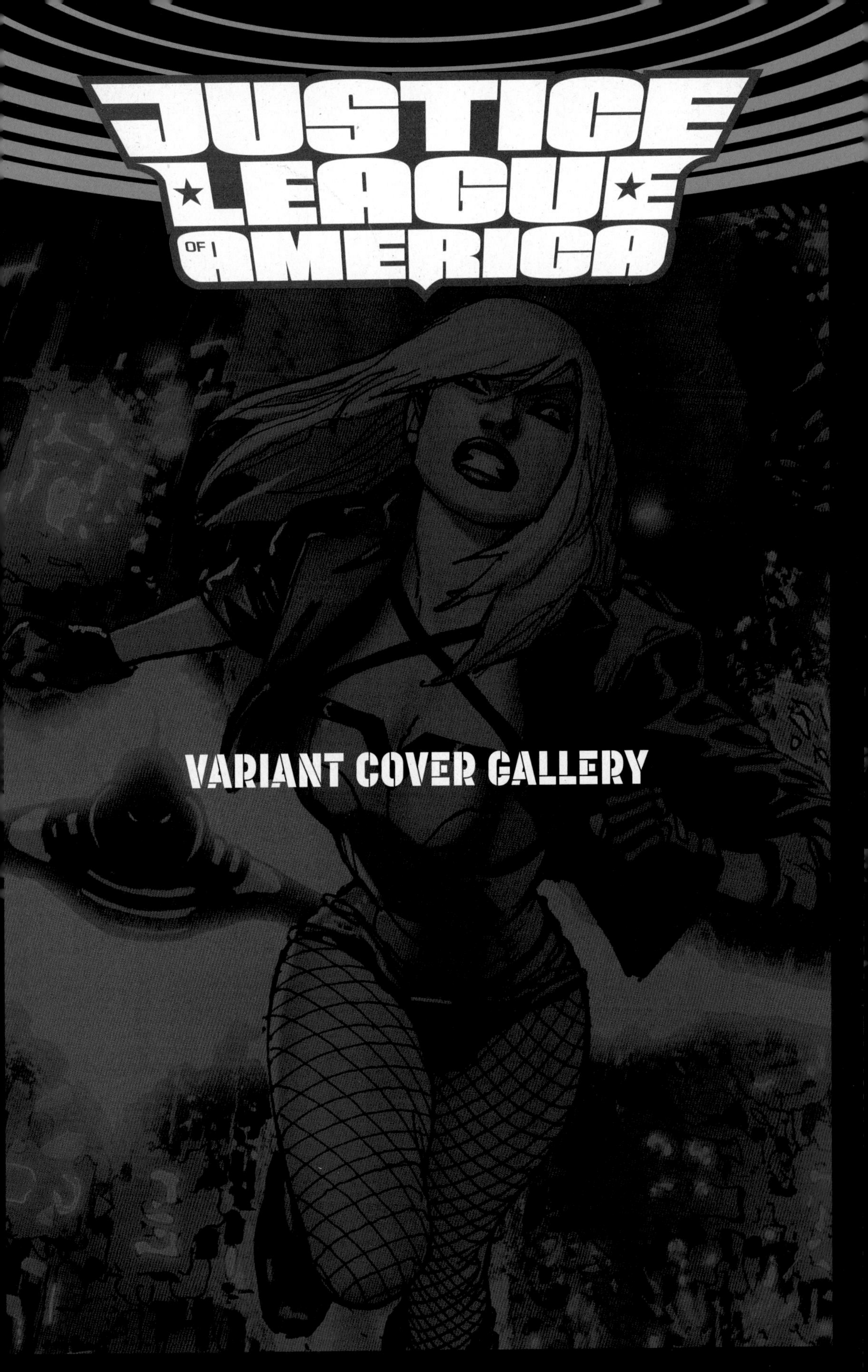
JUSTICE
LEAGUE
OF
AMERICA

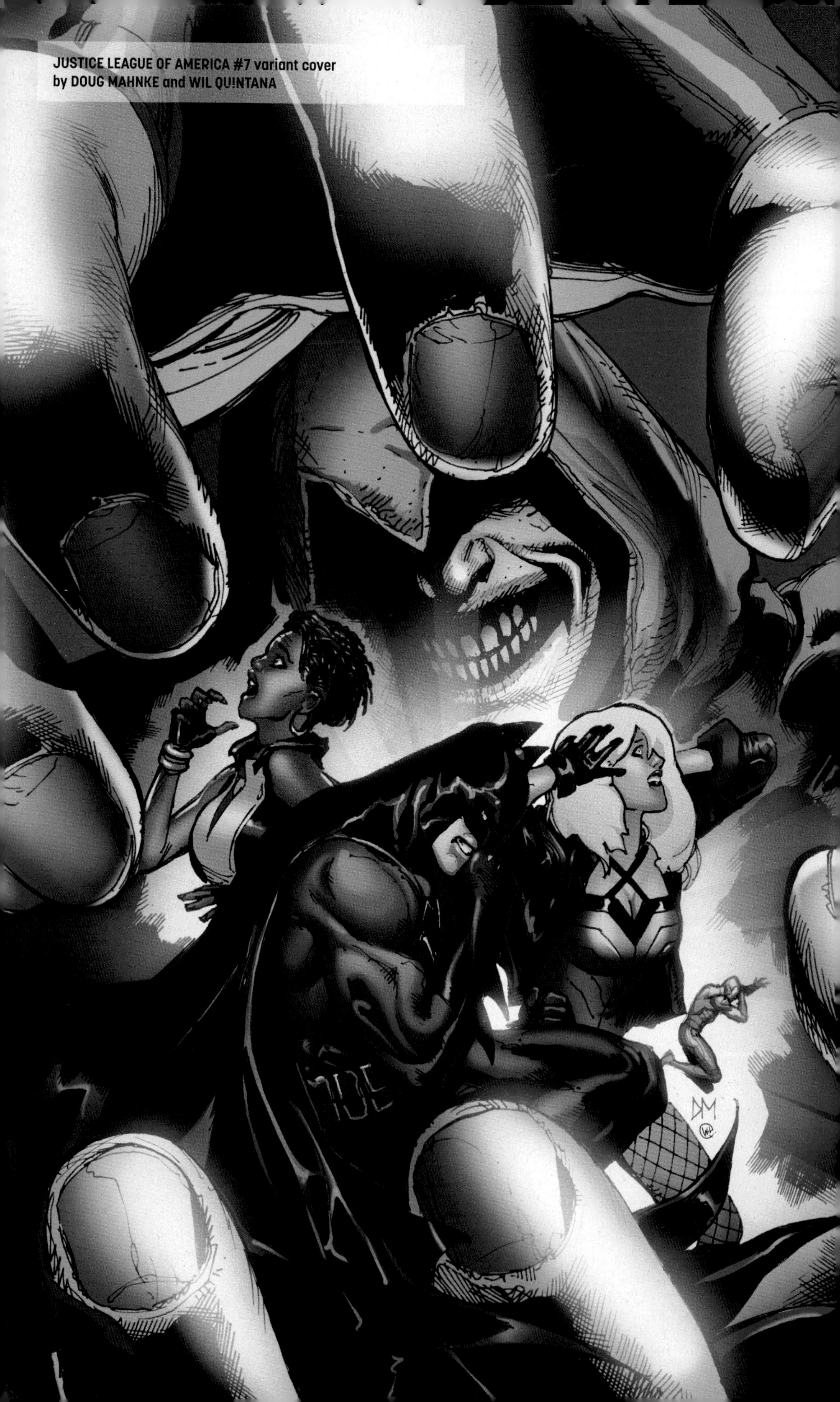

JUSTICE LEAGUE OF AMERICA #7 variant cover
by DOUG MAHNKE and WIL QUINTANA

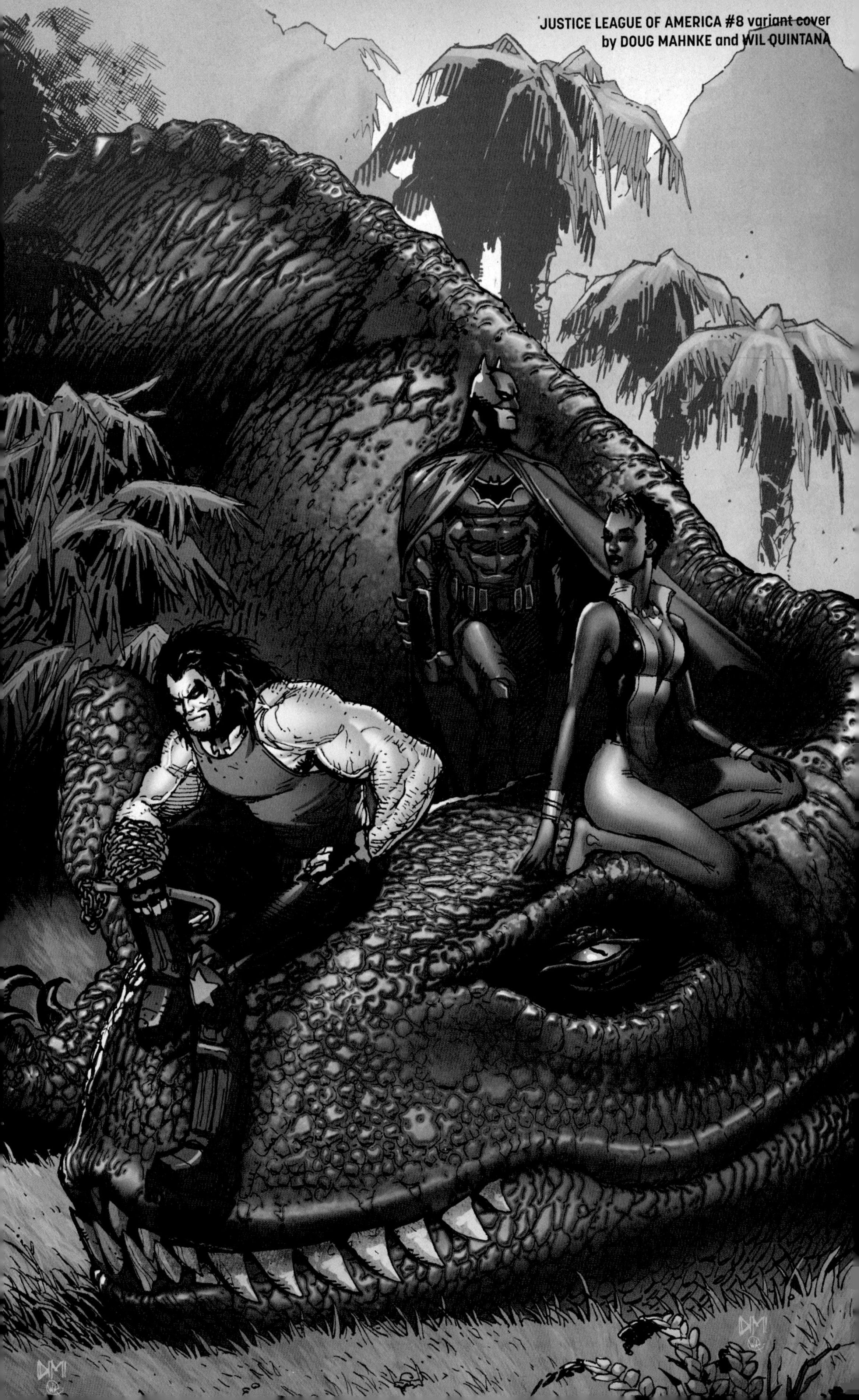

JUSTICE LEAGUE OF AMERICA #8 variant cover
by DOUG MAHNKE and WIL QUINTANA

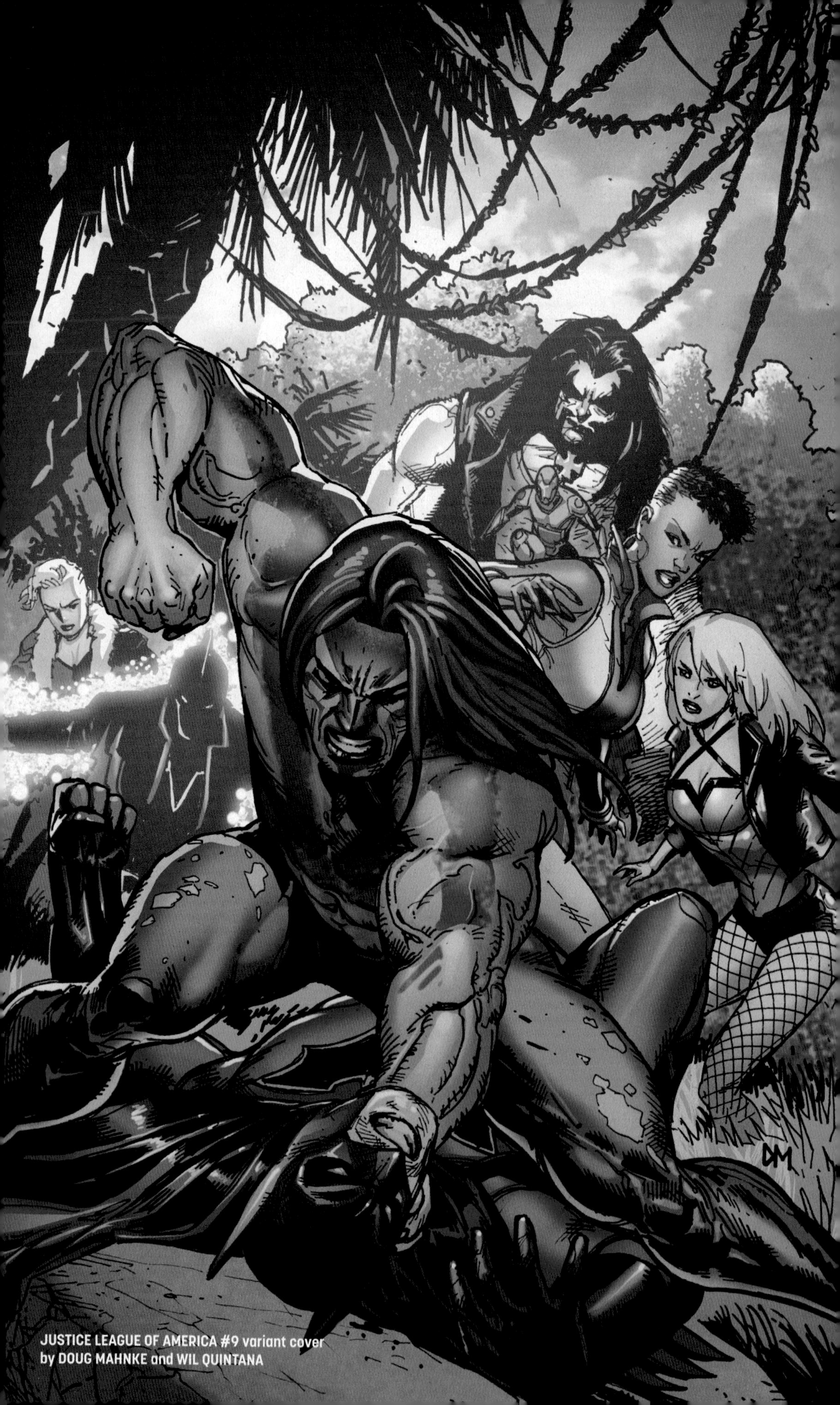

JUSTICE LEAGUE OF AMERICA #9 variant cover
by DOUG MAHNKE and WIL QUINTANA

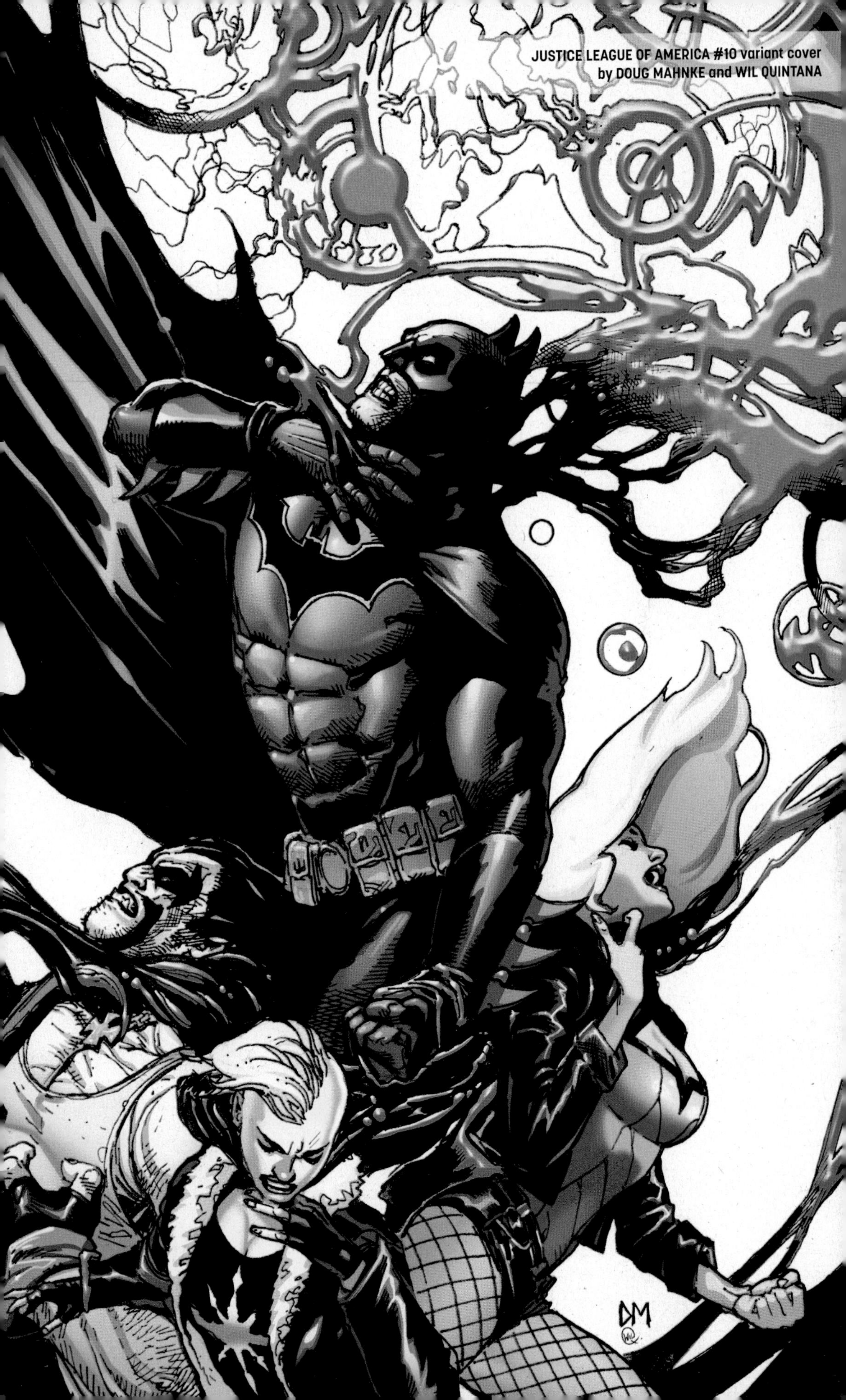
JUSTICE LEAGUE OF AMERICA #10 variant cover
by DOUG MAHNKE and WIL QUINTANA

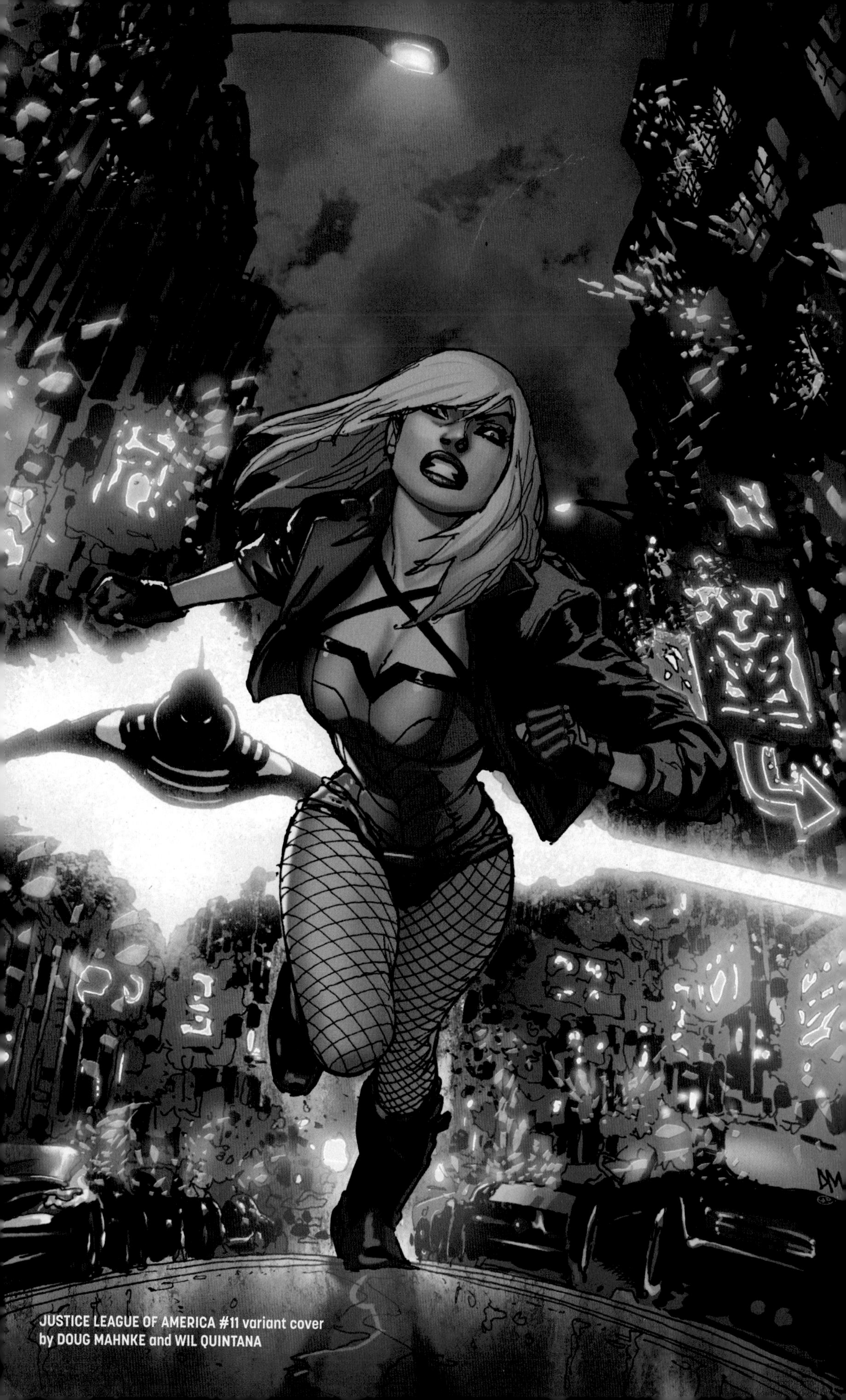

JUSTICE LEAGUE OF AMERICA #11 variant cover
by DOUG MAHNKE and WIL QUINTANA

MAKSON DESIGNS
by FELIPE WATANABE

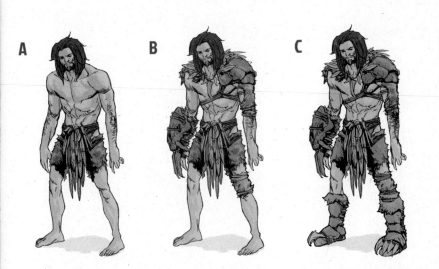

A

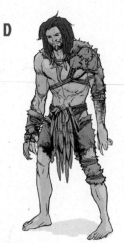

B

C

D

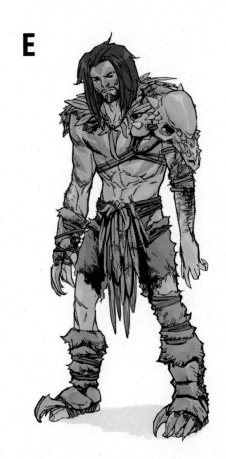

E

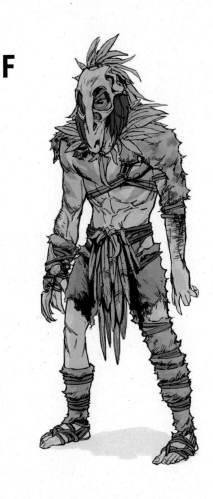

F

KINGBUTCHER DESIGNS
by IVAN REIS

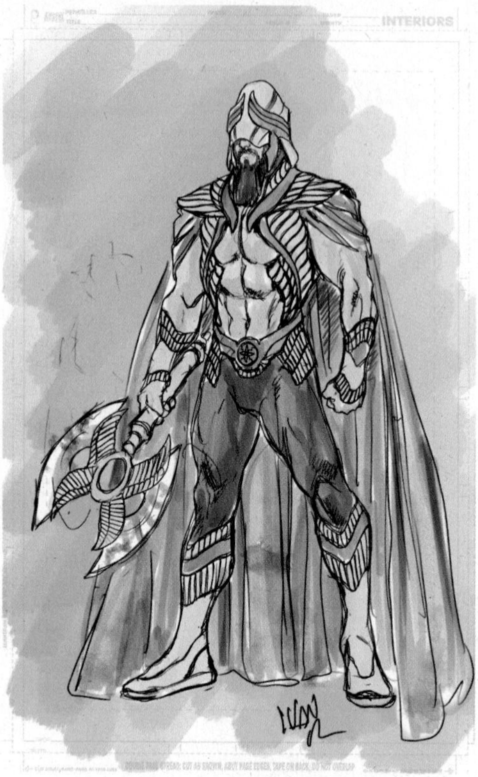
INTERIORS

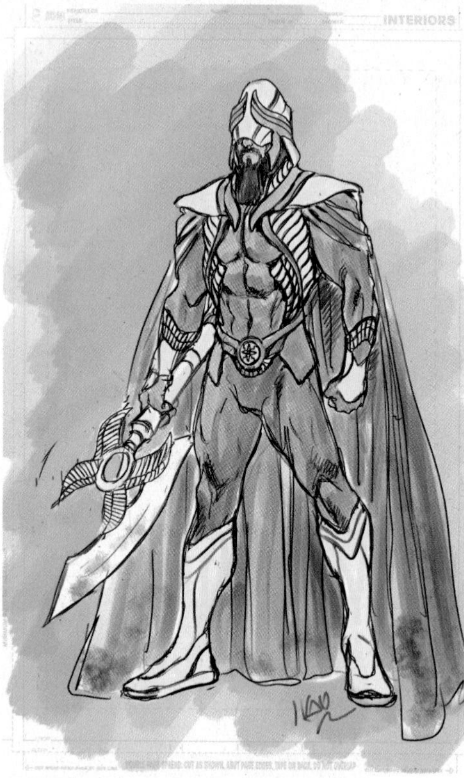
INTERIORS

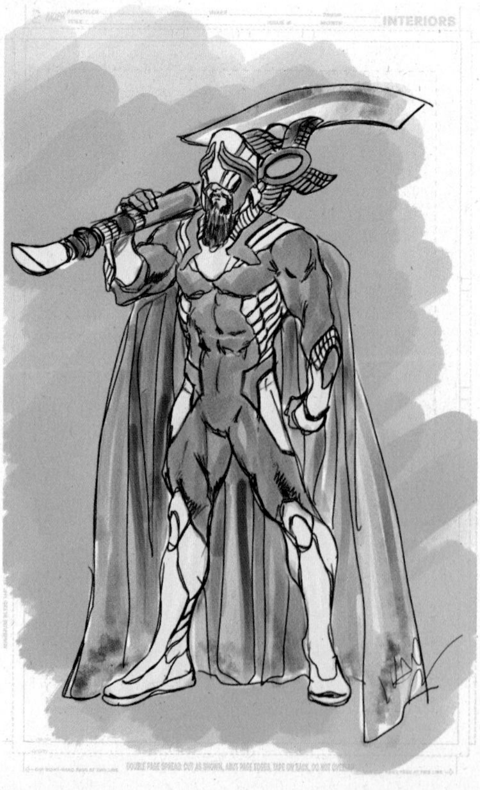
INTERIORS

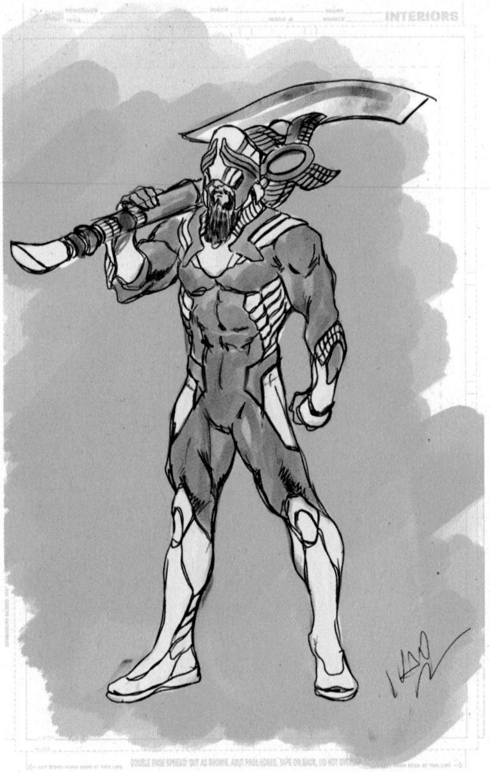
INTERIORS

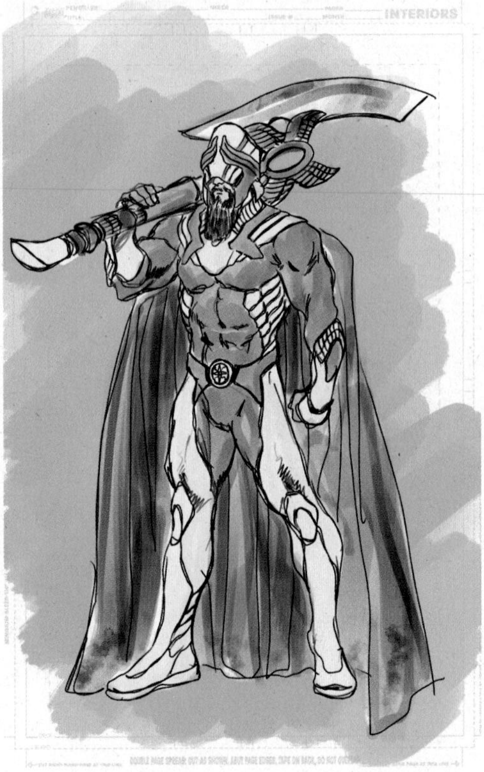
INTERIORS

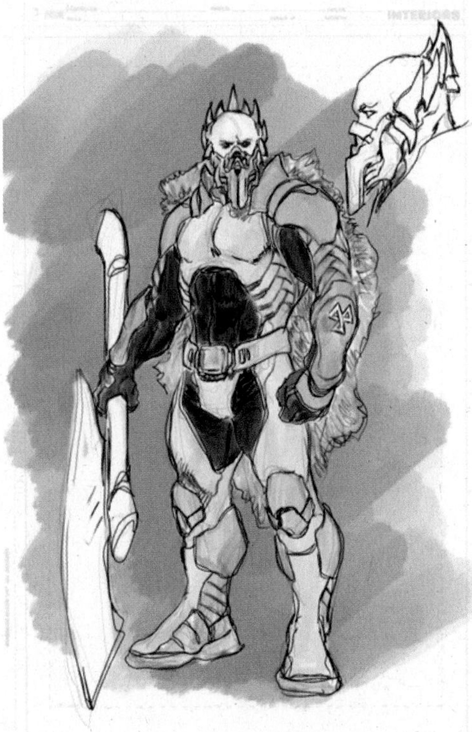
INTERIORS

JUSTICE LEAGUE OF AMERICA #7 COVER SKETCHES
by IVAN REIS

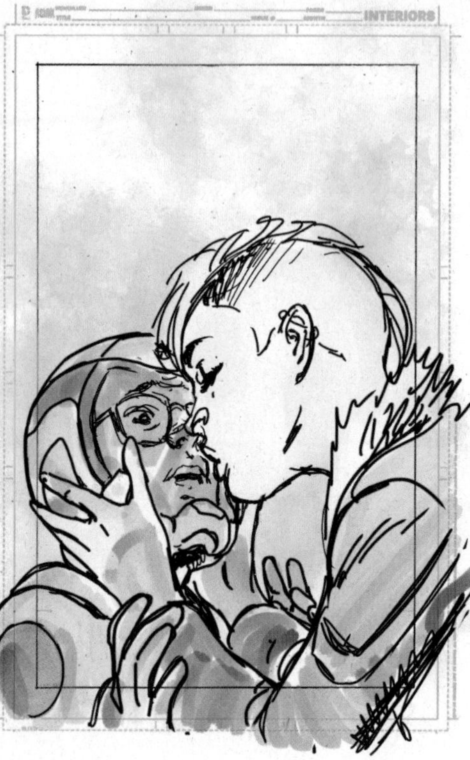
INTERIORS

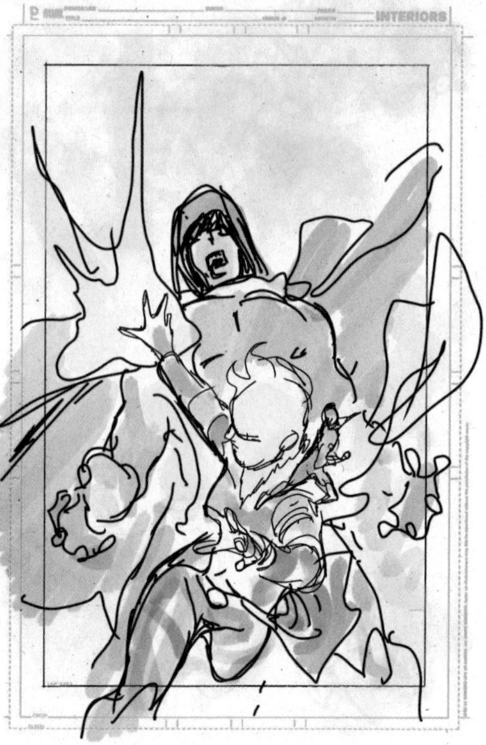
INTERIORS

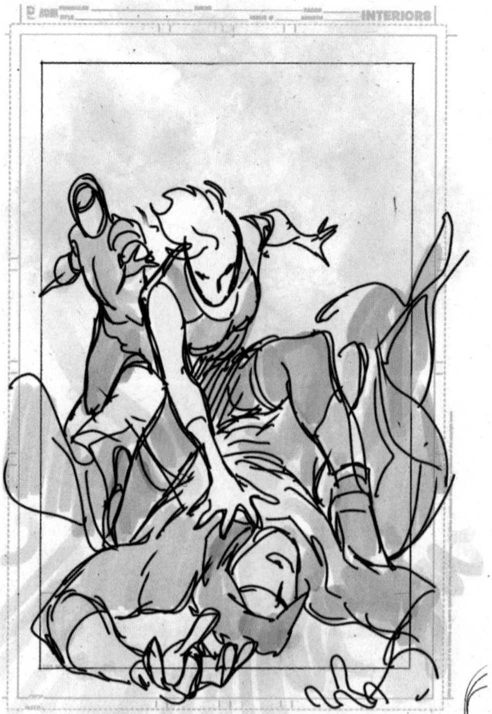
INTERIORS

JUSTICE LEAGUE OF AMERICA #8 COVER SKETCHES
by FELIPE WATANABE

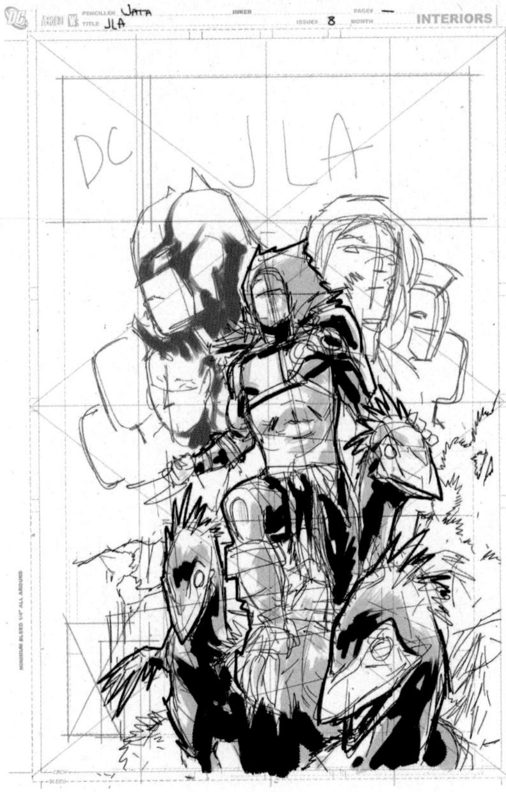
PENCILLER Wata
TITLE JLA
ISSUE 8
INTERIORS
DC
JLA

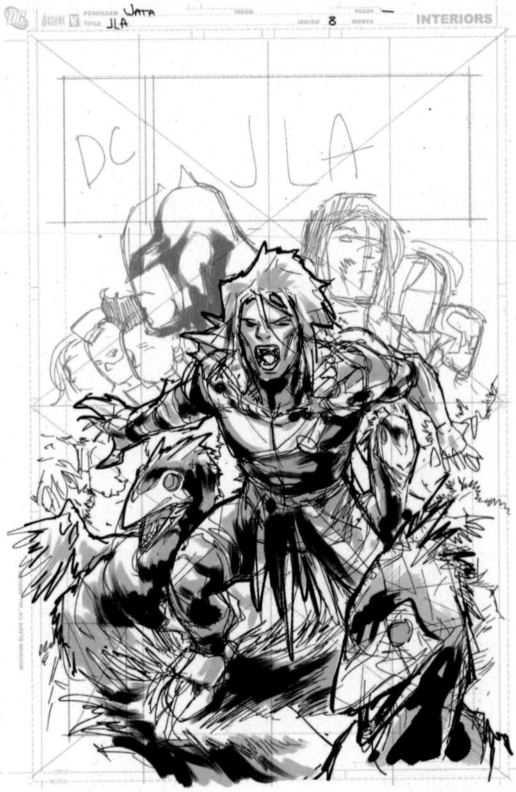
PENCILLER Wata
TITLE JLA
ISSUE 8
INTERIORS
DC
JLA

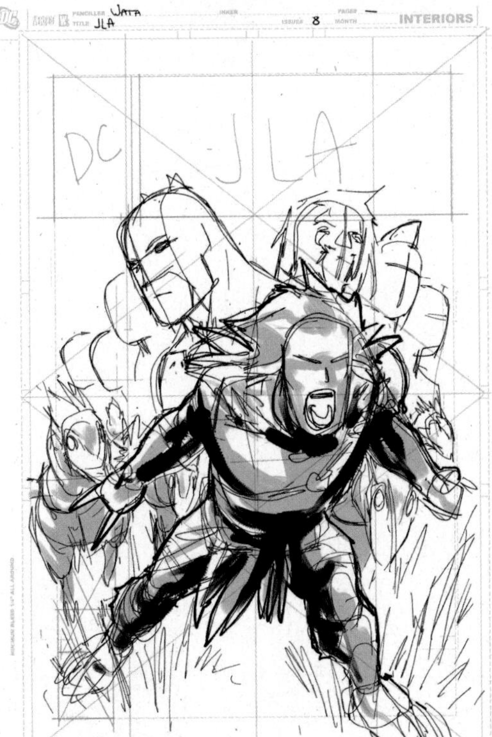
PENCILLER Wata
TITLE JLA
ISSUE 8
INTERIORS
DC
JLA

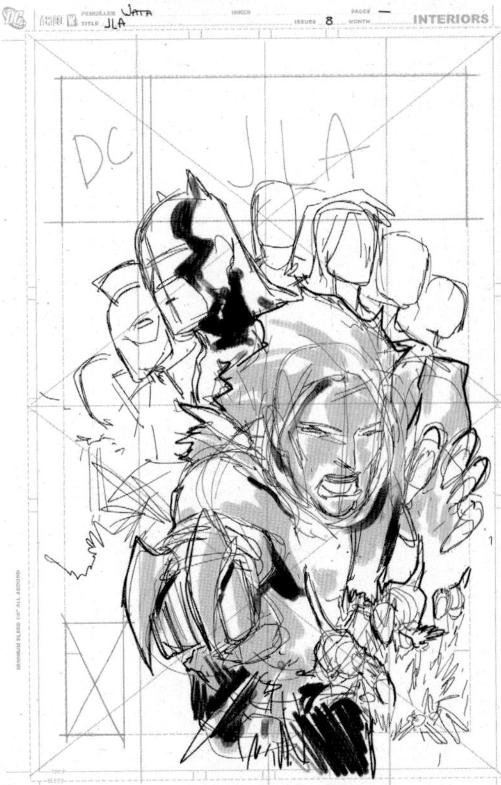
PENCILLER Wata
TITLE JLA
ISSUE 8
INTERIORS
DC
JLA

JUSTICE LEAGUE OF AMERICA #9 COVER SKETCHES
by FELIPE WATANABE

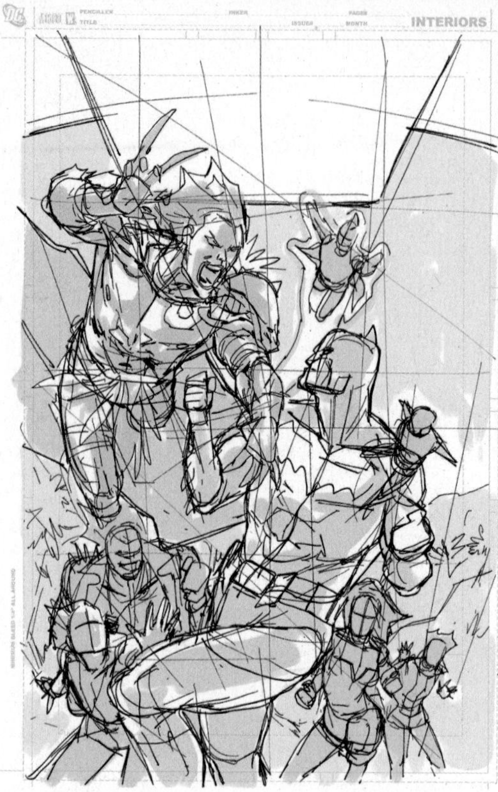
INTERIORS

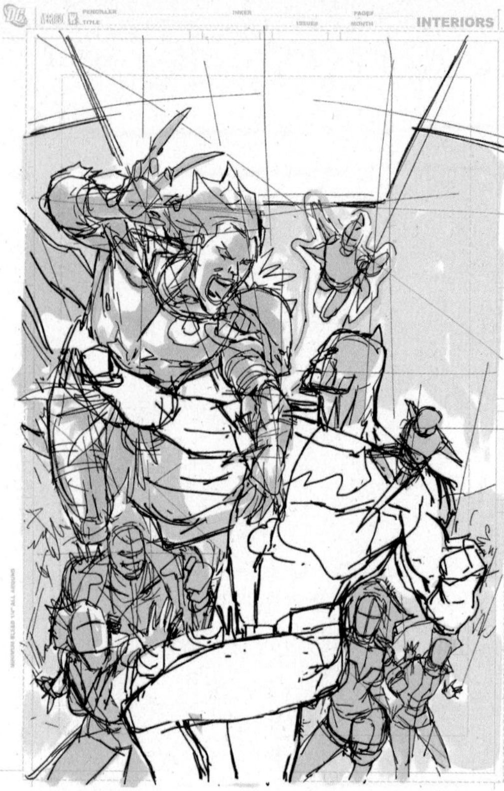
INTERIORS

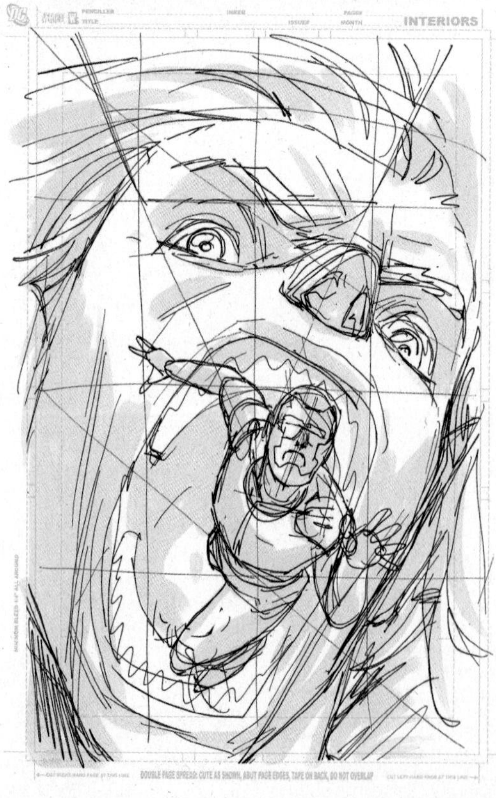
INTERIORS

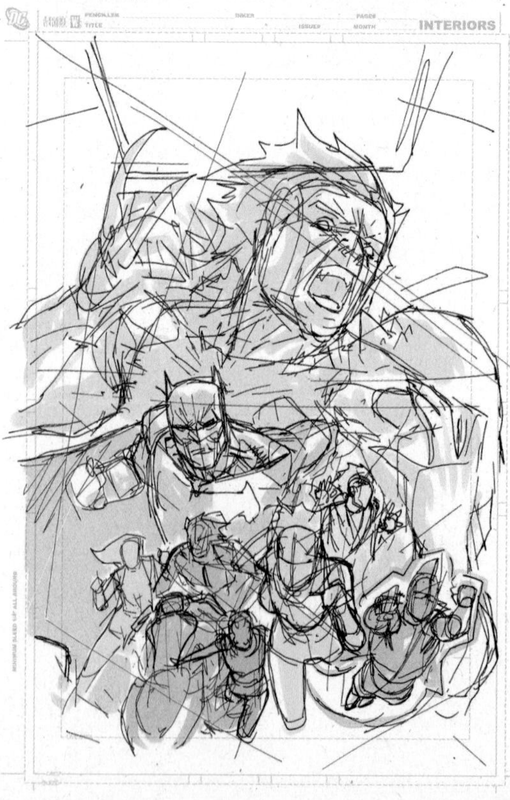
INTERIORS

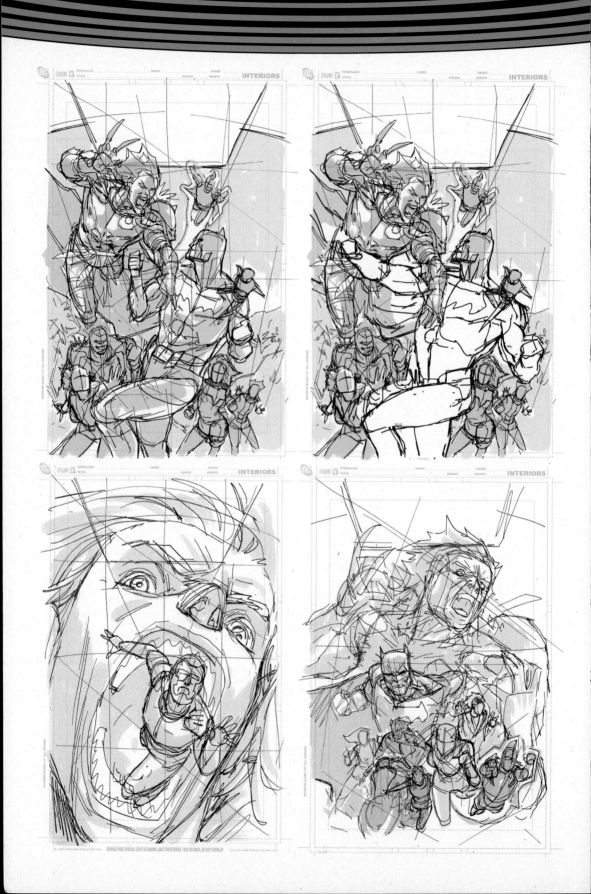

JUSTICE LEAGUE OF AMERICA #11 COVER SKETCHES

by PAUL PELLETIER

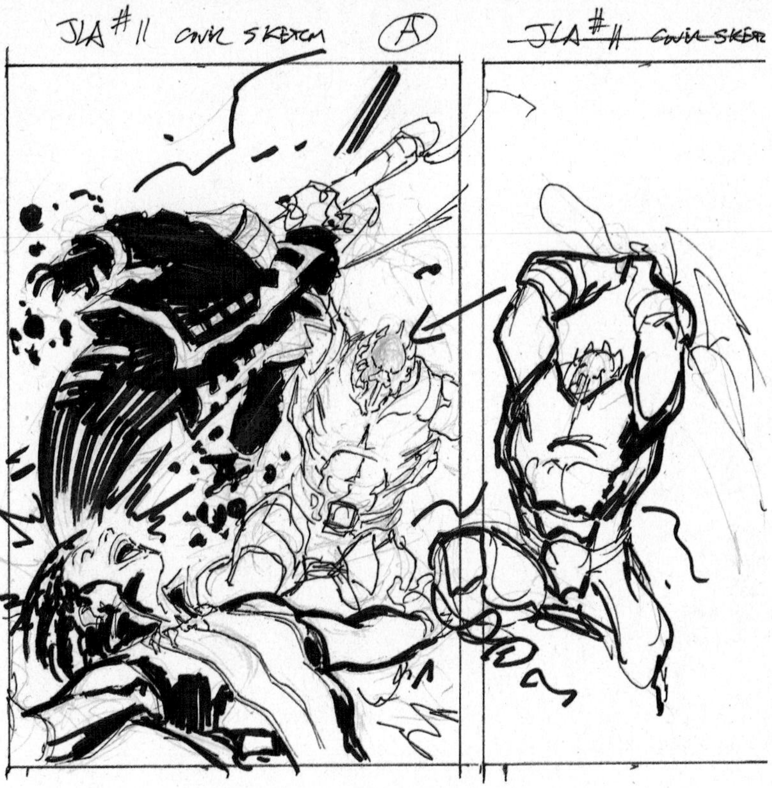
JLA #11 COVER SKETCH (A)
JLA #11 COVER SKETCH

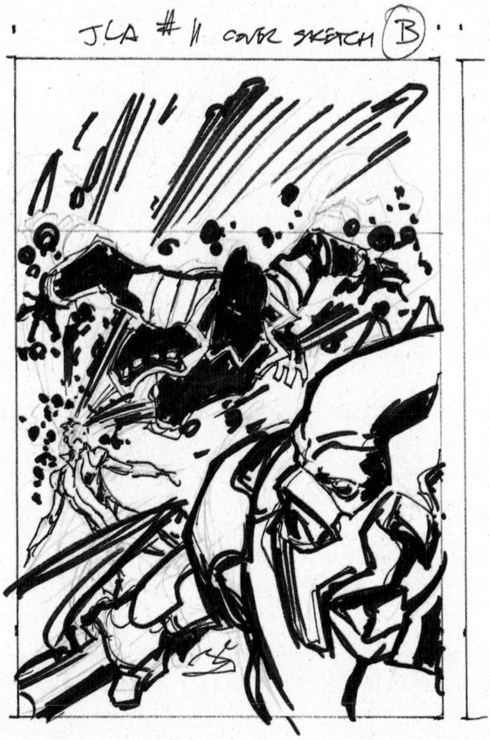
JLA #11 COVER SKETCH (B)

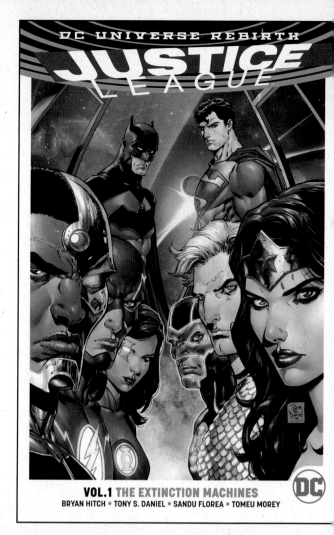
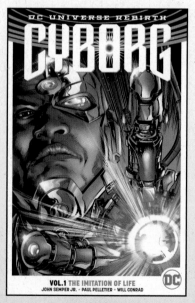